GUAVA DREAMS

A MEMOIR,
MOSTLY TRUE

MARY TORRE KELLY

OPHIR PRESS
1176 St. Louis Place
Atlanta. Georgia
30306
404-872-0934

ISBN 978-0-578-03978-7
Printed in the United States Of America

The characters, places and events in this book are both
real and imaginary. Most of the names have been changed
to protect the innocent, or are used fictitiously. Most of the
places are gone, or so changed as to never have existed in
the first place, except in the author's imagination.

To all the Noonie's,
and to Ted, who came for me...

"Children who watched their parents
blighted lives in the service of Venus
must punish love itself."

- Frank Bidart -

PART ONE

THE SEA BREEZE

1.

The first bud of remembering opens in a car, to the soothing thrum of the road, as we pushed south towards Florida to start a new life. It was a drizzly hot June afternoon in 1946. I was five—my life underway, but I felt I'd just joined in. The windows were half rolled down, and you could hear the wind wailing—my father said it was the lonely call of love. Usually I kept my ears shut, but I could hear that lonely call of love. I always would.

"Christ, somebody hit a skunk!" my father said, and he quick rolled his window up.

My brother Donnie, who was seven, reeled around fast and looked out the back window, but not in time to see anything. He made a face and growled, "ugh pee-yew."

I took a deep breath before I knew to stop myself, and that rank smell choked me, and shot out my eyes. There hadn't been any skunk on Cedar street in Nutley, New Jersey, where we were coming from. You might say that was the moment I came into full realization of a world outside my own head, that gas jolting me awake. I had inherited my father's great olfactory nerves and even the shape of his nose in a smaller girl-sized version, so my life had so far been a smell-fest, if nothing else. But this was like no other vapor on earth. My mother thought I was crying.

"What's the matter with you? get over it dearie, it's only a skunk. Phew." she said, holding her nose, and shutting her side vent, in no hurry at all. She probably couldn't smell it good and was just saying phew to be agreeable. She was a comfy pudding of womanly smells herself, layered over with the reek of Chesterfields and the Coty's face powder she patted on every single day. But I knew she couldn't smell much; otherwise, she wouldn't let our supper burn on the stove all the time, and she would know how much cigarettes stank. Mostly she could see good, and sense things. She saw the map of Ireland on my face, and on my little brother Andy's, but we couldn't see it. Andy was only three. He was on the floor pooping in his pants—that information hadn't reached the rest of the car yet.

Next minute, a ledge of fog slid over us like a surprisement, and my father had to slow our black '39 Ford 2-door Deluxe, that word deluxe made me feel rich, down to a crawl because he couldn't see a thing, and besides we were pulling a trailer weighted down with our belongings. It was to be our temporary home, until he could build us a real house. He had built the trailer himself, to look just like the Silver Airstream Clipper, only ours was made out of surplus airplane spruce and was painted a jaunty aquamarine color. It looked different. Most cars and trailers in 1946 were black, grey or white, sometimes navy blue or some other dull, stray color. My father promised we were moving to paradise. It was in Miami, the magic city. We would go to open-air schools and eat tangerines right off the trees. Mama still didn't want to go. You could tell she didn't believe in my father's paradise.

He started whistling a little song, warbling the way I liked him to. He was happy because we were escaping from the drab light and dirty cold snow of New Jersey. He was saving us. An awful bomb had exploded in Hiroshima and we were running from that too, although we had been nowhere near it. It felt like we were safe from the darkness of the war, our family of five enclosed inside this deluxe car with warm nappy seats, floating along on dumplings of fog. I wished my mother could see it like that.

When my brother Donnie sat still like this, I liked to study his perfectly shaped blonde head. From the side you couldn't tell his ears stuck out even though you could see they were gigantic. My mother said they were just like Clark Gable's ears. I loved how his neck smelled near his ears, sort of like a pink rubber eraser. Donnie's hair grew in a rounding pattern of light waves and trailed down his neck in fine hairs like lint. I wanted to touch it but I knew he'd hit me if I did. Sometimes, like now, he seemed there by me, but up on another floor in his mind that no one could get to. He just stared out the window and his body seemed a gentle thing that wouldn't hurt you, wouldn't strike out at you. He wasn't even biting his nails. I slid a little closer to him and thought my own thoughts. I stayed very still. If I moved too much, he would come out of the trance, punch me on the leg and say, "What are you looking at? Shove over!" I knew all his reactions by now.

"Do my neck," my father said. He meant me. I always tickled his neck as he drove along, to keep him relaxed. After awhile my mother looked back at me a couple of times. I thought she wanted her neck done too, so I slid over and

3

started touching her wavy brown hair and lifting it up gently. "Don't," she said, swatting her hand back at me without turning around. "I don't want to be fiddled with, it's too hot." She was intent on looking straight ahead, as if she alone was leading us out of the fog. She lit another cigarette and opened her vent back up.

"You can fiddle with me some more," my father said, and I went back to his leathery neck which was sweaty and crackled all over like a road map. My mother turned around and gave me such a look. I wished I knew her reactions.

We were creeping along now in a long line of cars backed up for miles. My mother clucked her tongue and said this was the worst fog she'd ever seen in her life. All of a sudden she screamed, "Hit the floor!" And it was like a firecracker went off. My head hit the roof, then I was on the floor wondering how mama saw it coming. We bounced and bumped against each other in the back seat, while up front my mother kept on screaming. I knew the world must be crashing to an end. Andy came awake hollering because Donnie and I were piled on top of him, but he wasn't hurt. None of us was hurt when the car finally came to a stop down in a ditch—just scared to death is all we were. First thing mama did was lean over the seat and check all our heads and bones. She was shaking and waving her arms around.

We got up on our knees and looked out the back window. A loaded produce truck had knocked us off the road, right into this muddy ditch. The back end of our trailer was laid open and all our belongings were slumming along the median in the company of soon-to-be rotting fruits and vegetables. It was a colorful sight even in the fog, like if Carmen Miranda dropped her hat. That was something I was always afraid might happen. My Carmen Miranda paper dolls were scattered all over the floor of the car, underneath Andy. Carmen had eight different halter tops with matching skirts that tied at the hip, plus a hat that was made up of piles of fruits; now I started wondering if I'd seen any vegetables on the hat, just to calm myself down. I was shaking, and I had that sick feeling like when we ran out of gas, which happened sometimes.

The produce truck was lying on its side in the ditch, smoking. My father jumped out of the car, leaving the door hanging wide on its hinges, and swiping his hair back with both hands, cussing at the driver. Mama was still waving her arms like she was swatting gnats. She lit up another Chesterfield to calm herself, and wouldn't let us get out of the car because she was afraid of things coming at us out of nowhere. We had to settle for looking through the back window, and we kept on steaming it up and wiping it off, straining to find out what was happening to our father who we could barely see out there, although we could hear him shouting back and forth, him and the truck driver, while car brakes screeched all around them.

Suddenly the car felt hot and crowded. Why did I always have to be in the middle? I knew it was to keep my brothers from fighting with each other, except they both just hit me instead. I could see it coming. Donnie was antsy, with a lost look in his eyes. His arm flew across and hit Andy in the back of the head. Wham! Andy started to tear up, and then he punched Donnie on the shoulder, and then they started slugging it out in a flurry of punches that were all rebounding off me. I covered my head and yelled loud as I could. Mama turned around, blew a mouthful of smoke at us and choked: "Stop causing trouble! Don't we have enough trouble now!"

Andy smelled bad and I shuffled on my knees to get farther away from him. "Move over!" Donnie yelled, as soon as I got too close to him, like I had leprosy or something.

"SHUSHHHHHH-UP" went my mother.

I shrunk down in the seat in the tiniest space I could make and hunched my scalding head inside my crossed arms where I could be alone. I tried to imagine my father's fight with the truck driver because I couldn't see it anyway through the clumps of fog turned the color of oleo by all the headlights. Skunkiness hung on us like oil.

Mama rolled down her window and pleaded: "George, please, the kids, for God's sakes...." As if she expected him to stop being mad just because we might hear a few cuss words while we waited.

The minute my father got back in the car he looked right at Andy, who had a guilty little look on his face. "What the hell'd you do that for?" daddy said to him, with leftover anger, like pooping in his pants was something Andy could help.

We had to stay overnight in a motor court right across the road from the accident while my father and the truck driver stayed up all night repairing the trailer. I had never stayed in a motor court before, or slept on strange beds with white sheets, crispy as paper. In the trailer we had woolly Army blankets on our beds, olive-colored. We were the pimentos, daddy said, and gave us a wink.

In the morning when we went outside, the first thing I saw were roses dripping with dew. They lined the walkways and hedged roundabout the motor court all abloom; pink ones in different hues and sizes, huge-headed red ones roaring open, and yellows big as cabbages, befringed with a dainty pink edging. They were drenched in fog like everything else. I lingered by the roses, put my face in close and took deep breaths, until I was dizzy from their scent. I thought this must be nature's sweetest air, the direct opposite of skunk.

The roses gave me a swanky feeling, so I almost forgot about our broke-down condition. But they were lost on mama, who was counting up her Community Plate silverware, and crying about her broken Golden Wheat dishes. Scavengers had come in the night and picked over our belongings before we could get them all back into the trailer, repaired and patched now, the back end slathered over with an ugly gray primer. Someone had even taken our pancake flipper and dustpan. "Where the hell's my pressure cooker?" Mama screamed out to the world. I could feel her pain, but I didn't own anything then that I cared much about except my paperdolls and the rag doll I held in my arms, so I didn't really understand why she carried on so.

So that's how our run to the sun began, with the reek of skunk, a foggy crash, and then the balm of roses wrapping round us. And I, Louise O'Neill, came awake as I had never been before to what was going on: I was in my parents' life just as my brothers were. We were all in their mysterious world. But even then I had a feeling it wasn't always going to be this way, that someday my life could belong to me. The

7

promise of that was in the wind too. All things seemed to lurk out there in the wind, like silent lightening.

The accident outside Baltimore became one of the events in my mother's life that she would later say shortened it, and brought her to the brink of a nervous breakdown. That, and The Great Depression, as she called it, which was over long ago, before I was born, but mama still suffered from it. "What I've been through, you just don't know," she would say, closing her eyes in agony and tsk'ing three times. But if you asked her what, she went blank and couldn't come up with anything. "Oh, never mind," she'd snap, shooing you away from her burden, clucking her tongue like there was a constant problem she had to work out in her own mind, something no one else alive could possibly understand. She had secrets, and she meant to hold onto them tightly.

I didn't know then that someday all the struggles of my daughterhood would come to a head when I found out my mothers painful secrets.

2.

Mama cried or pouted all the rest of the way to Florida, dabbing her eyes with a limp hanky she kept tucked in her dress between her bosoms. She looked back at me as if to say: "This is how it is to be a woman." It scared me. I didn't want to be like that. I wanted to be dry and brave like my father. After the accident she blamed him for every little thing, with the result that he catered to her and talked too softly to her for the whole rest of the trip. She was especially cranky in Georgia. "I've never seen so damn many shacks before. Where are you taking us? Jesus that red clay is awful." Once we crossed the line into Florida she squinted her eyes, "Gawd it's bright, somebody turn down the lights." And then she laughed, so we all did, and it was a relief. I could see daddy was eager for mama to like Florida, to like the house he was going to build her, to like him. He wanted to prove to her they had done the right thing, had come out of darkness and into light. She would keep him always trying to prove it too, prove something.

We were southbound on US 1, when daddy told us about the Indians, who were the only true Americans, everyone else had dropped in on them—and about how they had worked out a grand creation cycle. Turtle Island was the name the Indians gave North America, and the peninsula we were riding on right now was the turtle's head. Made it all seem small. Still, we drove for hours, and when it got hot he switched over to A1A and rode along the beach road for awhile, and when Donnie and Andy started socking me instead of each other, daddy stopped the car and let us take running jumps in the salty surf. That night, we slept in our trailer parked on Daytona Beach, a hard-packed sand road where the warm ocean rolled up to the door when the tide came in. In the morning mama opened the door and screamed when she saw how close the water came. We had to leave out of there fast.

The rest of the way to Miami, we were all salty and the car was full of sand. My father pulled up to five acres of land on Northeast Second Avenue in Dade County, that he had bought through the mail, and stopped. We sat in the car staring at the wide, flat expanse of solid-packed palmetto bush. No one said a word. The bugs were so loud it felt like we'd entered a bug world and were swimming in bug sound. There were jumbo trees in the distance, beyond our land, and way on down the road I could make out a single little house.

The place was called Uleta, twenty miles north of downtown Miami and ten miles west of Sunny Isles and the Atlantic Ocean. You could whiff the air and tell it had lots of skunk. Slowly we drove down second avenue, and turned a corner onto the main street, called the Golden Glades road. In the next block we saw a blinking light, and counted seven little stuccoed stores, including a beer joint called The Greyhound Inn that had big porthole windows like a ship on either side of the entrance. We passed the post office and after a couple of miles came to Biscayne Boulevard which was a wider road with motor courts, a drive-in movie, and a trailer park alongside the Oleta river. Here we would park for the next few weeks, while my father readied everything for the move onto our own land.

Uleta always seemed to me to have started when we got there. But in fact it was named after a river that ran through the jungly land called the Oleta that was so thick with snakes, 'gators and plantlife that it looked coagulated, not like flowing water at all but still and miry, congealed to a shiny black you wouldn't dare put even the tip of your finger into. In 1926, when the town had registered its post office, the people in Washington read the O as a U and Uleta it became and remained, a town in error—a mistake of a town that nobody cared enough about to correct. My father said it was without incorporation, an in-between place that attracted people who were unincorporated themselves: vagabonds, misfits, naturalists, circus performers and freedom-lovers like us. Then he laughed uproariously. And my mother scowled.

For me, Uleta was instantly home-sweet-home, a seedbed for the green shoots of my first understanding, a place where I would spend my deep deep childhood, and every day would be hard, and last as long as it could.

After he cleared some palmetto out of the way, the first thing my father had to do was dig a pit and build an outhouse over it. He had a model: every Sunday there was one in the *Miami Herald* in full color, Li'l Abner's outhouse with a crescent moon cut-out. When he was finished, ours looked just like it. I peered over the high seat and down into the cold, dark hole and imagined snakes living down there, like in the Oleta River. When I had to go, I squatted behind the outhouse instead.

Hundreds of feet away from the outhouse he cleared more palmetto and drilled the well. When he struck coral rock he pronounced the water good enough to drink. The next day my mother carried some of the water in a jar on the bus that came through Uleta every hour on the hour. The bus went to downtown Miami where she got the water tested. Sure enough, it proved to be good, though hard, potable water, full of minerals, especially iron which turned it yellow and gave it a strong smell and taste. It would make us all strong, my father said, it would make my red hair and Andy's even redder. Oh just what we didn't need.

There was a pump on the well with a big handle. We all had to learn how to prime it and pump the water up. I had to jump my whole body onto the handle to get it down, so by the time I had a bucketful of water my ribs were sore and bruised. Daddy rigged a shower stall beside the well, and finally he cleared a space and parked our trailer on the land. The last thing we got was electricity. A single new pole on the edge of second avenue connected us to Reddy Kilowatt, who daddy said was Miami's own electricity elf.

At night the crickets were so loud they kept us awake. The little trailer was hot and crowded. My skin felt like a fur coat. After we were all wilted and tired of slapping bugs a soft breeze started up and gradually got cooler and fluffier until it lulled us off to sleep. Daddy called it the Tradewinds.

When daylight came, we worked together to clear the land around where the house would be. Andy and Donnie mostly fought the palmetto down and trampled it instead of digging it out, and they yelled at me if I stopped working. Whyever do boys always have to threaten you with sticks and try to make you afraid of them?

For days we struggled with the palmetto and weeds, getting cut and bug-bitten, raw and itchy. Finally Daddy burned it out. We watched the wildlife running from the fire, jackrabbits and animals I'd never seen before and couldn't name, every species available from that latitude, and little black and white skunks, who added their reeking fume to the soaring smoke until it was a suffocating hellfire. Mama broke down and cried, saying this was a godforsaken place, and begging daddy to take her back up north. Instead, daddy took us all to Sunny Isles beach where we plunged into the salty ocean to cool off and heal our stinging cuts and bites. "Water is the best element of all, besides the element of surprise." he said with a wink.

As soon as the rafters, roof and outside walls were up, we moved into the house; mama was so anxious to get out of that hot little trailer. A long van arrived one day soon after and unloaded our dark northern furniture, maple beds and mattresses, golf clubs and lots of books. All our stuff from New Jersey looked heavy and strange in the glaring tropical light inside the unfinished house.

Windows and screens were the first thing my father had to hurry up installing, to keep the teeming bugs out. Then plumbing fixtures, a big tiled shower stall and a green tub separate from it, with the mistaken idea that two of us could wash at the same time without fighting. He made fancy built-in mirrored shelves around the green sink trying to please mama. Even the toilet was green. Lido green was the new color for bathrooms that year and this was the biggest bathroom I had ever seen, scaled for a man big as my father.

Then it was September and my mother enrolled Donnie and me in a Catholic school, a short bus ride away. I was five but I'd be six in November, so I could go to first grade. But within a couple of weeks the nuns told my mother to take me out, I was too immature and dreamy for school, and to also take me downtown for some hearing tests because they had tried everything to get through to me, even moving me to a front row seat. I didn't mean to cause trouble, but I couldn't understand their whispery voices, what they wanted from me or why. Everyone in my family shouted most of the time.

So downtown on the bus we went, through the suck and swish of a revolving door, I heard that alright, and up an elevator. Then I was in a little box of a room with rug walls, and I was supposed to hold up however many fingers I heard pings for. But what I heard was more like a cotton ball touching a blanket. Mama looked sad as we rode back home on the bus, and she didn't say one word to me. She wouldn't even look at me.

That first Christmas in the new house, it was so hot the candy canes melted on the Christmas tree and gave out a spicy pine-pitch-peppermint scent that made me feel a joy bursting alive inside. I twirled around the tree catching whiffs, dipping my fingers in the melting candy and pulling it in strings to my mouth like salt-water taffy.

I got a doll for Christmas as I always did, and I immediately clamped onto it, stared into its amber eyes, drank in its painty scent and started imagining a life for it. Andy got a sailboat and a peg and hammer set, and Donnie got a baseball bat and a glove. Before I could even give my doll a name, Andy smashed her plaster of Paris head in with his new hammer.

Donnie danced around in a circle, laughing, "way to go, Andy, way to go little guy."

"He didn't mean to do it," my mother said right away, when I started to bawl. That was a lie. Andy had taken aim and hammered the doll's head in like it was a peg. What she meant was Andy was surprised when the hammer broke the doll's head, that's all; it even surprised him, that his one little action could have such big results. I was surprised too, by his nerve. I could see then that boys were naturally mean and at the same time expected to be that way.

I cried for a long time. I felt small, my insides burned hotly. Finally I was so tired of myself I crawled onto my mother's lap and wiped my eyes on her gummy apron.

"Shut up that crying now," she dropped her voice to a whisper, "You're lucky it wasn't YOUR head."

"Dummy, you failed first grade, dummy." Donnie made a face, taunting me.

Mama nudged me in the ribs, "Get down. You're too big now, it's too hot." She dumped me off and Donnie laughed.

I went over to my father and climbed onto his big knee. He let me stay there, kept on reading his newspaper, as if nothing had even happened. My mother looked over at us a few times; her head seemed to shrink down into her neck. That was the last time I ever got on her lap.

3.

For years my father worked on the house on weekends, when he was off from his regular job. He had to do everything himself—that's why it would take so long. Sometimes I watched him for hours, waiting to be needed, listening to the sound of him driving nails into the wood in three resounding plunks. He set up a rhythm that could almost put you to sleep, and then a nail would plink-off, and he'd swipe it away and there would be a pause before he started up again and got back into his pounding rhythm. Finally he'd stop and call out, jolting me out of my trance: "Get me that chisel over there, hurry up."

"What's a chisel?"

"It looks like a toothpick for dinosaurs."

I found it right away and handed it to him. He grinned and said what he always said, "There ya go."

He made me feel like his best ally. My brothers were not as close to him as I was, but I knew that was something I should never say to anyone. His own father had died in the first World War when he was a little boy, and fathering sons was confusing for him—my wild brothers scared him. I was easier, more pliable, and besides, he was the most important person in the world to me, and he knew it. He lifted up my heart, he always did.

I liked to watch his hands at work. They were usually chipped and bloody from all the things he did with them, but they were beguiling tools that smelled of machine oil and Cashmere Bouquet soap, and scratched my back every evening too, while he read the newspaper. He could even bake cakes and form pastry, and draw wonderful pictures, as well as make anything he wanted with those hands.

Most of all, he wanted to make our house hurricane-proof. To him, Miami was a magic place where a tropical jewel of nature had emerged from a primeval swamp. He said we weren't really pioneers, or pilgrims, we were tropists; but I thought that was just a word he made up. He was always making up words. He said we could learn to live in this tropic so long as we respected and outwitted our biggest enemy: the hurricane. So he drove steel rods down into the coral rock, and fitted cement blocks over the rods, poured concrete inside them, and set the house up three blocks high. He said because the house was up on pilings, the wind could circulate under it, and it wouldn't become a pressure box that might explode in the shear of heavy winds. It could sway with the wind, like a palm tree did. The shutters were hinged and had latches on them, to close over the huge windows during storms. It was one story with a sloping roof, lashed on with metal straps, and faced East and the Atlantic. All summer long we were cooled by the ocean's breezes coming in the huge windows.

He painted it white with aquamarine shutters, and named it The Sea Breeze. Mama said he should name it The Sticks, and she laughed like a banshee. She was trying to get him to knock down the outhouse because she was ashamed of it, but he wouldn't. He liked to go out there still, on Saturday mornings with his newspaper.

The Sea Breeze had polished hardwood floors and plaster walls dividing the rooms, all painted in crayon shades of green, blue and coral pink. All of the doorways had Roman arches with no doors on them, except mercifully the bathroom had a regular doorway with a door that you could push a button in and lock. My mother hung flowerdy curtains in the arched doorways of the three bedrooms and that was the only privacy. George Lincoln, which is my father's name—he was named after two presidents—told us solemnly that he didn't believe in closing doors within a family. He was after togetherness in his architecture, a unity of the Roman temple and the cozy Indian tepee.

My room was the smallest room in the house, but it had the biggest closet; you could walk through the closet and come out into the kitchen hall. Sometimes I hid in that closet, or escaped through it to get out the back door, and leave the house. When you're powerless you get sneaky.

In the ell of the living room there was an alcove with a built-in bookcase jammed with grown-up books like "The Barefoot Mailman," which I intend to read, soon as I learn how. There was a holly-green davenport, a silky maroon and cream-striped chair, and a mahogany drum table with the telephone on it. We sometimes listened on the party line. It was my favorite room in the house, the only peaceful room, where I could go to escape my mother's wrath and the "hitmosphere," which is what Donnie calls the space around him. If you get too close, you get hit.

18

The bookcase made me feel rich. In this room we watched sundowns, and played Big Casino. Sometimes my father showed us magic card tricks by the moon's light, long before there was any television in the world. It's the room where I would ride out our first hurricane and experience a sensational new kind of love.

4.

Our second September in Uleta, mama enrolled me and Donnie at Fulford Elementary public school, a short bus ride away. When I told my father my teachers' name, he laughed and mimicked me: "Mithsus Austin." I could hear my lisp, and feel my tongue popping through where my two front teeth were now missing. It surprised me so much I felt foolish and blushed. "At least you escaped the nuns." He whispered, trying to cheer me up.

My father's regular job was as a high iron worker. In the mornings, some of the men he worked with came by for him in a truck, carrying their aluminum hats and black lunchboxes and wearing stone brown, steel-toed work boots. They all had on dungarees and blue work shirts, with white t-shirts underneath, the same as my father wore. They were big, strong men, mostly Mohawk Indians who'd come down from Canada, all part of the same raising gang my father was in. The raising gang hoisted up the steel girders, set them in position and bolted them, so the fitting-up gang could come after them and get everything in plumb and bolt it some more to get ready for the riveting gang who came in and replaced all the bolts with red-hot rivets, buttonheaded with a pneumatic hammer—a bone-shaking job my father told me. He said he liked walking the naked beams five hundred feet in the air, pretending it didn't mean any more to him than walking on solid ground. He liked you to think he had some Indian blood in him too. Our bookcase included an old scrapbook of his family. They had lived in Rhinebeck, New York, up around the Hudson River since the 1750's and before that had come over from Tipperary, where his ancestors could be traced back to the king of Ireland, A.D. 148. I didn't really know if he was part Indian, although he could be; he had good instincts like an Indian.

I started to have a crush on one of the iron workers. My father said he was a Mohawk, whose Indian name, Oroniakete meant: He Carries The Sky. But no one could remember his Indian name so he was called Blackie. Probably because he had cat-black hair and black eyes, deep and shining. He was tall as my father, with high cheekbones and smooth walnut skin. I had never noticed before how handsome a man could be. My father didn't look handsome to me, even though he probably was. With his black hair, blue eyes and pink skin like mine, he just looked comfortable.

I daydreamed fuzzy, soft, floaty feelings about Blackie but couldn't make a picture in my mind of him and me close together touching, or anything like that. My insides just went squishy when I thought about him. When I found a stray tiger cat I kept it and named it Blackie. Then I pretended to talk to him all the time.

I took over mamas job of making lunch for my daddy, and always put in an extra sandwich and dessert for Blackie. I'd spread all the food out on the new formica table daddy had made with a built-in eating booth around it, and make Dagwoods, like I'd seen in the funny papers, with egg salad and tuna fish or thick bologna with lots of mayonnaise and cheese, onions and pickles and lettuce and tomato, and for dessert I'd make peanut butter and guava jelly, or cream cheese and grape jelly sandwiches, all wrapped up in double folds of waxed paper so they would keep good, and packed in daddy's black lunch box. I wished I could give them Rhubarb pie, but there wasn't any Rhubarb in Florida. Rhubarb was my daddy's favorite thing in the world and he was always talking about it, craving it. I guess I was courting my men with food. It must have been some kind of instinct. My mother watched me doubtfully, slurping her coffee, frowning and tsk-tsking away; I don't know whyever.

While the men waited for Daddy to finish his breakfast, I slipped outside, reeking of onions and peanut butter, and padded over the rocky driveway barefooted, to watch Blackie, who always sat on the running board of the truck whittling a piece of wood. He filled the cool, dewy mornings with Mohawk words mixed in with English, waiting for me to hear them. He was a peaceable man you could count on.

One morning my mother screeched out the window, rudely breaking into my bliss: "C'mere Lou! you get in here right this minute!" I didn't know what I'd done, but it had to be bad. I hobbled quickly across the driveway stones hurting my feet, but I didn't want Blackie to hear her yell any more like that. She was waiting in the doorway in her bathrobe, clucking her tongue. Even though I stood right before her, she still screamed, scalding my ears: "You shouldn't be going near grown men in your nightgown. It's disgraceful hanging

22

around outside like that. Don't you know you can see right through that flimsy thing?"

I was mortified. I hoped Blackie hadn't heard her, but I knew he had. Up to that time, I hadn't noticed my body much—it didn't bother me or get in my way any. Now it felt icky to have a body, like it had a meaning I was too dumb to know anything about.

I stopped making my father's lunch and he complained and begged me to start up again. But I wouldn't. My mother slapped a single slice of bologna between two pieces of bread with mustard on one side, and threw in a banana, hardly ever wavering. Let her keep on making his lunch if she wanted to so bad. Everything I did sooner or later made her nervous and mad. That's why I had to keep so much from her. Sometimes when I tried to tell her something she'd say: "That's neither here nor there." and she'd act disgusted with me. Or she'd say, "Speak up dearie, what is it you're trying to say?"

All through first grade, I passed it this time and that's about all I can say for it, and through the second grade which was no better, I watched Blackie from the window, keeping my distance. I wouldn't budge in the early mornings, but stayed in bed like my lazy brothers, peeking out the window to look for Blackie, until my father and the truck was gone and it was time to get up and get dressed for school. Fulford Elementary was a two-story, dark red-brick building. There was nothing open-air about it, and there were no tangerine trees either. It didn't matter though because after school I liked to get out and run and come alive again. My true nature came out then. I didn't like being folded in a chair all day

23

long or staying put in a line, either one. I was fluid and open and growing avid.

Blackie stopped coming around and I didn't see him anymore. The first of many loves to come and go—the very way of love demonstrating itself to me, although I didn't know it then. I preferred my tomcat Blackie anyway. He was easier and my mother left us alone.

5.

Although I knew I had a body, and now I had to keep it covered, I still didn't feel very solid. More like I was flying apart, air-soluble, like I was only floating in place. I had long, coppery hair—mama said it was my best feature, ignoring the fact that it's so red. She braided it and tied it up on my head every morning and called it my crown of glory. It embarrassed me, and soon after I left the house, if I remembered to, I took the braids down and plain let them hang. I was pink-complected with the kind of skin that always got sun-burned; I blushed if someone unexpectedly talked to me. I couldn't control it. I didn't like to be looked at either. My insides seemed exposed, because of my transparent skin, and I was sure everyone could read my thoughts.

All through the summer my freckles multiplied until I was almost one solid freckle, and in the winter they faded, and I got pale as waxed paper. It was like I had a skin disease. I grew more conscious of my skin than my hair even; for one thing I could feel my skin. My blazing red hair was different, and set me apart from other kids, except Andy—he wasn't much better off, except he was a boy at least.

Sometimes I felt like a pile of stones; if you kicked me, I scattered, inside. Donnie kicked me all the time. He thinks he has a right to do it just because I was born. But I'm trying to change all that by keeping away from him. He has a hair-trigger temper. Everyone in our family has a bad temper, but Donnie's is the one I'm most afraid of.

My mother billed herself as a big city girl from Boston where she was a sweater girl and a nurse. She said her family had come over on the boat, escaping the poverty the potato famine had caused, and it gave her a terrible fear of the poor house, wherever that was. We weren't supposed to tell anybody. "This doesn't go outside the family," mama said often when she told us things about her Boston family, or "this is a secret now, don't tell strangers."

The saddest part was about her sister Claire who had died of Diphtheria, but who had never stopped dying for mama. She brought her up from a deep dark well of memory and could hardly tell us about her before she'd get swamped in tears. And there would be a lilt in her voice almost like she was talking Irish only it was still English. Sometimes she'd sing Tor a lor a lora then, and it could make you cry.

That summer mama started taking me and Andy on the bus to downtown Miami. She liked the bus. She made Donnie stay home because he made trouble, and was always hitting. You didn't have to do anything to get hit. If he just felt like it, he hit you. And however hard he hits you, you're not hurt. He's blameless. I think he's crazy. I feel sorry for him though, and sometimes my heart aches because he hates me so much.

Downtown we always did the same things. First we ate lunch at the S & W Cafeteria, where I got the macaroni and cheese and green Jello with cream, and Andy got chili and chocolate cake. We walked around and looked in the

26

windows, and finally my mother stopped and studied her reflection in a store window. She patted her soft brown hair in place, opened her eyes wide, licked her middle finger a couple of times and rubbed it across her eyebrows so they'd show up better. She touched the corner of her hanky with her tongue and dabbed at me and Andy's faces to clean the food off. Andy squealed in protest. I liked how her spit smelled like her Coty's face powder; even so, I always pulled away.

And then mama said, "Okay, let's head for Byrons now," and she held our hands a little harder and got this huntress look. She was street-smart way beyond downtown Miami's need for her to be. She said Byrons reminded her of Filenes in Boston, because the basement had wood floors and there were bells going off all the time. I wondered if it smelled the same too, sort of a stale cosmetic, rubbery smell, very pleasant and cool. She always liked to buy something in Byrons, even if it was just dishtowels. If she went downtown alone while we were in school, she'd bring home pajamas for everyone. She was big on pajamas. She said she never had any when she was a kid. She had to wear old ragged hand-me-down dresses to bed.

After Byrons, we went straight home. On the bus ride she seemed let down and lost in memories, her brown eyes wistful. I sat across from her and thought; if only she could see how pretty she is, she'd never feel sad again, and she wouldn't need to scream and holler so much. I never asked her what was wrong because I was scared she'd tell the whole bus. Anything to do with someone in my family always seemed to be about me too. Especially my mother—it was like

27

I was her as well as myself. All Her emotions were loud and raw and full of gusto. They surprised and baffled me all the time, and made me want to keep very still to balance her out. She had resentment—a bitter memory, about something missing or regretted, that made her dislike her own children. Anyhow, that's how I felt.

Just before we got off the bus mama said, "Now don't tell your father we went downtown." I don't know whyever. Also, I didn't know where Boston was, only that Uleta was a foreign place compared to Boston and that my mother was not adjusting. She told white lies and the bugs and heat tormented her. She always looked confused by the flat land covered with palmetto bushes everywhere around Uleta. There were thick stands of tall old pine trees too that went on for acres and acres, and random banyan trees that were for climbing and merciful shade, and palm, mango and avocado trees dripping with fruit. Some of Uleta was planted in rows of citrus groves, broken by barren flat scrub land with nothing on it but weeds and sandspur patches, or palmetto. There were hardly any houses. Daddy said because of the coral rock everything here would have shallow roots including us. He laughed about that.

Mama looked out the window at the glowing white light around our house, bewildered, and whined, "But where's the shade? there's no shade?" Mostly she stayed indoors all day long with the excuse of doing housework. She chain-smoked Chesterfields, read the *Ladies Home Journal* and wrote letters at the kitchen table to her older sister, Molly, in Boston, which she sometimes tried out on me first. I could hear a little better now, but I still read lips. One letter bragged about how clean the air and the ocean was and how nicely her hurricane-proof house was coming along. But when Daddy came home from work that night she started right in complaining about living in the middle of nowhere, and never mentioned how clean the air was. The only thing that calmed her down was this golden brown liquid she kept in a jelly jar on the top shelf of her clothes closet and took sips from whenever she needed to. It smelled like fruitcake.

In the front yard Daddy planted a ficus benjamina that would grow big fast and give generous shade. He circled the house with coconut palms, and named his little dory boat after mama: The Ellie-Nora. We planted a patch of strawberries, her favorite fruit. And finally my mother was cowed by love; she wouldn't leave us and go back up north even if she could.

6.

One moonless night a cow came up to the screened door in the kitchen while we were eating supper, peered in and "MOOOOOOED" LOUD. My mother screamed and we all scrambled over each other trying to get to the door to look. My cat Blackie screeched like a tiger and the cow trotted off. We rolled on the floor laughing. "Oh that's a good one," mama kept saying, with her legs crossed so she wouldn't wet her pants, "that's a hot one."

The next day there was a goat in our yard from out of nowhere. It was a windy, hot day in the middle of summer and you could see midget storm clouds squatting out over the Atlantic. Still, the goat couldn't have blown in. My mother was hollering for me to find out who it belonged to because it was wrecking her strawberry patch. "Get him the hell out of here!" she yelled. I think she suddenly felt threatened by wild animals she couldn't control. I didn't understand that. Compared to people, animals were so unthreatening they made me sleepy.

As soon as I took the goat in tow he tried to eat the rope, so I let it drop and he followed me, nibbling all the way on junk and weeds. I decided to give him a real treat and led him down the road to the guava bushes. Goat heaven. He sucked up ripe and rotting guavas off the ground while I marveled at his capacity, ate a few myself, and lost track of time.

Now the bouquet of guavas, especially rotting ones, is both beautiful and pungent as different layers of the gas reach your nose. I was in a nimbus of that scent, flying high on it, and thinking there is nothing so filled with life as the guava, when I noticed the goat looking like he had a watermelon in his belly. He'd stopped eating and was staring into space. I poked his belly. Hard as a watermelon.

I thought about the time my mother was picking out a watermelon at Badgers Grocery and she was poking them. Old man Badger said, "Lady, you can't tell a thing about a watermelon thataway. Ain't no watermelon I ever knowed poked back."

I led the goat away from the guavas fast. By now he was giving off a rough odor, enough to make your eyes water, and I had to stop a few times so he could return to the earth some of the digested guavas which had already skedaddled right on through him.

I decided to find Bicycle Bill. If I could get him to talk, he might tell me where this goat came from. Bicycle Bill was this man who wore too much clothing and practically lived on his bicycle. Even though he was probably old he had a young face that could have once been handsome and made you wonder why he went around like a bum. I had seen him pedaling along, with goats tied onto his bicycle, among other things. There was no hurry. I wanted to keep this goat as long as I could anyway.

A gentle sun shower was falling making everything sparkle. It was just enough to cool you off and make you feel like you were swimming in the air. I had a hunch Bicycle Bill lived around the guava bushes somewhere. Sure enough, there it was back in behind a banyan tree, a little shed covered with branches and scraps of rusty junk for camouflage. His bicycle leaned against the shed adorned with palmetto branches to hide it, except you could still see the wheels so it looked like a traveling bush. There was some lightning now and wind and little burps of thunder but the sun was still dazzling up there through the tickling raindrops. It was the rare atmosphere just before a storm and always excited me. I couldn't understand why nobody else was out enjoying this magic.

I stood across the street staring at the shed, afraid to go closer, afraid of crossing some invisible line of no return, where I would be sucked into Bicycle Bill's fearsome world forever. I knew if I stared long enough, he'd feel my eyes and come out. Directly he did, got on his bicycle, and pedaled right over to me. His big brown eyes covered my whole face like a wave of cold mud. I'd never been looked at like that before. His mouth was turned down at the corners in a tragic frown. I started jabbering nervously about how I'd found this goat and did he know where it came from? When I blushed, he yanked the rope from my hand and rode off with the goat in tow.

I ran after them. He never even turned around to see if I was keeping up. Down the lanes of dirt and black asphalt we went—it must have been miles—until finally we were in Ojus. Now Ojus was a place we thought of as just a spin-off of Uleta, only junkier. It was closer to the Oleta River, therefore more dangerous. Besides a scattering of tenant farmer houses, it consisted of three and a half square miles of pineapple patches, growing and ripening, squat to the ground. In Creek, which is the Seminole language, Ojus means juicy. Mostly, though, we looked down on Ojus—Uleta was the place.

Right beside the pineapple patch I could see a whole goat herd sloppily fenced in with some chicken wire. About thirty goats, a regular goat farm. Goats must not like pineapples or there wouldn't be a one left. I'd been to this place a few times before with my brothers and feasted on hot sweet pineapples and wallowed in the cool muddy ditches between the rows, but I'd never seen the goats here before.

I pranced right over, determined to show Bicycle Bill I had followed and was not afraid of him. And that's when I saw Goatman for the first time. He seemed to come out from underneath the goats until I saw his low wagon parked in amongst them, and realized he'd been sitting up under there trying to keep dry. He was a short little man with burlap sacks draped around his shoulders for a raincoat, and a long beard the color of goat hair. There was a lumpy person under there with him but she covered herself completely over with burlap sacks, and I couldn't see who she was. I knew it was a woman though because I heard her tingaling voice.

Although Bicycle Bill hadn't spoken one word that I knew of, Goatman seemed to know everything and walked right over to me and took my two hands in his and thanked me gratefully for finding his goat. That's when I saw he had yellow eyeballs like a goats, and he smelled fragrantly of goats too. He took the rope from Bicycle Bill, untied it, and smacked the goat on the rump so it jumped inside the fence with the others. Then he showed me his wagon which had pots and pans and all kinds of stuff hanging on it, falling out of it, dented from goat nibblings. A sign on the side said: PREPARE TO MEET THY GOD. The lump wiggled around but she didn't come out.

He led me over to a group of baby goats who were bouncing and strutting around while their parents gazed blankly. He gave a command that sounded like "Andalay, Andalay!" and the baby goats jumped up high and turned full circles before they landed. Goatman laughed heartily, so I laughed with him. Bicycle Bill pierced us both with his brown mud eyes and then turned and rode away like he was disappointed about something.

Goatman talked in a loud southern drawl thicker than anything I had ever heard before: "Ever year I come down from Nawth Calina. I come through Dallas, Georgia, and Mayretta on Highway 120, and on down through Macon, seein' lots of folks. Twenty of these here goats pulls my wagon and more git born on the way. It takes a long time to get here and then a long time to get on back. You wont to know why I do it?"

Goats nibbled at my dress and licked my legs for salt. I was afraid one would just bite out a big chunk of my leg before I knew it so I had to keep jumping and darting away from them. I hollered, "Why?... okay, whyever?" not because I was so curious to know, but because I saw he had to tell me, and that was the only way to wrap things up and get out of there.

"Well, we are sin-strippers, these little goats and me," he said, with confidentiality in his voice. "The Bible tells of atonement, how God took a bundle of human sins off man's back, tied it to a goat, and sent the scapegoat to a solitary land. That's where we're at now. In the very act of forgiving in Florida. Our job, and we're a doin' it, is stripping man of his sins, forgiving him and finding a new way of looking at someone who's done wrong. You see?"

I said yes, I did, and thanked him and left out of there, quick as I could, my legs tingling with goatspit. It got clearer to me as I walked toward home. Goatman had a job to do, one he'd found himself that nobody else was doing. It might look funny but that's because it was deeper, not easy to see or understand like Daddy's job which at the time was putting the top on the Columbus Hotel in downtown Miami.

When I was about halfway home, angry clouds started gathering overhead, like the hot-dark beginning of a big squall. Loud thunder claps jolted me and a heavy rain started pounding down. Usually I didn't mind walking in the rain because I knew I was waterproof, like my father said. But this time, a wind came up that I could hardly walk against. The trees were bent double. Things were flying by me. Could this be one of his famous hurricanes? When it began to really rage, I started thinking about taking shelter somewhere for a little while, until it blew over and I could get home. It got so bad I ran up to the next little hut of a house I saw. A woman's skinny arm jerked me in through the door, disgusted with me for being out in that storm, calling me a little lost sheep out of the fold. She made me get under her kitchen table where

35

her three daughters were already huddled. Then she knelt over it with her hands pressed together and led us in prayer: "Our Father, who art in heaven..." We all knew that one and said it together. Then she started reading scripture from the Bible and pounding on the table, sobbing. Pretty soon she was rearing up and slapping her palms on that table, throwing back her head and begging the Lord to please SAVE us. Her voice rose in volume until she was as loud as the storm, and then she went completely berserk and screamed: "Oh my su-weet, su-weet Jesus, SAVE us NOW, DE-LIVER us,"

The wind whipped at the windows and rain poured from the heavens pelting the roof. I thought the world must be ending. I'd never witnessed such a reaction to a natural storm before and I was scared, not about the storm, but of this woman. I tried to escape out from under the table but her daughters gently held me back. They knew their mother wouldn't let me just run on home now, as I had a mind to do. So we all shivered under there together.

When it thundered she got worse, yelled like she was hurt, beseeched the Lord and wailed her disappointment in him when the storm kept on going. I thought she was crazy to think that would work on a storm. And of course, it didn't and I saw I was going to have to ride this whole thing out under that table. I felt sorry for her daughters who were silent, embarrassed. They seemed sorry for me too, witnessing insanity maybe for the first time, while they were used to it. We didn't have to talk much to understand each other.

One of the girls was a three-year-old they called baby Linda. Another of the girls was folded over in a much larger body than usual, and the third girl seemed ordinary sized like me, only a couple of years older. The large girl said her name was Shelby. I said my name, Louise, and the older girl said hers, Rene. Baby Linda said "Boo" and covered her face with her hands. We huddled together underneath that table for a long time trembling, while their mother and the storm raged over our heads.

Shelby said she was a giant like her father, the Great Earl Wauldin, who worked in the Barnum & Bailey circus. He was seven feet four inches and still growing. They looked modestly at my face for some reaction. Shelby was eight, like me, and already looked to be about twice my size. Her hands were large and chapped, and dangled, like she didn't know what to do with them. In her bigness she was fragile somehow, like a straw scarecrow. In a little bit I said to her: "Will you please scratch my back? It makes me feel better."

And this calm giantess tenderly scratched my back for a long while and I relaxed. The storm started to ebb, so I knew everything would fall back into place. "Where's your daddy?" I asked, and Rene said, "He ain't here; if he was, she wouldn't be a-doin' all that." She poked her thumb up at her mother, rolled her eyes, and went on telling more about her family.

When it was nearly over, Mrs. Wauldin collapsed on her bed and fell into a deep sleep. We crept out from under the table. I started for home wondering if the storm had blown any other animals into our yard. Outside the sun was blazing and tree branches were scattered everywhere. The air was bright, washed fresh and clean as glass. We stood under trees rattling the branches flicking rainwater on each other to cool off, giggling, trying to forget about Mrs. Wauldin. Shelby and Rene took turns carrying baby Linda, and walked me home so they could see where my house, called The Sea Breeze was at.

When I got home my own mother was taking an afternoon nap—her hand moving rhythmically under the covers. No doubt she had slept through the whole thing, which was like her. She knew better than to try to stop a storm, that's for sure, and I was glad of that.

"Where were you?" she called out to me groggily, "I was worried about you."

"Oh, I was at a new friend's house," I answered, covert as ever. But there was no way I could have told her about Goatman and the Wauldins' because then she would have gotten alarmed and warned me about being careful who I associated with and who was influencing me and all that, and then her panic might build until she went berserk too. I wasn't up to another one of those that day.

Mrs. Wauldins' religion was like a storm, and I was attracted, fearfully so, like a duck might be to thunder. I wanted to hide from it and peek out at the same time. My heart pounded just thinking about the intensity of Mrs. Wauldins' plea. Blackie purred and chugged loudly as I told him about where I'd been and all that had happened. He could feel the same excitement I was feeling. He was big and thick, more like a tiger than a cat. He made passes by my face, rending the air with his substance and thunderous purr. Most of the time we communicated without words. I thought about how animals don't care about words or sins or religion. They don't care about anything unless it's alive, or they can eat it.

I decided Shelby was going to be my best friend from then on. She needed me. I wouldn't be able to take her home because she was too big and my mother would stare and ask her too many questions, like what descent was she? mama always wanted to know everybody's descent—and then she might start talking about glands and medical stuff and take down her nursing books. I didn't want all that. I already knew that Shelby and Earl were pituitary giants and that they'd grow until they died. Rene explained it to me under the table. I hoped it took a long long time no matter how big they got. I felt safe around Shelby. I'd like to see my brother Donnie try and get me in a headlock with her around. She could pick him up with one hand if she took a notion to.

7.

Every day during that long summer I went out with the expectation that something good was gonna happen to me. My brothers and I left home early in the morning and wandered around all day in the continuous heat, exploring paradise. And I had the same argument with mama everyday, before I could go.

"Where do you think you're going?"

"Up to Uleta, with them." I meant my scowling-to-get-moving brothers who would never let me hang around with them, but had enough sense to keep quiet about it now.

"But you're just a girl!"

"So what! I can do anything they can." This to my brothers was outrageous bunkum. To my mother, it was highfalutin, vain even. But I knew she secretly liked it when I talked big.

"Well, you stay with them, Miss Smarty Pants. I don't like you wandering around all by yourself, and where are your shoes?"

"It's too hot for shoes."

"You're turning into a Florida cracker, don't even know the value of shoes. You'll get worms in your feet. Put your shoes on, all of you."

It was her duty to say that, but she'd given up, and knew we wouldn't keep them on for very long. Soon as we were out of sight, we hid our shoes behind a bush and went on.

We had worn our own shortcut, by tromping through the palmetto bushes to get to Badger's Grocery and the Youth Center up in Uleta. It was a test to get through the hot sand, choke-full of stickers. Sometimes we pretended it was quicksand and the object was to run through it as fast as possible, planing just an inch above the ground. Now and then there was a green snake basking across the sunny middle of the path to jump over or try to go around. Every kind of bug seemed to be waiting to ambush us. Hoppers and lizards and palmetto bugs big as Baby Ruth bars. Donnie said Bicycle Bill roasted them over a fire and ate them for supper. When I believed him he laughed. "You dumb cluck," he said and put both his hands on my wrist, twisted them in opposite directions, and gave me an Indian burn. I couldn't wait to get away from him.

As soon as we got through the shortcut, we split up and I headed over to Shelby's. She was helping me figure out what everything meant and who I was in the scheme of things. She had a whole different point of view than anyone else because she was already sure of who she was. She was a giantess.

Shelby and I started walking all around Uleta, holding hands, pretending we were invisible. We practiced how we would fade into the background, or disappear in the middle of a group of people should we ever come upon one. We moved very slowly when we played this game which we called "Fade." If we saw someone coming down the road we could evaporate into thin air, even Shelby big as she was could do it. This game usually began after we had been eating guavas. Guavas made you think you could leave your bodily concerns behind.

Shelby's peaceable brown eyes reminded me of my mother's in a picture she kept in her bureau drawer, from when she graduated from the Bayonne School of Nursing in 1938. She had on a white uniform and a white cap with a little black ribbon running around it, and she stared out calmly, untroubled. She must have been different before she had her children, quiet and tranquil, like a queen. Maybe she was happy then.

Behind Shelby's house there was a ramshackle storage hut that became our playhouse. There was an old black trunk inside, and one day we broke it open and found damp, mildewy clothing, heavy wool, silk and satin from another time and a much colder place. It was all black stuff, ancient like I imagined graveclothes, with pearl and clear-glass buttons, and a few dull-colored neckties. There were black shoes and hats and purses, all very old-fashioned and dour. Shelby said they were her parents' clothes from when they were first married. Mrs. Wauldins' dresses fit me perfectly because she was so skinny, but they dragged the ground when I walked, even with her high heels on. The only things that fit Shelby belonged to her father; an old black tuxedo with suspenders that buttoned onto the pants, a tall hat, elevator shoes that were too big, with five-inch soles that made her loom up there even higher. When you're a giant you can never be too tall. After putting the clothes on and off a few times they softened up; the mildewy smell bloomed and became a stimulus for our pretendings.

Rene and baby Linda played dress-up too, and one day Rene brought in a new girl named Sandy Yates who thought up the idea of makeup. She was ten, like Rene, and pretty too. It took all morning for everyone to be ready at the same time, but the last thing was the makeup, and Sandy put it on us one by one. First some talc for face powder, then cherry juice for lipstick. She stuck her hand out the window and plucked the cherries from a Surinam bush, where a stray goat was grazing. The Surinams were big that year. Real lipstick was forbidden in the Nazarene church which they all belonged to. So we worked around that.

When we were all ready, Sandy said, "Let's tote baby Linda on over to the house now." When she said it, I turned around too fast and said, "What?" Shelby laughed softly and explained in her kindly voice, "Lou likes words." That was the first I thought about it, but I guess she was right, I did.

"Well, anyhow, let's carry her then," Sandy said sleepily, tieing a musty necktie around the goats neck.

And so we walked, or it was more like we straggled together down the road like a black swarm, a punk of mourners, under that red-hot sun, leaning on each other and passing baby Linda, who barely even said boo, among ourselves, toting her, stopping to stick hibiscus behind our ears and the goat's, and tearing the flowers apart, sucking the stamens for honey. Along the way we lunched on more cherries, guavas, and mangos, sashaying onward, getting all fruit-sticky and sweltry hot in our woolly, velvety black raiment.

By the time we got to the Yates household, we had run Mrs. Wauldins' shoes over at the heels, collapsed the arches

43

and had them slung over our shoulders so we were barefooted again, our footskins frying on the pavement.

The Yates lived in a rickety old wood house with lots of add-ons and a run-down yard, across from a cow pasture. It was surrounded by orange and grapefruit groves. They came from Alabama. Sandy said her daddy was a carpenter during the week and a lay preacher on Sundays. We sat in their dark, cool kitchen at a huge table that took up three-quarters of the room, and was covered with a slick, faded oilcloth, topping off our fruit lunch with saltines skimmed across with Blue-Plate mayonnaise, and ice water in jelly glasses. Lots of little boys wandered in one by one and joined us at the big table—bare, brown-chested boys with raggedy pants that were cut off above the knees and feet so coated with dust they were furry looking. They looked related but there were too many the same age to all be Yates. Still, Mrs. Yates fed them all in her gracious way, that made you think you were hers too—all children were hers to feed. Sandy had a couple of older sisters, but they were usually at work or out on dates.

I started going to Sunday night revivals at the Higher Ground Nazarene Church with the Wauldin family, and all the Yates'. Mr. Yates did his preaching at the Higher Ground. Everyone went, except "THE TALL DARK AND HANDSOME EARL WAULDIN"—that's how Shelby's father billed himself. He didn't like church. Just like my father. Shelby told me he had gone over to Fulford Elementary once and complained that her desk was too small. She was embarrassed and proud at the same time, that he took up for her. I was a little afraid of Earl Wauldin, of his huge size, but Shelby said he was just a gentle giant, quiet and easy-natured as a cat.

We walked to church—it was around two corner blocks, behind the Wauldins' house. We wore a shortcut through their backyard because sandy dirt was a few degrees cooler than black tar and we didn't have any shoes on. We could go barefoot to church, but we had to wear dresses—shorts weren't allowed.

It smelled like Easter lilies and daddys shellac inside the church. There were big fans on so it was breezy and cool, until things got started good, and it heated up, and filled, slap to the walls, with sweaty people, all hopped up about something. First there was singing, a tinny piano, tons of singing. Songs that turned over and over again until my ears felt drugged: "Do Lord, oh do Lord, oh do remember me; oh Lordy, do Lord oh do Lord oh do remember me; look awaaaaay beyonnnnnd the blue." I sang it too, endlessly, and fell into a kind of song trance for awhile, until the yelling began.

Everybody had just been getting primed up with that singing, for the joyful noise and shouting out yet to come. It was suspenseful, starting slow and building up like that. Some of it was dim, in a language I'd never heard before, and wasn't hearing too good now. They were probably making it up, with wrought-up actions to match. Soon, everybody started beseeching the lord like Mrs. Wauldin had done in the storm, yelling, pleading, braying at God. Then a call went out for all sinners to come forth and be saved. People got down on the floor and rocked back and forth crying, losing their breath, and rolling up the aisles to the front, where Mr. Yates,

45

who was called brother, and another preacher-brother were saving them by slapping their foreheads, stirring them up even more.

The brothers hollered: "Volunteers, come forward and give your life to Jesus. Forget your past sins and give all your burdens to Jesus, and he'll carry them for you."

It sounded good. One night when I was beset real good I went forward with all the others. I waited in a long line of people that was swaying and sobbing, on the way to getting saved. When it was my turn the brothers looked down, laid their hands on me and called me Little Roman Sister, declaring me saved just in the nick of time. Some of the faithful were even crying and I could see they all felt sorry for me. They called me a Papist volunteer, whatever that was—I started feeling more like a victim. The cluster of sweaty people was suffocating as they pumped my hand one after another and squeezed me hard. I didn't like being congratulated for doing something everybody else was doing too. I blushed red as a Surinam cherry.

Shelby took my hand and led me back to our seat. Now the church was stifling hot, and my neck hurt. Shelby said I was just resisting Jesus. I crawled on the bench in the midst of it all, rested my head in Shelby's lap and fell out, while everything around me swirled.

When I woke up Baby Linda was getting dunked under water. The blue velvet curtain had been pulled aside, and behind the pulpit there was a little square swimming pool, deep and spooky looking. The regular preacher stood in water up to his waist, holding Baby Linda, dressed in a white dress, under the water while he prayed. I couldn't help squirming in my seat and grunting for him to hurry and pull her up. Shelby whispered: "It's okay, it's her penance, for original sin."

Baby Linda's arms and legs were thrashing as she tried to grab the curtains, anything, to get up. It definitely put the fear of God before her in the form of the fear of drowning. When he finally brought her up, she coughed and yowled and swung at him and I didn't blame her one bit. For her past sins, now she was baptized clean, the preacher said. I wanted to ask what past sins? But I kept quiet.

The pulpit and the pool gave me the willies and conjured up images of the coldness of the rock pit where I sometimes swam with my brother's, and other kids too, even though we weren't supposed to. Once I'd almost drowned there, and Donnie had pulled me out just before I went unconscious. I remember it was a pleasant experience once I started to give in to it. But afterward, when I was alive again, I was shocked at the thought of death getting so close to me. I didn't want Baby Linda to be afraid of drowning, but what could I do? a little redheaded cracker girl.

When everyone started hollering again, praying forcibly, like Mrs. Wauldin, I said goodby to Shelby and slipped out of the church, longing for home. To my great relief, it wasn't dark yet. Naturally, I had been sneaking out to church all this time, even attending Vacation Bible School weekday mornings with Shelby and them, where we did my favorite thing: art. The church my mother sometimes took us to didn't have Vacation Bible School and, besides, you couldn't walk to it.

I dreaded the questions I might face if my brothers were already home before I got there. They could go wherever they wanted and no one cared. I envied the freedom boys had. There was less heat to take if I wasn't the last one coming in for the night, so usually I wasn't, but this time I got caught. My mother knew, I don't know how, but she did—she was waiting for me. My weary heart went right into my mouth as she dragged it out of me like a confession, that I'd been going over to the Nazarene Church.

"Holy Mother of God! You're a Catholic!" she shrieked. "It's a sin to go outside the one true Church." Right off, I didn't believe it was a sin. Whyever would God, who was good, make some people sinners just by the church they happened to be going to?

"Where does it say that in the Bible?" I mumbled. She slapped me across the face. Tears hazed my eyes, but I stood before her and tried to keep my face as blank as I could while she hollered her answer: "In the EYES of the CHURCH! In the eyes of the church." She emphasized her answer by saying it loud the first time and repeating it in a whisper the second time, like it was secret information. Just the way she ground that word EYES out, and the way she emphasized CHURCH like it was the highest court of judgment on Earth sent shivers down my spine.

But I wasn't buying it.

From his chair, my father rolled his eyes and winked at me. He knew I was a rounder and a sneak, but he admired me anyway. I saw my mother was afraid of the Catholic Church as if it had secret powers. I didn't like her wanting me

48

to have the same fear she had—or any idea that came with so much force. It made me feel sick to my stomach and even more determined to believe whatever I wanted to.

What would my mother do if she knew I'd been saved and now belonged to Jesus instead of her? What kind of sin was that in the eyes of the church? I heaved a heathenish sigh and looked up at the ceiling.

"Don't be so fresh. You don't even know anything dearie." She shook her finger in my face. My father rattled his newspaper, his way of slowing her down without butting in.

I had to promise to stop going to the Higher Ground, but I was finished with it anyway. I did not believe God wanted me to get so panicky about him, like Mrs. Wauldin and them did. Sitting in the Nazarine church I had realized how different our family was. My face must have shone with sadness, because people had looked at me with pity.

A new song I'd heard at Vacation Bible School kept running through my mind: "Jesus wants you for a sunbeam, a sunbeam, a sunbeam." I thought that was a way I might be useful, if I could just figure out what one was and how to be it, all day long.

After that, mama started taking us to mass every sunday and catechism afterwards which was questions and answers like: Who made me? God made me. Who made God? God made himself. We were in training for first holy communion.

At the dinner table, Donnie suddenly started turning into the Lone Ranger. His hands galloped across the table, fingers intertwined like a rider straddling a horse, the horse whinnying up in the air while the Lone Ranger rocked up with him. Donnie's fingers did a horse and rider dance to his own hummed rendition of the William Tell overture: da num, da num, da nun ta ton, da num, da num. . . And we all laughed and got our hands on the table too, trying to do it as good as Donnie. Especially my father thought it was funny, and to Donnie that was love and approval—it was the kind of attention he always craved.

So Donnie started doing it every night, enlisted Andy and me as Tonto and the enemy and we all traipsed across the dinner table da-numming away, my father roaring. Until one night we knocked over a glass of milk and mama yelled with a pent-up fury that took my breath away, all directed at Donnie: "What did you do that for? Look what you started, you're always making trouble, you're driving me crazy!" She slammed her fist down on his plate of hamburg, spinach and mashed potatoes and said, "Eat! Just eat! I'm going to have a nervous breakdown because of you." Then she ran from the table crying.

Donnie started crying softly, blinking so a piece of spinach would drop off his eyelash. He kept his rider mounted and finished the overture in a low broken voice, riding up the back of his seat.

My father rolled his eyes and started chewing his food harder, clamping his huge mandibles down, making a loud noise so she'd hear it all the way back in the bedroom.

I got the dishrag and started mopping up the milk. I felt sick, so I told myself this was just my family. There was a whole nother world out there.

8.

One day Andy said he wanted to show me something. I knew it was a person because Andy sort of collected people. They liked him because he was quiet and shy. He took me over to Marie's yard, right around the corner from our house. I had watched the building of this row of little boxy houses so close to our own and was excited about having neighbors, although my daddy wasn't.

It was plain to see that Marie doted on Andy; she tousled his curly red hair and made him blush terribly. It was as if he were turning me over to Marie to take his place, giving her a substitute. He liked her and didn't want to waste her, but she was too demonstrative for him to bear. We weren't used to displays of affection like Marie's.

She oozed, "golly day, aren't you the sweetest thing!" and attempted to pick my brother up but he ran off. "He's so cute I could just eat him up," Marie said.

I knew as she beheld me, that even with all my blushing and shyness I was a cooler cookie than my brother, and Marie underneath her gushing might be worth a closer look. She had Jesus sandals on her feet for one thing, and her long thin legs had good tone and shape. She wore tailored shorts, and hitched up in a halter top just like Carmen Miranda's were large breasts. As my eyes traveled over her body, I had the certain knowledge that mine would be like that some day too. Her face was framed in short, brunette curls I would later find out were the result of something called a Toni home permanent wave. Her face had red, patchy places covered over with a flesh colored cream, tiny beads of sweat, and something else: freckles, lots of pale brown freckles, just like mine, in full bloom, all over her.

It was 1949. The aqua-painted cement-block bungalow she lived in was brand new. Beside the walk leading to the front door was an inky blue gazing globe mounted on a concrete pedestal. Marie said if an evil spirit starts to enter her house he sees his own reflection in the gazing globe and is frightened away. That was the first time I'd heard anyone mention them out loud. I knew there were evil spirits. I just knew it. They were in the world invisibly, but if they could get inside people, like Donnie and mama, I guess they could get inside houses too.

Marie knelt down and finished digging out weeds with her spade while I watched. All around the house she had planted beautiful hibiscus flowers in assorted colors. Radio voices floated out the open windows: "'Gone with the Wind' will forever be the longest playing movie in the world," the announcer said, and he played the theme song, "My Own True Love." It wafted over the airwaves and Marie sang along, while I swooned beside her at the romantic sounds. When it was over, Marie looked at me with tears in her eyes. "Oh, to hell with the wind," she said. Then she stood and pulled off her gloves. "Golly day, I don't know how you keep yourself up, you're such a little bird. Let's go in now. The sun's too hot."

She poured us "Co-colas" in tall glasses over ice. She acted like it was a tonic for my growth. We never had Coke at home because my mother said it was bad for our teeth and made us drink milk instead. Coke was exotic to me. So was Marie's cool, clean house. I'd never seen such a spotless place. I had assumed dirt was everywhere, I was surrounded by it in its many forms—scum on sinks and bathtubs, the dirty sour laundry, stained mattresses, stinking garbage pails, dusty dirt roads, everything rusting, and the gritty heat. It all added together to give me a feeling of being dirty myself sometimes, even though I was not. Every evening I washed my feet before I went to bed. The rest of my body didn't seem to need it as often but I couldn't sleep without washing my feet first.

My mother hated housework and she always did it in a big hurry with a scowl on her face. Once when she was vacuuming, a bloody pad dropped on the floor. She just picked it up and jammed it up under her dress again and went on vacuuming. There was terrible peril in being a woman, and having to put up with a leaking body was the part I dreaded most. But Marie seemed to have it all under control, and even to enjoy a simple purity and order inside her little oasis. It was heaven to go there, like going to Carmen Miranda's house.

That first day she started right in teaching me how to sew on her black Singer pedal machine. I made a halter top by sewing two rows of casing across a strip of cloth and threading elastic through them with a safety pin and then gathering it all together in a little band that I could slip over

53

my head and wear across my flat chest, the coolest way in the world to cover my button-sized nipples. She made me shorts to match. I retired my hot dresses and went over more and more to shorts and halter tops as I got on to the knack of making them from Marie's bright-colored scraps. She made sets for herself that matched mine, only her halter tops were more complicated: two big cloth diamonds with straps that tied up around her neck and across her back like a harness.

Marie had been an acrobat, a dancer, and a trapeze artist, before she retired to marry her most recent husband, Gus. She showed me a picture of herself, taken when she was a nineteen-year-old belle, swaging a silky, black fringed shawl between her long bare arms in a dancing pose. The picture had been taken in Atlanta, Georgia behind the house Marie was born in.

"I grew up sitting on laps." She said with a faraway look in her eyes.

In the picture, her creamy, bare shoulders and the way she gazes over them hinted that she was naked underneath the shawl. What I thought was: Even people with freckles can be dancers. I was overjoyed because that's what I wanted to be. She knew the Wauldin family from her days in the circus and she loved Shelby too, just like I did.

Soon Marie was teaching me acrobatics. Whenever she was concentrating she filled her cheeks with air, making them round like a blowfish, and then slowly she'd let the air escape. It was how she practiced patience. She did it when we were sewing too. As I learned more, she did the blowfish less. Every day, while her supper cooked on the stove—it had to be ready the minute Gus got home—we got out in her side yard behind the fushia bougainvillaea that ran riot up a trellis, and she taught me.

First she stretched me: as I leaned against the house standing on one leg, she took the other one and raised it up higher each day until I could get it over my head and touch the back wall. Gradually I became as limber as a flamingo's neck. Splits became my specialty. I could do front and side splits, walking splits and rollover splits. I had flips and cartwheels down pat too. Backovers were harder. That's where you do a backbend and then flip over and when you get good you do about four in a row, fast, so you look like a wheel rolling backwards over bumps.

The bougainvillaea gave the yard privacy from the street, so whenever Gus came home from work I ducked into the kitchen and then out the front door, as he came in the kitchen door.

Once I didn't make it, so I hid behind a chair in the living room and tried to listen to the conversation while they ate dinner. Marie talked about her sister Skeeter and what she had done all day long in the house. I didn't hear her mention me. Gus never said anything—he just grunted, while Marie chattered away as if she was there to entertain him, whether he appreciated it or not.

She told Gus her real name was Lilly Marie, and she laughed her high-lilting laugh: "I was named after both my grandmas. Why they'd lay that on an innocent baby I don't know. Just as soon they'd 'a named me Minnie."

55

I giggled, and Gus said, "What was that?" Then he came over and caught me as I attempted to dart out the door.

"Oh, that's just little Lou, she lives across the street." Marie seemed nervous.

Gus picked me up and sat down in his big lounge chair, plopping me on his lap. "Well, well, what have we got here," he said, tickling my chin, his big face grinning so close I could smell his stewy breath. When I blushed horribly, he loosened his grip and I jumped up and ran. Marie covered my flight by saying, "You run on home now, honey, your mama wants you for supper."

After that, I made sure I kept my distance from Gus. I didn't like a person who thought he could grab me up like that just because he was bigger.

9.

Marie was a bountiful teacher who passed along on the wing all she knew, and I was glad to have her. So far, my knowledge had not come from school but from out in the world, from people. God had not been in church, but outside in nature, in superabundance.

God's creation was unmistakable to me the first time I climbed a turpentine mango tree and hung in the cool thick branches like the primate I was and picked a ripe, juicy mango, dropped out of the tree, sat beneath its shade and sloshed my face in hot, sweet mango meat, getting all sticky, stained orange, and sated with an almost drugged contentment; then finding a spigot in someone's yard and washing up, the cold water drying instantly in the hot sun— and it was unmistakable the first time I saw Lentini too.

I had dallied up to the Uleta post office to get the mail for my mother. She was always hoping for a letter from her sister Molly in Boston. The post office was on the Golden Glades Road, where the rest of the stores, like Badgers Grocery, were too. I crossed the two-laner and looked through the large plate glass window as I entered, and there he was—an old, but handsome and dignified man, wearing a brown suit in all this heat, and sitting on a stool by himself reading his mail. I must have surprised him because he jumped up and hurried out, the stool following after him. And that's when I saw that what he had been sitting on was not a stool at all, but a third leg, brown-suited just like the rest of him.

I worked the combination on box 264, grabbed our mail and hurried out to follow him. He was way up ahead of me, his third leg bent and bopping in the air, like a tail with a shoe on it. I ran to catch up, and then I saw Bicycle Bill appear from out of the bushes and pedal protectively alongside the three-legged man. They seemed to know each other. Bicycle Bill was always given a wide berth when you passed him on the road. There was something fearsome in the dense loneliness that surrounded him like fog. It looked like he was carrying everything he owned on his bicycle: tools, pots and pans, baskets of food, rolls of clothing and blankets, trash pickings. He had a sign across the back like a license plate which said "FACTOTUM." It was like he'd found a word that belonged to him too, like all the other pieces of junk tied on his bicycle.

They stopped outside a gate, the three-legged man went in, and Bicycle Bill pedaled on up the road. As I drew nearer, I saw through the fence, behind high, thick weeds, a pretty little villa. It was a corner lot and when I came around the third side of the property a huge trailer-truck that I had never seen before loomed up, and painted on it in jovial letters was: THE GREAT LENTINI - THREE-LEGGED MAN - THE RINGLING BROTHERS BARNUM & BAILEY CIRCUS. I stared at the truck for a long time, wondering what was inside and what, exactly, happened at a circus. I'd heard about the circus from Marie, but had never been to one.

That night at the dinner table I asked what factotum meant. "No such word," my mother snapped, "you're dreaming things up again.

You been eating guavas?" Donnie said, and got me in a playful headlock and wouldn't let go until my father yelled at him. Then an argument broke out and finally Andy got out a dictionary and looked it up. It was a real word. It meant: a person employed to do all kinds of work.

"Oh sure, a jack-of-all-trades," declared my father.

So that's what Bicycle Bill was too, without being anything at all like my father. They didn't believe me when I said I saw a three-legged man either, and I wished I hadn't even told them. They all laughed, and Donnie resumed his headlock. I'd have to find out on my own about the circus. Then about a week later, after everyone in Uleta had seen Lentini too, they believed me.

By that time there had been sniggering in the post office when he came in, and kids hiding in there to make fun of him. I knew who they were, Platts and Whitfields, and I didn't like any of them. They lived up in Ojus and were all interrelated. One of them was named Didge Platt, because he was always in trouble and his mother was always asking him, "Didge you do that?" So after awhile she just called him Didge. His real name was Donnie, same as my brother's. Donnie sometimes hung around with Didge and Charlie Whitfield, although I don't know whyever, and I wished he wouldn't.

Charlie Whitfield's father, who we called old man Whitfield, called everybody Pie Face, like he couldn't remember even one single name. He was a wino, always staggering and slumping up against the post office where he slept. He had an indelible appearance of sottishness that never changed. I always walked widely around him. Otherwise he'd give me his pitch which he used on everyone: "Excuse me, Pie Face, I need your help. Some a your money too. Now, I ain't a gonna lie to you, I'm gonna spend it on whiskey. You wouldn't believe me if I said I was savin' up to go to college anyway, would you?" He'd laugh, showing a green mossy mouth, and huff at you so you got a big waft of his poison gas breath.

Charlie Whitfield and Didge Platt always had wounds and bruises on their bodies, in various stages of infection and healing. For sport, they rode off the roof of the Youth Center on their bicycles and landed, sometimes perfectly, on the basketball court below. When they didn't land so good their antiseptic was spit. "Put some spit on it," they'd say, "spit heals."

Sometimes Donnie was up on the roof with them—watching—he wadn't that crazy. Besides, they wouldn't let him use their bicycles anyhow. He learned bad things from them though, like how to squirt a string of spit through his teeth and how to chew tobacco, and how to piss the farthest.

Once I heard old man Whitfield try to panhandle his own son, with the same old pitch. After Charlie refused, the old man asked pitifully, "Then what am I gonna do about this bump on my head?" Charlie kicked him in the leg, looked into his eyes real hard and said, "NOTHING. Just wait until it busts and kills you." Oh I didn't like any of them.

But I was curious about Lentini, and one day not long after I'd first seen him, while I was staring through the weed-covered fence at his house, the french doors opened and before I had a chance to run away a white-haired lady walked right over to me carrying a tray of teacups. She caught me gawking like a goat and I badly blushed. I couldn't even tell what she was saying, my head was so on fire. I was being invited in to tea. She opened the gate and beckoned to me. Tea? Kindness was out in the world too, just as wild as evil. I had never been to tea and thought it was a made-up thing from *Little Women* which my aunt Molly in Boston had sent me to read, a book that presented a whole other foreign world to me, far different from Uleta.

She laid the tea tray on a glass table outside the open french doors. We sat in cold iron chairs that looked like they were cast from grape vines, sipped from delicate china cups and ate triangles of toast with marmalade on them. I felt clumsy and exalted at the same time. Exalted is a word I learned from catechism class.

From where I was sitting, I could see that those weren't weeds by the fence at all, but a garden of beautiful wildflowers, backdropping this little patio, and giving it privacy. Faintly I could hear opera music coming from inside the house.

The lady had white hair, streaked with yellow, and a soft, furry upper lip to match. Although she was old and plump she had pink skin that looked velvety and she smelled like the Lavender soap mama got for Christmas. She wore a house dress, faded blue like her eyes, and told me she was

61

The Great Lentini's wife. I said my name, Lou, and felt ashamed by my own bulky nothingness. How could I tell her who I was when I had not become myself yet? I was practically invisible, and seeing her there where she belonged and fit so well made me realize it.

While she talked quietly about her flowers, every once in awhile, I'd catch a whiff of the inside of her house, cool, clean, and musty, like the insides of old books, combined with Marie's washed sheets flapping in the sun. I peered into the darkness of the living room, and made out the glow of white druggets on the furniture—I knew they were called druggets from *Little Women*. Where was The Great Lentini I wondered.

Mrs. Lentini said, "You know, my husband is physically different from you and me, but he has exactly the same feelings as we have. He's just a human being and he doesn't really like being treated differently. Our one regret is that we never had any children."

I wanted to volunteer, "I'll be your child, I'll protect him and watch out for him," my mind raced with possibilities, but my mouth was locked shut.

She went on: "He gets his feelings hurt so easily now, he's more sensitive to teasing since we found out about his heart condition, and since we've been back, some of the children around here have caused him great pain."

Oh, no God, did she think I was one of them? When I'd have married him too in a minute? I held still and bore up, hoping with my silence and a dignity I'd actually copied from Mrs. Lentini to melt any suspicion in her mind.

But she started crying softly, and her voice rose as she told me, "They threw sticks at him, and chased him up a tree and kept him treed there while they taunted him. He won't come out of the house now, it's been two weeks." Then she gasped: "One of them peed on his leg." She broke down and sobbed while I sat there dumbly. I thought I knew who'd done it and I just hoped Donnie wasn't with them this time.

I had an awful sinking feeling. And then anger. I wanted to be an amazon and go and beat up all those Whitfields and Platts, avenge The Great Lentini. But to my own horror when Mrs. Lentini looked over at me, I only blushed and didn't say one thing.

Pity is not what I felt for Lentini, not then, and I didn't feel superior either. Oh God no. To me, he was endowed, special, like Marie's double hibiscus. What I felt was awe and plain curiosity, but now I saw that this had a terrible price for the Lentini's to pay, and I knew as I left her garden that day, I couldn't ever come back unless I had a good reason. Otherwise, I was just an ogler with nothing to offer—too puny to avenge her husband, and unable even to tell her how truly bad I felt for what had happened to him in this world of mean people.

That night at the dinner table I tried to find out who had tormented Lentini, and if Donnie was in on it.

Donnie exploded, "What's it to you? What do you care? It's none of your business anyhow, dummy."

I could tell by this purple vein on his temple that popped out, if I pushed, he was going to lose his temper, something I lived in fear of all the time, so I kept still. But I knew that

63

Donnie always put anger up for his protection, and he got behind it and hid whenever he didn't want you to know him, or the truth.

He didn't have a big closet to hide in like I did.

10.

The next day, I ran right over to Marie's. I had bad dreams about Donnie to get over. I peered into Marie's gazing globe so if the evil spirits were surrounding me they would scatter. It was a relief to bask in the cool harmony of her house. I was quiet for awhile, but my face must have shown the knotty way I was feeling, because Marie started prodding me to tell her what was wrong. I didn't have the words to tell it. Would she even believe there was a three-legged man? Finally I blurted out it was because a lady named Mrs. Lentini was so sad.

"Lands," Marie said, "when someone is sad, girl, what you have to do is distract them."

That never would have occurred to me because I didn't know I had the power to distract anyone from anything. But I knew there was something missing in me and that must be it. I wanted that power. I wanted to have an effect on people.

Turned out Marie knew all about the Lentini's. She had been their friend for years, been in the circus with them. She told me, "Lentini has a weak heart, an extra valve or something, like his extra leg, and he isn't supposed to get overly excited."

She put on her halter top and shorts that matched the set I was wearing and said, "C'mon, hon, we're goin' jukin'."

I knew I wasn't supposed to go off with anyone in a car, but Marie sang "I've got you under my skin" and opened the door on her little cantaloupe-colored Nash so fast, I just jumped in, squinting at the hot sun, hoping jukin' meant a cold "Co-cola." Her little chihuahua named Gravy jumped in too, and then it seemed okay.

She drove us up to the Greyhound Inn in Uleta. I'd walked by it many times on my way To Badgers and noticed the smell that wafted out when the door opened—a bubbly, yeasty, adult smell, smoky and mysterious. Marie lifted me onto a bar stool, even though I could have climbed up by myself, and then she sat lightly on the one next to me, and Gravy curled up by our feet. It was like we were the queens of the place. All the men paid us a visit, one by one, and Marie sort of showed me how to flirt, which was lots of fun, even though I was scared one of my brothers might see me through those porthole windows and tell.

I had a nice bottle of ice-cold Coke in front of me, and Marie had a draft beer. Hank Williams singing "I'm So Lonesome I Could Die" wailed from the jukebox. I'd heard him before at the Yates, who were from Alabama. I linked his sound with what Alabama must be like. Sandy Yates had told me that Alabama was from an Indian word, ALIBAMU, and meant to Clear the Thicket. I imagined Hank Williams clearing the thicket right out with his voice. And I could tell being lonesome was a very sorrowful thing.

Everyone in the bar was in high old spirits, pretending to believe Marie when she introduced me as her daughter. I was secretly proud, even though a little guilty feeling about my real mama nagged around behind my ears. I knew if mama found out she wouldn't like this at all.

After a couple of beers, Marie started talking about her son again. She had told me this same thing many times before, about how he was grown now, a Captain in the Army in Washington, and married to a girl that Marie didn't get along with very well, so she never got to see them. It was the girl who couldn't stand Marie. Marie could accept her, anything, just so she could see her son once in awhile. But no, the girl had put her foot down and forced the Captain to choose between his mother and his wife. The surprise to me was that he chose the wife. I didn't see how anyone could not like Marie, could not want to keep her around for all her knowledge and talents. The girl must be dumb as a goat.

I looked at Marie, her head and neck were straight like a dancer's, but there were tears standing in her eyes, like some old spongy dump of a nightmare memory was pent up in her, about to burst out. And then it did, a flood of tears like none I had ever seen before splashed on the bar and in her beer. Gravy jumped in her lap and began licking them up.

In between sobs, she told me, "I had twin baby girls, they were born dead, and I never even got to see them, to be with them, because you see they took them away and I was only a young girl of twenty myself and didn't know how to ask for them back, just to say goodby to them, and today they would have been twenty-one. It's their birthday and I never will get over this."

67

Her grief made her repeat herself over and over again, but the burden of it never lifted any. Her sorrowing was like a wheel spinning in sand.

I thought about how irresistible it is to stare into the face of a baby and just look and look, as if you could somehow get to know that baby and who it was, what it was like, its personality and all. Even when it had its eyes closed and was asleep. And how if a baby of mine died I wouldn't want them to take it away and bury it until after I had looked at it for a long, long time.

Marie's face drooped and melted but she fought to smile. She heaved a sigh and said softly to me, "Ah'll Swanee Lou, you do bring a person out," and she reached over and squeezed my hand. When she saw I was crying too, she said, "I'm sorry, I'm so sorry I made you cry."

I looked into her tear-filled but still twinkly eyes and her pert doll face that was red with weeping and realized that whatever I was feeling, she was feeling something bigger and deeper, something so tenderized after all the years, that I would never understand it, no matter how hard I tried, unless it happened to me too. I had a new fear now, that someday that might happen to me. It could.

I wanted to distract her someway, and to distract myself, so I mounted my hand horse and da-nummed across the bar, over her beer glass and right up her arm until she giggled up a storm.

That was the first of many honky-tonk afternoons with Marie, and it was the first time I understood that a lot of life was about sorrow and disappointments.

11.

Autumn is a strange color here in Paradise. Everything stays regular green except it's tinged with a chartreuse that makes you blink. Maybe the light changes when the air cools and that chartreuse has been there all along just waiting to show up—maybe my hearing had been there all along too, just waiting to show up. Anyway, this was when it did.

I was crouched behind the chair in the ell, the bookcase room, hiding from Donnie who'd just hit me in the head with his bat. I was a little dizzy, and I started wondering where I came from because I couldn't be Donnie's real sister, and why was I here? deep in this house that was beginning to live in me as much as I lived in it, both of us smelling like fresh wood, when something happened. My ears went tata tat tat tat, and I felt a spike of heat and a hot POP, and suddenly what had once been the soft sensation of sound RANG in my head. I screamed in pain. It was only the phone, but the sound filled the bones in my ears like never before. Sounds had been distant and buffeted, and I'd have to think awhile to figure out what was said and if someone was talking to me or not. "You hear what you wanna hear." mama accused me. But it wasn't true because I'd heard the nuns when they said: "She's a little slow." Now I heard birds chirping, LOUD, the buzz of electricity on the poles, pings and pongs and everything shouting and startling the echoes. What a racket! I wanted my inner world back but I could not get it. I covered my ears, but I was still taking a blasting.

I ran to my mama, who was at the stove cooking dinner. "I can hear!" I shrieked too loud, my voice gave out, and I had to clear my throat and start again. "I can hear." I planted my head in her apron and sobbed.

"What happened?" she looked in my ears, dug a wax plug out of each one with just her finger. "I'll be damned," she said. She held me out from her by both shoulders, and looked into my eyes with a smile on her face: "Don't cry. You're lucky you can hear dearie, jeeze I thought you were gonna be deaf and dumb."

Lucky? Mama always said I was lucky, but this was the first time I felt it—and then the feeling passed like a shiver. Donnie had been my luck. I had him to thank for hitting me in the head, but I'd never be able to do it.

School was starting and I was filled with dread. Now that I could hear good it was going to be even more boring. The set-up and routine of it was alien to my nature, but I had to go anyway. Mama said it was the law. I'd survive if only Shelby Wauldin would sit behind me in class and scratch my back sometimes. Her gentle paws lulled me into a dreamy forgetfulness of my surroundings. I didn't expect much from school besides a lot of lining up. I hated to line up. Sometimes we had art. That was good. Hardly anything interesting ever happened though, unless someone threw up, wet their pants, or had an epileptic fit. That was the most excitement you ever got.

No sooner had school started when we had a hurricane warning and were sent home. Hurricane Bess was whipping up out in the Atlantic, giving everybody time to get ready.

"Land is where hurricanes go to die," my father said, giving me his dangersome look, as I helped him nail the shutters closed over the windows. He alone understood how loud everything was now. He showed me how to hammer because he said if I was making the sounds myself they wouldn't bother me so much, it would even things out. And sure enough I started getting used to the racket.

My mother wanted to go to a shelter, but daddy said no, we were better off in our hurricane-proof house, and something about the proof being in the pudding heh-heh-heh, which made my mother bite her cuticles the way she did when she was nervous.

Bess made her landfall in Miami about six that September evening in 1949, and moved wickedly across the state of Florida with winds at one-hundred-forty-eight miles an hour. There was no call of love in these winds. Every little while you could hear an explosion. One thing a hurricane does to you right away is destroy any ideas you might have about safety. You are at the mercy of the dangerous wrath of nature. My instinct was to hide. So I sat cross-legged on the floor behind the chair in the ell, a big maroon and cream striped chair, with my favorite cousin, Willy, and his portable radio. He was eleven, two years older than me, and was my daddy's, sister's, son. He had smooth, white skin, calm brown hair and blue eyes, just like daddy's. He looked like a saint, or maybe a sunbeam.

His family had just come down from New Jersey and they were staying in the little trailer that was still parked behind our house, washing out in the sun to the color of water, so it looked like a huge tear. Even the outhouse was still out back. They all moved into our house for the hurricane, where daddy assured them they'd be safe.

During the hurricane there was no running water, telephone or electricity. Reddy kilowatt was disconnected at the fuse box and we were cast in darkness, except for candles. Daddy said that light attracted motion, so we had to keep it as dim as possible. It felt like we were hiding in the dark from the cyclone. We filled glass milk jugs with water for drinking, and filled the bathtub with water that we could use by the bucketful to flush the toilet. We had a full tank of propane gas outside the kitchen, so the stove still worked.

Our two big families, eleven people in all, crowded together in the loud darkness and waited for the worst. The smells of an oniony pot roast, split pea soup and something chocolate, cooking on the stove, whiffled through the house on little puffs of wind that seeped in around the windows.

I was worried about my friends, Shelby, Marie, the Yates' and the Lentini's. I hoped they were all warm and dry, in a hurricane-proof place like I was in, with something good to eat, especially my big sweet Shelby. I could feel the excitement of the cyclone like it was a mammoth animal moving over us. Could Lentini's heart stand it?

We huddled behind the chair, my cousin Willy and I, and held hands and didn't move for a long, long time until they got sweaty. I leaned my head against his shoulder and it felt like a place I had longed to come to all my life. The candlelight flickered. We pressed our dry lips together and kissed, both of us for the first time ever. We were like explorers, amazing and wonderful. We merged there, for hours, in our own private world behind the chair, a tenderness between us that was opposite from the raging storm, calming each other, listening to Hank Williams and The Drifting Cowboys, on Willy's radio, and the faraway sounds of the other cousins, in other rooms, laughing, yelling, playing hide-and-go-seek, and the adults in the kitchen playing poker and drinking beer, all jolly.

We listened to the trees cracking and splitting apart. It felt like the house was going to lift off at any minute. We kissed again and again until we felt weak, and blended together, with a shared, open feeling, and a secret that no one else knew. It was that we alone, the guardians of the storm, with our concentration, were keeping the roof on the house, and the walls up. No one bothered us, not even Donnie. It was as if we were in some hallowed place, where nothing beyond could reach us.

My father was about to discover that he had made only one mistake in building The Sea Breeze. He had hung the front door so that it opened out. The aluminum screen door, featuring a flying duck with a curlicue winding around it, also opened out. Daddy hated doors anyway, so in a whimsical moment he had hung his doors to intrude on the outside world, instead of into his own living room.

At around midnight, when we were all used to the continuous wild beat of the storm—some of the kids had even fallen asleep in pushed-together chairs—a loud water and wind racket full of thundering booms bombarded the roof and shook the house to its footings. Willy and I could feel the tremors all the more, sitting on the leeward side where the window always had to be left slightly open to prevent the build-up of pressure inside the house. We peeked through the shutters and watched the funny light, all golden and dark at the same time, like the flickering light at the end of a movie reel. The house swayed and see-sawed, the sound coming in violent bursts so everyone came awake screaming.

Suddenly the window slammed shut. It was like the crack of doom. The walls quivered. Willy and I clutched each other and looked out from behind the chair just in time to see the front door fly open with a great sucking sound. The screen door with the flying duck had already taken wing.

The whole house went into a panic, everyone running around screaming, as Daddy and uncle William tried to grab the thrapping door without getting sucked outside themselves. Gravel cracked against the house like buckshot. Water cascaded in on them in a sluice that was more like ocean waves than rain, washing away the sweat as fast as it sprang out on their foreheads.

The wind pulled violently against their best efforts and tore the door away from them over and over again, but they wouldn't give up. Everyone in the house was holding onto them in a human chain that reached clear into the kitchen.

Finally in a lull they got the door closed, and nailed to the door jamb. Then my father went out the back door and came around the house, hugging its sides while coconuts and palm fronds, and even small animals sailed through the air. Goatman had already started back to Georgia, otherwise his goats would be flying through the air too. Everything loose in the world was blowing in the wind, pelting daddy as he nailed two-by-fours across the front door so it would hold forever. My mother carried on the worst of anyone, tearing her hair, screaming: "The wolf's at the door, George, the WOLF, the WOLF, oh don't go out there, no George, don't go, NO, NO NO." And the whole time he was gone she wailed, "he'll get killed, oh Jesus, Mary and Joseph help us!"

It seemed like there was always something at our door. We peeked through the cracks in the shutters and watched his progress. It was bright and magical outside, lightning flashed while the quiet lull of the big eye passed over. In the flickering light we saw a smile on my father's face as he relaxed and began to take his time then. That's when I knew this was not the end of the world. Not yet. More than anything I longed to be out there with him.

In the quiet of the lull I heard him whistling "Over the Waves," soulfully, in that trilling way he had that sounded like there was a tiny gurgling motor in his throat. "When you are in love, it's the loveliest night of the year...." Willy and I sang along softly. Daddy took his sweet time coming back into the house, but I wasn't worried for a second. He was indestructible and I knew it.

This time when the adults resumed their game of poker in the kitchen they upped the stakes and started drinking hard whiskey. And the Hide'n Seek game accelerated to smaller, more intense hiding places. Willy and I, the guardians of the storm, again took up our position behind the chair, but we were changed. We'd gotten older in a short time, and wary of having roused the Gods. Somehow though, we knew that we existed as a force alongside of nature, however middling. We didn't kiss anymore, but stayed close by each other, good and tired. By and by we fell asleep. There was something easy about cousin love, as if a part of me knew how to love a part of him, knew it in my blood.

By morning Hurricane Bess was through with us. We all came outside and opened the shutters. The outhouse was blown to sweet Ojus but the trailer was still there. A palm tree had fallen on it anchoring it down. Parts of roofs were lying in our yard and the landscape looked soppy, wind-wrinkled. The Sea Breeze was undamaged except for the doors, and all we had to do was pick the clothes and junk out of the trees, clean up the yard, and take up our everyday life again.

I ran over to Shelby's, jumping over downed lines and trees, to see if she was there. But their little hut of a house had blown clean away, our dress-up hut and Bicycle Bill's lean-to had faded too. Stuff was strowed everywhere. Rabbits, chickabiddys and bawling goats grazed the tree dander on the ground. There was the smell of skunk, ditchwater, and burnt wires in the air and something sweet on top like frangipani. But no Shelby anywhere.

12.

It took all day but I found her. The Wauldins' were safe. They had gone to the shelter at Fulford Elementary School, like a lot of other people. I could just picture Earl, the tall, dark and handsome, with no chair big enough to sit down in, and Shelby with her soft brown eyes smiling as she slid delicately into a desk, every inch of her touching it and able to stand up and take it with her if she wanted to. And Mrs. Wauldin screeching like a magpie at the cyclone. Bicycle Bill probably carried his bicycle with all the junk on it right inside and scared everyone.

The first places I went were around to all the houses of the people I knew. Marie's block house was okay, except most of the windows were broken because she didn't have any shutters to close. Inside, there was water damage, and Marie was mopping up. Gus had gone off to get some window glass.

The Lentinis' villa and truck looked untouched. Marie had told me they'd gone to a hospital to ride it out. Boards had been nailed across their french doors. Even the Yates house was still there, add-ons and all, only a jot more aslope. The Yates' had ridden the storm out at Fulford Elementary with the Wauldins' and Bicycle Bill, where a lot of praying must have gone on.

Willys' family skipped out right after the hurricane and drove back to New Jersey, before I could even say goodby. So

I lost track of him, although I would never forget—we had been through a tempest together, and seen how life might be changed forever in an instant. I would think often about how we had tamed our fear, and changed it to love.

It was amazing to see part of a roof lying on the post office floor with about an acre of broken window glass around it, from where it had come sailing in, and right outside the door beside that, a hibiscus bush, completely unharmed. The hibiscus were all wound shut; the flowers had scrunched themselves up and held onto the bush through the whole hurricane. They were in no hurry to open back up either, like they hadn't gotten the all-clear signal yet.

I volunteered for clean-up, scrambling on every busload that left school to go around greater Miami and pick up trash and stray objects, like broken bottles, nails, lawn chairs, parts of houses, and people's personal belongings—things like underpants were hanging in the trees. I kept an eye out for our screen door, but I never found it. The clean-up took most of the rest of that year, gratefully interfering with school routine.

Now Goatman is back, signaling summer. I saw him ambling down the Golden Glades road with a herd of goats pulling his rickety wagon, and about twenty bleating kids straggling behind. He has a big new sign on the wagon: JESUS WEPT. Oh he is a sight and a stench to behold, yet he brings a loosening up of things somehow. Suffering the boiling heat is our atonement, and trying to stay cool and downwind of the goats takes everyone's mind off sin.

78

All the big windows stayed wide open at The Sea Breeze. Daddy was adding on a front porch with jalousies. I had my freedom back to roam the roads of Uleta—what could be better than a road?—and maybe discover beauty. I was always on the lookout for it, and for something good to eat. The Wauldins' had moved into a frame house behind the Brown/Holt compound, between the Higher Ground Nazarene and the drug store. So there was this shifting, and it brought new people into my gypsy life. The Brown/Holt compound was a little village of houses all made of coral rock. It was like a reservation with swept dirt yards instead of grass. The Holts were half Seminole Indian and half something else—alligator, my brother Donnie said. The Browns and Holts always married each other so about five families of them lived in there, all related, somehow. I wondered if cousins could marry cousins but I was afraid to ask anybody.

I rarely went into the Brown/Holt compound except to cut through to get Shelby. There was something cave-dark and unfresh in there. I trusted my nose as the best way of knowing anything. It reeked in there of wet dog, smoke fire and fruit garbage combined and brought to a pinnacle by the heat. There were always a lot of trucks in the yard, an ugly forklift that scared me. I usually walked right on by, unless I saw tall Paul who was my favorite Holt.

He was deafer than I used to be, and spoke with sudden halts, clipping the beginnings and ends off his words. Most of the time he was mute—it was easier—but he would talk up a storm to me and Shelby because we made an effort to understand him. Everything he said was important. His stories usually were about things he cared about that agitated him, like alligator fights and other fights in which there was always an underdog that he would build up our sympathy for. "Me he haw" was "me and him saw," talking about Billy, his cousin, "em" was them, "raunch" for rolled "dis gator over and cut her eggs out." Tears prickled in his eyes. I liked tall Paul, even though he always looked sad, and there was no way to cheer him up. He was smart, and good too, a walkabout saint. He always went around with his cousin Billy Brown who protected all of us, if we needed it, from the Whitfields and Platts, even from Donnie. Billy was about a hundred pounds overweight for his age but what looked like fat was really muscle. He was the strongest, and best fist-fighter in Uleta. He learned it from his big brother Cecil who was much older than the rest of us, was the owner of the forklift, and who's eye I never wanted to meet.

When they got to be about six, Cecil would take brothers and boy cousins over to the Tamiami Trail and show them how to put a gator to sleep. That must be when their eggs got cut out. Cecil believed that wrestlin' gators built character. After them, no puny fistfight was ever a problem.

But Shelby and I knew Billy and Paul in a different way, their gentle, playful sides which they were free to be only when they were away from the other boys. We swung through the mango trees together, playing Tarzan and Jane, Billy yanking down the heavy vines for ropes, and hunted up soda bottles to return at Badgers Grocery for two-cents a piece. We'd get enough bottles, if we had to walk all over Uleta, to each have a Pepsi and a bag of peanuts. These were five cents each. Then we'd sit outside Badgers so we didn't have to pay deposit, and dump the peanuts in the Pepsis and fizz them up and eat out the soggy peanuts. After that, we poured the flat Pepsi on the ground. Or else we'd get RC's and Moonpies, Shelby's favorite. She loved chocolate better than anything. Occasionally Billy came into some big money. The kind that bought banana splits for a quarter each at the soda fountain in the drug store. The terrazzo tile floor was cold to our bare feet, and seemed to harbor the smell of vanilla. We sat up on red twirling stools, in luxurious air-conditioning, scented with the dizzying mix of medicine and vanilla, and Billy, proud as a gator, treated us.

It was on one of these rare days that I first saw the Mole Lady. We'd come out of the drug store with our bellies full of cold ice cream, feeling air-conditioned from the inside out, with big chocolate grins on our faces, when she walked right past us, slow as a turtle. She had moles in great numbers all over her body, moles on top of moles. You could see bumps showing through her thin cotton dress. On her face there were clusters of moles and a nose that looked built out of them. Dumbfounded, I turned around and stared. She felt my eyes on her and scuttled away. I knew instantly that she hated herself. I saw it in her face and eyes—and I imagined the agonizing slowness of her learning to hate herself, like it was the daily lesson of her life. I was scared and had a feeling of dread. I thought the Mole Lady was so strange somebody might try to kill her.

Bicycle Bill appeared and pedaled along close behind her. He had the strangest way of condensing out of nowhere.

Shelby knew the Mole Lady from the circus, and even Paul and Billy had seen her a time or two before. I seemed to be the only one who was laying eyes on this exotic specimen for the first time. I said, "see ya," and ran towards home. Whenever things seemed to be too confusing, or new, or happening too fast I headed over to Marie's. I'd get down with her in the yard and pull weeds for awhile, or do acrobats, and get distracted. She always came up with something for us to do. Now I was a year older so she was teaching me how to do pedicures.

While she took her afternoon nap, I sat at the foot of the bed and swabbed her toenails with cuticle remover, then I clipped and filed them and washed her feet in hand lotion. I polished the toes with bright red Cutex enamel, and by that time Marie was snoring softly. So I went inside her closet where it was dim and cool and sat down on the deep carpet and arranged all her high-heeled shoes, as she'd shown me how to do. They were already in order but I lined them up exactly, and I think she knew that I also tried them on and walked around the room, and dreamed of when I'd wear high heels and be another person. Marie had little shoes, size six, and my dusty feet, splayed out from going barefoot all the time almost filled them.

I took all her underwear out of this little three-drawered cardboard chest with huge pink and red roses all over it, just like the real ones I'd seen in Baltimore, and refolded everything and put it all back in, just so I could look at it, and inhale the pungent rose sachet that she kept in the drawers. Marie called her underwear lingerie and seemed very proud of it. It had names like Van Raulte and Vassarette and Vanity Fair. Silken V's with lacy trims, the kind I'd have some day, instead of the white cotton from Byrons I now wore.

That same day I saw Mole Lady, Marie gave me an old pair of high heels to take home. I wore them while I set the table, enjoying the clunking sound they made on our kitchen floor as back and forth I went. My mother, cooking at the stove, cut her eyes over at me a few times but she didn't say anything. Her eyes were shrunk, like cherry pits, the way they got when she sipped too much of that medicine on her closet shelf.

I had been worrying about Marie's skin on which she was constantly applying a flesh-colored salve. She told me she had a rare skin disease that wasn't catching, but still, it had separated her from people all her life. I felt sorry for Marie, but not as much as the Mole Lady. I mentioned Marie's skin problem at the dinner table and made the mistake of bragging on her for all her many talents.

"That's no rare skin disease," my mother said, "it's just eczema. She aggravates it by drinking too much. She's a nervous wreck. She's had four husbands. What do you expect? You always like outsiders better than your own family, don't you? Where'd you get those shoes?"

Made me wish I'd never mentioned Marie at home, that I'd kept our friendship a secret. No way was I going to tell about the mole lady now.

The next day when I said I was going over to Marie's, my mother wouldn't let me. Then she called Marie a cracker and a drunk, and said I should stay away from her.

She sent me to Badgers instead for a bag of potatoes, a pack of Chesterfields, and the *Ladies Home Journal*. I took my sweet time just for spite and when I got home I got a slap in the face. But I didn't care because of who I'd seen in Badgers. In fact, when my mother slapped me, it woke me up from the dream state I had lapsed into after seeing them.

First I saw this tall brunette lady with big brown eyes, fair skin, and long long legs wearing short-shorts. She swayed and tapped her foot on Badgers concrete floor while she sipped on a Co-cola. She was the most beautiful creature I'd ever seen in my life. She looked like Moonbeam McSwine in Li'l Abner only she wasn't dirty and didn't have that lazy look in her face that must come from sleeping with pigs. She was droll like Moonbeam, at her best. She leaned over and talked pleasantly to her little daughter, another baby Linda, who was planted on the soft drink chest, pretty and blonde just like Shelby's baby Linda, with nice tanned skin and little white teeth set in a bashful rosebud of lips. She had a tiny brown mole on her cheek, the kind Marie called a beauty mark, and Moonbeam's own big brown eyes. Dangling from her hand was a little Indian papoose doll. And just then, from out of the shadows stepped the Mole Lady, and Moonbeam said to her, ever so sweetly, "You ready to go, mama?"

I have wondered whyever, with all the space in the world, two dragonflies will come and settle right beside you on the grass, and allow you to witness their mating as if you are merely a moving mountain they know they can fly around. They are so sure of their speed, and completeness; they're superior to people in self-confidence. I felt like I'd seen justice and it was perfect, sweet, and confident. It lulled me like a dream, like the dragonflies did. I felt lucky for the things I saw, and I was in a reverie of this when mama slapped me awake.

After that, I saw them a lot, always together, never with any men. Who were their husbands? Who had mated with Mole Lady to produce the beauty that was her daughter Moonbeam? She towered protectively over the Mole Lady, and Baby Linda, clutching her doll, took her grandma's hand on the other side, and nobody looked at the Mole Lady, nobody teased her. Nobody dared do anything but look in awe at the beauty God had created out of the Mole Lady. And she was proud, content, self-possessed, like she had secrets. I wished I could have made my mother feel that way.

Hard as I tried, I could not get the Mole Lady's eye. Her self-hate was healed by the majestic beauty she now reflected in. There was even a little smile on one side of her mouth. I had felt a link with her, that we had something in common. Didn't she see that my skin was covered with freckles and my hair was red? I'd been teased too, and made to feel miserable in my own skin. "You look like the shit hit the fan and splattered you. Or Red head wet the bed." My hands got clammy thinking about it. I felt dirty sometimes and different, and I was sure the Mole Lady would understand. But she didn't even see me.

It was a more-or-less world. My freckles weren't even anything close to what she had to bear. I saw that I was presumptuous to think I could get next to her because of them. I wondered about beauty. There were times when it was easy to recognize, especially if people made it, like Marie's underwear—but when God made it, I wasn't so sure. People always said to me, "Your freckles are so cute." But they were lying. Now I wondered if anyone could see the Mole Lady the way her daughter and granddaughter did: they thought she was purely beautiful.

13.

I had just come in one evening and was washing my burning feet in the tub, picking out the stickers, when mama asked me: "Where do you traipse around to all day long? Why won't you wear your shoes?"

"Oh"—I shrugged—"around, you know..."

"No I don't know. Where?"

I told her I'd been playing with the Yates in the cow pasture. You had to wash your feet good after that, or you really would get worms.

"The next time I let you go off to spend the night at the Yates I want to see you first thing the next morning."

"Okay," I said.

"Do you hear?"

"Okay Okay."

"God knows where you're galavantin' around to all the time, popping in and out of people's houses, like you haven't got a home of your own."

I thought about where I'd been, the truth. First I spent the night with Sandy Yates, as mama already knew. Sandy was two years older and sort of took care of me around boys. But we had camped out in the cow pasture across from their house. Her parents let us when it was too hot to sleep indoors. Rene and Shelby spent the night too, and lots of little stray boys, some of them Yates'. We made bedrolls out of holey old Army blankets and towels and watched where we stepped, although in our part of the pasture the cow buns were mostly already dried and turned to smoke when you kicked them, which we had a good time doing all night long. The fragrant dust made us all smell like a barn but kept the skeeters down. For supper, we cooked Campbell's Pork 'n Beans over sterno-can fires and roasted vienna sausages on sticks. Tall Paul and Billy Brown stayed with us too, for protection. They stood guard like Indians, in case the cows got mean and decided to charge, or something like that. They scrounged up an old tire and set it on fire. The smoking tire also kept the mosquitoes away—they'd learned that from Goatman.

All the Yates boys could fall asleep anywhere, in trees, piled against a fence or just laid out in the middle of a field. We had a big camp of people finally when everybody settled in at around midnight. All night long we had run back and forth between the pasture and the house getting what we needed. Ma and Pa Yates sat in the house on beat-up chairs drinking a clear liquid from a Mason jar, while all us kids ran in and out, getting water, peeing, jumping on the beds, rummaging in the cool closets for things we needed. The doors and windows of the Yates house hung open, the sounds of Hank Williams singing, "Hey, good lookin', whatcha got cookin'" mingled with our screaming and playing, as Ma and Pa Yates got fulsomely drunk, sitting there smoking long Pall Malls. Pa Yates seemed to have forgotten he was a preacher. I liked their contemplative look—they seemed made of smoke, and hardly moved. They never said a word to us and almost disappeared sitting there. It was tons of fun at the Yates'.

In the morning Sandy's mother fixed biscuits and this thick white gravy which everyone glopped on them. Sandy and I put sorghum syrup on ours instead. The Yates house always smelled like kerosene and biscuits– a comfortable smell to wake up to. Sometimes there was a dark red meat with a rind on it that was impossible to chew but you could hold it in your mouth and suck on it for about an hour. It tasted salty and delicious, like bacon, only better, but seemed to be scarce so I never took much. The Yates' were the poorest family I knew yet they always fed the most people. It was like the Bible story of the loaves and fishes over there, always enough for one more.

Although she had never been there, for some reason, the Yates' house was a safe haven to my mother. Once she asked me what nationality Sandy Yates was. I said Alabama. And she laughed, "Another cracker!" But she didn't seem to fear their influence on me, whatever it was. She always acted like she had to protect me from what she thought was my fatal flaw: I was too impressionable. She hardly missed a day telling me. So now I thought I'd better not tell her where I'd gone after I left the Yates'. Besides, Marie was now my SECRET friend.

I got to her house around noon. The first thing Marie did was put me in the bathtub and scrub me with Ivory soap. I had to wear an old dress I left there once when I changed into a new halter top and shorts set Marie had made me. Next she braided my wet hair and tied it up in a crown. I let it stay. We had grilled-cheese sandwiches and bread n' butter pickles for lunch. Then she drove us to her sister Skeeter's house in Biscayne Gardens, and we stayed for hours. Her sister was named Skeeter, Marie said, because she was such a tiny thing.

Skeeter's little villa glowed with careful, domestic grace, like I had never seen before, not even at Marie's. It was spotless and sprawled with comfort and the glamorous smell of gardenias. It reminded me of a miniature Roney Plaza, the most luxurious hotel on the beach which had a magic atmosphere of palm trees and fountains. Under the cocoplum trees at the entranceway, Skeeter had a gazing globe too, like Marie's, only hers was silver.

We sat out in the Florida room, a glassed-in, cuban-tiled jungly room, with three different seating areas like a hotel lobby has. There were bowls of floating gardenias on the tables, and rattan furniture with a big pattern of palm-fronds splashed across the pillows. Three walls of the room were glass, so you could look outside and see corn-yellow oleanders blooming in the shade of huge old ficus trees that had staghorn ferns sojourning in them, like witnesses.

I was served ginger ale over ice in a crystal glass that Skeeter graciously refilled every time I took a little sip. I never had service like this before. Skeeter didn't have any children, that must be why. She handed me a gigantic photo album to look through, and I pretended to be invisible so they could talk freely.

Skeeter's husband made them lots of highballs with bourbon and ginger ale, and we all had cherries and pieces of orange, cut like medallions, floating in our drinks. They talked and teased each other, Skeeter's husband egging Marie on about something I couldn't hardly understand, until finally she balled him out, shaking her finger in mock anger and all of them laughing at the same time, in high spirits.

When we were leaving, Skeeter's husband took a picture of us outside on the gravel driveway. Marie, standing the tallest in her striped tailored shorts, looking devilishly happy; little Skeeter, in gabardine shorts and a panama cotton blouse, grinning like she doesn't understand even one thing that's happening; and me in the middle, between their sheltering arms, barefooted, besotted with ginger ale, and wearing a DRESS. I'm holding a silver colored jeroboam of Champagne they had given me for a prop. The sun is so bright I have to force my eyes open. I squint. Marie squeezes me. I look up and see a big, wide-eyed smile across Marie's red face and I think: What courage. Then I look back at the camera. CLICK.

I didn't know that picture would mark a green bud of time—what life can be for one moment, and then it isn't that way any more. One day I would think of it as the time BEFORE—before the unstoppable fall into real true sorrow.

I gave my mother the gardenia I had picked for her in Skeeter's yard. It was a little yellowed because I breathed on it too much. She looked at it without interest, the very proof that she couldn't smell.

At the dinner table, which was too quiet, something was up, my father made an announcement: "Your mama has to go in the hospital tomorrow for a little D. and C. operation." It sounded simple.

91

Mama clutched her belly low, so we would know it was something in there, in her female parts, and she was in pain.

"She's gonna be all better afterwards, but you kids have to take care of things around here while she's gone, you hear?" We all nodded our heads.

The table was quiet after that, everyone felt jangly, unable to talk. Mama was nervous, a glum look on her face. She was cutting her mashed potatoes with a knife.

While me and Andy did the dishes, she paced around listing things we were not allowed to do while she was gone. She told Donnie not to swing the bat in the house. Then she said, "And no guavas for you, young lady." She thought I acted funny after I ate guavas. When I tried to tell her things that were going on in Uleta she would say, "Where'd you dream that up?" After awhile, I just gave up. Until the way things were now, I wasn't hardly telling her anything at all.

I thought she would be all right. But what if she wasn't? She was too strong and fierce ever to die. But what if she did? I would have to take care of Daddy all by myself. I had a little feeling of pleasure, yes I did, I have to admit, and it horrified me. I felt so ashamed. I forced it out of my mind. Suddenly all the stored up love I had for my mother flooded my chest and I could hardly breathe. I wanted to run to her and hold on and tell her I loved her so much and not to ever die. But when I looked in the living room she was reading her *Ladies Home Journal* and I knew if I interrupted her she'd say: "Don't bother me now," like she always did, and shoo me away.

I was sorry she didn't like her life, that something was missing in it and I was helpless to supply it. I had the strangest feeling of regret and longing for her. It was inconceivable that my mother could die. I wasn't up to death yet in my understanding. I tossed around worrying about it all the night long and hardly slept a wink.

Next day I went to the bookcase and took down my mother's nursing books and looked it up. D. and C. stood for dilation and curettage. It was an operation where they took this loopy tool, and scraped out the uterus. Sounded awful. Whyever do women have to get tortured just because they have the wombs?

14.

Since mama had not mentioned Marie in her list of things I was not allowed to do while she was in the hospital I practically lived over at Marie's. She brushed my long, thick hair pretending I was her little girl, putting it up ten different ways to get it off my neck.

"lands, your hair makes me sweat like a teabag just to look at it. You should have gotten the curly hair instead of Andy," she said, and did a couple of blowfish. "You ought to have it short in the summertime, like mine is, and curly too, instead of hanging down your back, so hot and heavy."

I agreed. So she cut it off and gave me a Toni home permanent wave right there in her kitchen. It took about four hours and when it was all over Marie handed me a mirror and I peered in, expecting to see myself looking just like her. But I didn't look like Marie at all. I was so shocked I turned gray as Gravy, who started barking at my new look. Then I turned green and threw up in the sink. Marie said it was probably the ammonia in the permanent wave that did it. I reeked with that smell and felt scalped and shorn to a powerless state—and I was full of dread.

I didn't know what I was dreading. Marie kept on saying how cute I looked. I studied her eyes. I was okay as long as I didn't look in a mirror. I liked how cool and light my head felt. "It's cuuuuuuute." Marie hooted.

When I went home my father laughed and said I looked like Little Orphan Annie. Then he showed me her picture in The Miami Herald. Donnie and Andy were rolling on the floor. I tried to laugh too. "It'll grow out fast, don't worry," Daddy said. Blackie didn't seem to know me or like how I smelled— he wouldn't come near. I shampooed it a few times to loosen it up and get rid of the smell but it must have to wear off. The next day, after I cleaned up the house good, my father and I baked a cake for mama, applesauce, her favorite. We wanted everything to be real nice for her homecoming. I almost forgot about my hair. But when mama came in the door and saw me, she went wild.

"What in the name of God happened to your hair?" she screamed, like she couldn't believe it. She turned me around and around roughly. "Where is your hair?" she kept on demanding over and over. I didn't know I was supposed to keep it, or how to answer her.

"Marie gave me a Toni," I mewed out.

"Are you crazy? You let her do this to you?" Then she started tearing at the sides of her own head, and her eyes bulged out. "It looks like the wrath of God—Jesus, Mary and Joseph. That was your crown of glory she cut off, that son-of-a-bitch, it was your best feature!"

She tore at her head and danced around in circles kicking things. I jumped out of the way. She was venting all the gasses she had built up in the hospital on just that one little thing. She raged on and on and I blushed so much I almost passed out from the build-up of heat in my head. I was sure

Marie could hear mama all the way over to her house. This must be what I had been dreading.

"I forbid, forbid, forbid you, to ever go near that woman again." She ordered me, stamping her feet. Then she clutched her stomach and doubled over, like she'd hurt herself.

I ran into my room and crashed onto the bed sobbing. How could I ever show myself again if I looked that bad? I was crying so hard I couldn't get my breath. My mother hollered for me to shut up and stop being so damn melodramatic.

Everything was ruined—crumbled to dust. I plunged into hopeless despair and a climbing dread like I had never felt before. "I wish you had died in the operation." I said, not loud enough for her to hear it. The words shocked and scared me as soon as I said them. I wanted to run away, disappear and never see anyone ever again, especially myself.

Blackie started nudging me and mewing. He was scared too. I heard someone moving outside the window and then my father's voice whispering, "Poor little Cinderella, the mean stepmother won't let her go out." He said it over and over again, until it began to soothe me. I raised up and looked out the window at him standing there smiling and acting like there was another outlook, like he represented another point of view and everything was going to be all right. He was purely brilliant.

My face, streaked with scalding tears, began to cool and dry. The earth stopped rocking. Daddy looked at me, icky and vile as I was, with such love and a smile so sweet that I had to try to smile back. He lifted all my troubles. He always did— him and Blackie. I couldn't live without them.

The next day, Rene came over and told us Lentini had died in his sleep of a heart attack and I plunged into deeper darkness, like the ground was cut right out from under me.

The funeral was the following day at the Higher Ground. I put on my Sunday dress, and shoes, and tied a scarf around my head to cover up my hair. Then I hid in the closet until it was time to go. When I headed out the door, my mother was tipped off by my appearance.

"Where do you think you're going all dressed up?"

"Lentini's funeral," I said, picking up speed and trying to sound casual at the same time.

"Oh no you're not!" she yelled, "get back in here."

But I was already way on down the road and now I ran like the wind. She sent Donnie after me but I had a big head start and I cut through people's yards and lost him. I could hear him yelling behind me: "Get your ass back here, you dumb nincompoop."

I had to go. I just had to, even though I was afraid and didn't know what to expect. I'd never been to a funeral before—I never knew anyone who died before.

When I got there, it was already going, people were sitting down, looking straight ahead. There was music, a song being sung over and over by everyone, their lips barely moving: "Just like a tree that's planted by the Wa-a-ters, we shall not be moved." I sat in the back, off to myself by a window, and looked over the crowd of people hoping to spot Marie. Everyone was dressed in purply colors, some of the circus people in costume, and clowns in full makeup. I kept turning around expecting to see Donnie snarling at me. My nose sniffed the air like an animal's, trying to get used to the strangeness of a funeral. I looked up at the ceiling fans turning slowly, and then I followed the big white lilies up the aisle with my eyes until I froze at the sight of two shiny grey caskets, one open, with Lentini lying in it, in his brown suit and another, child-sized one that contained his third leg. It was closed but everyone knew. I couldn't believe it was Lentini lying there dead. I couldn't hardly believe in dead.

The music got sadder and woebegone and then stopped altogether, leaving everyone in a kind of shock at the sound of silence. The preacher started talking, trying to make us believe in dead, that it was good and peaceful. "The lamb's blood... has washed him clean... He shall wear a crown... Precious Lord, take his hand... take him to the city that is four square." He talked like that with words from the Bible, and long pauses of his own. Then he called for silent prayer. I heard Mrs. Lentini sobbing up front, and I started crying too. I thought about my mother. I took it back wishing she was dead and asked God and his son Jesus to forgive me because I didn't really mean it.

What everyone knew was that Lentini had decreed that his third leg be separated from him at death, and buried in a separate box. This way when he was reincarnated he'd come back as a normal man. He just didn't want to take the chance if there was any connection between body and soul after death. In life he had experienced a great connection. What if, I wondered with horror as I stared at the little coffin, what if his soul was in his third leg and he'd separated his body from it? I closed my eyes swirling in confusion, and the room disappeared. I heard a jungle of bird songs outside the window, like a separate bunch of mourners scolding us.

I relaxed then, and daydreamed about Lentini, how I used to sit up in a banyan tree and watch him mow his lawn. He never knew I was there. He had a Sears and Roebuck push mower and he always let the grass get long and spindly before he mowed it, so his rows were clear, wide swaths through the fierce and buggy grass. The bugs just went a-flying as he blazed through, his third leg, brown-suited as usual, dangling and bopping up behind him, doing a dance on his body that he didn't try to restrain. Then when he got tired, he would just take a seat on that third leg, turn it right into a stool and it would disappear under him and he would take his handkerchief out of his back pocket and mop up the sweat across his brow and under his collar the same way ordinary men did. I thought he had a great design and wondered why God had not given us all a built-in chair.

Just as I sat staring at the little coffin, the lid started to raise open, and I could see Lentini's third leg was doing the job of lifting it. Everybody in the church went "Ooooh" and "Aaaah" at once, in surprise. Then Mrs. Wauldin, sitting up front right under it, let out a shriek and came running up the aisle, her hands covering her face.

In an instant the man in charge of the funeral was up on his feet trying to calm us. He held down the lid with one hand and patted the air with his other hand saying, "Now, now, it's just a little post-mortem lividity. Nothing to worry about. It's over now." He signaled for the funeral march to begin, and the piano started up while he closed both of Lentini's coffins and latched them shut. Roustabouts from the circus came forward and carried the two coffins outside to a black hearse, and the rest of us followed. Everybody got into cars and limousines and formed a line that crawled off for the cemetery, slowly, like a long, droopy black caterpillar. I stayed behind and watched until they were out of sight.

After that, I don't know where I went. Just wandered around, letting the sun beat down on me and wishing I had a pool of cool water to fall into. Water, the most wonderful element of all, besides the element of surprise. My shoes ate up my socks, so I took them off and carried them. It was so hot my knees were sweating. I daydreamed about looking through a keyhole and all I could see for miles and miles around was cool blue water and flowers: roses, gardenias, hibiscus, oleanders.

I was afraid to go home, but I was too tired now to care much what happened. When I straggled in, my mother didn't even hit me—as though she'd decided to forget where I'd been, and everything that had happened before that too.

"Come on and sit down now, dearie," she said, "and take that face off you, supper's ready."

That night I dreamed of twins that were joined by the hair, but every time they tried to cut the hair to separate them, they shrieked because it hurt so bad.

Also, that night I wet the bed.

15.

I could not find "Post Mortem Lividity" in any of my mother's medical books, but I wasn't sure how to spell it. There was *lividity*: discoloration on a cadaver, and in the dictionary, *levity*: lightness or gaiety of mind, character or behavior. I chose that one. It was a lightness of leg, a bopping up, a past habit of the nerves not yet forgotten. I could see how it might happen. Maybe death was not the final movement.

We had barely gotten over Lentini's death when Andy found a man dangling from a banyan tree, right near our house. Poor Andy ran home howling and mama called the police and tried to calm him down. In minutes, the street was blocked with police cars, and an ambulance. First time I'd seen either one in Uleta. Here came another black cloud over us. I was glad we didn't know the man. Death is easier if you don't know the person that died I'm finding out. Still, new sorrow loomed, latched onto me.

I kept my distance while they cut the rope and took the man away—his body stiff as a hollow log. It made my flesh creep to watch. I moved up to hear what the people milling around there who knew him had to say about it, and what I heard them say is he had finally done it, taken his own life. I didn't know there was such a thing as self-murder. It was a strange, untellable idea to me. The gist of what I heard was

101

that the man's adding machine for sins was not geared to subtract. He had been unable to forgive himself or anyone else for anything ever in his whole life.

It felt like there was a pall over all of Uleta.

I went looking for my Blackie because I hadn't seen him in a day and a half. I suddenly got a panicky feeling, like an alarm clock was going off in my stomach. I took the shortcut up to Uleta, cutting through Shirley Hanley's yard behind the Greyhound Inn, outran Badger's mean geese and came out on the Golden Glades Road.

I kept calling, begging: "Kitty Kitty Kitty." Then I saw a cat lying still in the alleyway between Badger's and the Greyhound Inn. I smelled a tang in the air and backed away. I stood staring at the cat for awhile, trying to deny it was Blackie. Blackie wasn't this big, was he? This cat just had the same stripes. My mind tried to blot out what I was seeing with a big horrified NO. I went in closer and knelt down and touched him and that's when the realization that it was Blackie crawled over me like a black shadow, and I started crying hard. He was already stiff. His beautiful tigerish coat was cold and impersonal, like he'd left it behind. He'd left me too. He had no wounds so I couldn't understand why he was dead. Was I being punished? I lugged him all the way home, crying harder as I went because his body was so thick and heavy. I'd perceived his value because of his thickness and substance and now he was empty. He didn't care about himself anymore, or me. He was gone and left me this heavy shell that was cold as ice but still made my arms sweat from the weight of it.

102

My father said Blackie had been poisoned. But why? How could someone kill a beautiful cat just like that? I felt an unfocused hatred that I longed to have a target for and wanted revenge so bad I tasted iron. Instead, the sweetness that was Blackie kept on feeding my heartache every time I thought about revenge.

Daddy dug a hole back in the yard. "Bend," he said to me. "Be bendable like a tree in the wind. Let the bitter grief fly away."

I held onto Blackie for a long time, babbling, "I shouldn't have taken it for granted that you would always be here. I shouldn't have wished mama was dead. I shouldn't have ignored you just because I was upset about Lentini. It's all my fault. I shouldn't have loved you so much either."

Daddy said, "Nobody would ever love anyone, or do anything at all, if they knew what they were in for."

Then we buried Blackie and daddy left me alone.

I lay on top of Blackie's grave way into the night. It was Lentini's grave and that unknown man's grave and the grave of my hair too. I felt I had to understand something about death so I could leap up out of this black hole and fire back at it, outrun it somehow, make it stop happening, or this pain would never end. I was in a pitch black tunnel of grief so deep and dull it had to be the end of the world.

But no. The next day the sun came up again.

It was a Sunday and mama took us to Mass. She did that whenever she felt attacked by outside forces, or whenever there was a lot piled up to pray about. What we really needed was another good hurricane to blow all this bad stuff away, to distract us. Instead, there was only a little afternoon sun shower.

After Mass, I dawdled in the guava bushes, eating the little pink and yellow guavas until I was full as a goat. I clapped my hands in the wet bushes and rubbed the guava juice off my mouth with the rainwater. Life had leached me out already and I had no way of knowing if there was any future at all or what was going to happen next.

My world had come down, and now at the same time I felt something starting to build up inside me. I saw that I had to change, that I had to do something myself, even if it was reckless, or things would just keep on getting done to me until I was buried alive.

I walked toward the Wauldins', where their old house used to be, and wished I could see Shelby. Sweet Shelby, who thought with her body—her slow movements revealed her understanding of life, showed her deep knowing.

I saw the gate open to the Lentini's, and people gathered on the veranda amongst dead and dying flower arrangements plopped everywhere. All the special people were there swarming around Mrs. Lentini, who sat in the center, looking downcast: my Shelby and all the Wauldins', Bicycle Bill, the Mole Lady, Moonbeam, Baby Linda, Marie, Badger, Billy and Tall Paul, clowns I didn't know, the Yates'. Everyone, even Goatman, was there, goatless. I saw that I had never belonged to these people and they had never belonged to me. They were all there by some plan and I just happened to come along. They had their own secret club and I was an interloper. Shelby could never really be my best friend. I was the one who was different.

I watched them standing around Mrs. Lentini in a half circle, with long, hang-dog faces, some of them in full clown makeup just like at the funeral the Sunday before. They were acting as if the roll had been called and they were in attendance, ready to be dead themselves. Made me mad. I wanted to yell at them, "It's a mistake, the roll hasn't been called yet. This is recess. This is the time BEFORE the roll is called up yonder. Don't give up." But my words were buried deep within me, tangled up in fear, and other itchy feelings; I knew I couldn't say a convincing word.

So instead, without even thinking about it, my body took over and I did three cartwheels down the middle of that walkway to the veranda and presented, hands in the air, as Marie had taught me, I even smiled. Everyone looked up. My stomach went all swimmy-trembly, so I did three quick backovers and slid into a couple of traveling splits, brought my legs together, toes pointed, slowly eased over and stood on my head, X-ing my legs in the air to heaven a few times, and then leaping up to a full balanced handstand. I dropped over into a backbend from which I slowly rose up and faced my audience, hands on hips. Now I saw they were distracted, especially Marie. I was in position for running flips but first I did some slow cartwheels so they'd come as a surprise. When I had everyone's attention, I took off for the finale, flipping in the air, first one, then another and another, light as can be, like a whirling, baby goat. I made it look easy. Then I bowed low, panting and breathless. The applause was thunderous. When I

105

raised up I burped—I couldn't help it—a loud bilious guava burp, and everyone laughed for the first time in a week.

PART TWO

THE BEAT IS ON

16.

I stayed in action for the rest of that sorrowful summer, trying to beat back the dark shadow of death. Somehow my only thought was to keep moving. If Light attracted Motion, like my father said, then maybe Motion could attract Light. And that's what we needed in this lightest of all places, so hot-bright it fried your eyes like eggs—we needed more light. I never got to where I understood death any better either, this mystery that had struck so hard, and I really tried too. I decided it was outside my knowing, something you couldn't understand until it happened to you, and maybe not even then. I might have been too young to die but if my life had ended then it would have seemed a full one to me. I would have been happy to go to my understanding.

Shelby and I wandered around Uleta looking for where the Mole Lady and them lived and never were sure we found it. She was slippery, that moley lady, and led us on many a wild goose chase, only to vanish just when we thought we had her. She knew FADE too. We narrowed it down to a place behind the Higher Ground, deep in the mango trees. It had to be back in there, where the pongy air hardly moved and it was easy to hide out in privacy, with no paved road leading to it, the light mingling with the gloom, no chance for rainbows. We both shuddered as we stood looking into that dense shade. It was hard to imagine Moonbeam and Baby Linda back in there with her, but they must be.

Shelby had to go out on the road with her family to work the circus and wanted me to go with her. She didn't know my mother at all. All she knew was that I was afraid of her and didn't want to be like her. Shelby and I had that in common; she didn't want to be like her mother, either.

After Shelby left, I sneaked over to Marie's every day and we did acrobats in the side yard. Marie was grooming me for the circus—said I would be ready in about a year or two. The high wire. She didn't know my mother, either.

One day while I was practicing I asked Marie about the Mole Lady, who her husband was, who Moonbeam's father was, facts like that I had been wondering about.

Marie laughed. "Moonbeam? Who's that?"

"That's what me and Shelby call Mole Lady's beautiful daughter," I said, and did three one-handed cartwheels.

"Oh lands!" Marie said, "Well, her name's Delora-Delora the Divine- she's an exotic dancer. Not in the circus though, in fancy clubs, over on the beach,"

Marie thought out loud while I stood on my head in the grass wondering what an exotic dancer was. "I don't exactly know who Delora's father is, or who Nola married if she ever did marry. Maybe Divine. Maybe that's a real last name, Delora Divine. I just don't know, but she is Nola's real true daughter, she birthed her, we were all there for that. And now Delora has retired her mother. It hasn't done Nola one bit of good either—she's just gone and gotten all shy again. Watch out for that dog shit."

"Who was Nola in the circus?" I asked, taking a seat beside Marie on the steps, for a rest.

"Why, she was billed as The Great Nola The Untouchable. The barker would yell, 'Not one square inch untouched by moles on her entire body.' And it's mostly true, too. She always drew a good crowd."

"Did she take off her clothes and show everybody?"

"Oh no. She wore thin, see-through veils, Virgin Mary blue, and she modeled back and forth inside a tent for the audience. With some tricky lighting, you could see the moles good without her having to strip."   Marie was doing the blow-fish while we imagined it. Then she said, "I may not ought to say this, but maybe she don't even know who Delora's father is. She sure won't tell anybody if she does. Not even Delora who wants to know real bad—asks her mother all the time. It's a mystery. I'll swan, you have hit on one of the greatest mysteries in Uleta, little Lou."

So I asked where the Mole Lady and them lived and Marie said it was in a tiny little house in the mango grove behind the Higher Ground. Just where we thought.

"She has it looking like a witch's house," Marie said, "worse than the house Hansel and Gretel stumbled upon in the fairy tale. Does that to keep people away, especially kids. She hates little kids. Now let me see some slow back-overs. We have to keep your back limbered up good."

A week before school started, my mother took Andy and me downtown to Byron's to get some school clothes. We could each have two new outfits and a pair of shoes. I wanted penny loafers so I could put dimes in them and wear white bobby socks. I picked out a purple skirt with large pockets and a white blouse that had an eyelet ruffle around its elastic neck so you could put it off your shoulders, which I never would. Mama talked me into an emerald green dress with a sash and puffed sleeves for my other outfit. She said green was my best color. I helped Andy choose two plaid shirts. He looked real good in plaid. Mama picked out Donnie's shirts for him.

After lunch at the friendly smelling S & W Cafeteria, a delicious soup, pudding and floor wax combination, my mother took us to the movies with the warning not to tell our father. Whyever? I don't know. The film was called: "The Boy with Green Hair." It was about a sad little war orphan who felt different when his hair turned green, so he joined the circus. Green is the color of hope, spring, new growth, they tell him, and he looks right at us, the audience, and tells us that his green hair is to remind us that war is very bad for children. I sympathized with him, since I've always felt like sort of a Girl with Green Hair, and I wondered if Andy did, too. Mainly though, the movie was strange and scared me, even the circus was gloomy. Still, I was glad I had the green dress because of what green stood for.

On the bus ride home we sat across from some colored kids sitting with their mama's. Our mama liked to sit as far back in the bus as we could get and that's where the colored people sat too. It was like she already knew them—they were from Boston to her, familiar and comfortable. I thought everybody was colored someway. I was pink. I stared, wanting them to look back at me but they wouldn't. I knew they felt bad about their skin, that bad things had happened to them because of it. I wondered if they had to go to school too. I decided I liked their beautiful brown skin even if they didn't. They looked like Egyptians I'd seen in this book we had on the Pyramids. They had that sideways way of standing, with eyes shaped like the mango and lips like Surinams. When I whispered to mama that they were Egyptians she said I had grand ideas. The reason I wanted them to look at me was so they could see I felt bad about my skin too and understood. Didn't they see how I clashed with everything, how gaudy my freckles were, how naked I was in my pink skin? We all sat there feeling like the boy with green hair, but none of us talked. We had no trust, nothing to do with each another.

Just before Little River all the colored people got off the bus, and it continued on to Miami Shores, North Miami and finally Uleta, the end of the line, where we got off, and the bus turned onto Miami Avenue and went back downtown again. There were no colored people in Uleta, only the circus people and regular people like us.

Mama didn't want to know anyone, especially the circus people. They weren't serious to her, didn't live real serious lives. I was the opposite. I wanted to know everyone, to know how life was lived outside my own skin. I wanted to go right inside their houses.

17.

It's morning. I'm in the fifth grade. Shelby is sitting behind me scratching my back with her wonderfully chapped paws. Tall Paul and Billy Brown are sitting nearby, silent as panthers napping. I hope Shelby won't have to go out on the road again for the rest of the year because she hates it, and I miss her. I tell her everything I found out about Moonbeam and about the movie, "The Boy with Green Hair."

The big thing this year is bomb shelters. In school we have weekly air-raid drills that make me feel sick. We crouch under our desks. Everybody talks about building bomb shelters next to their houses and stocking them with canned food and guns to keep other people out. My father laughs at this idea and doesn't do one thing to get ready for a bomb. He says it is not a real war but a race to see who can build up the most arms, us or Russia, who can be the most threatening, a "cold" war. He says if we're not either falling behind Russia or getting ahead of her, we don't know where in hell we are.

I asked him if the colored kids went to school. He said they had their own schools. He said it was a long sad story, but mostly it was because everybody was afraid that if the races went to school together they'd amalgamate. I had to look that one up. It meant to unite, to merge, to mix. Whyever was anyone afraid of that?

After three o'clock, when school let out, I came alive again. We all went over to Crofts Ranch and drew Shetland ponies for hours in the cool autumn afternoons, trying to forget the air-raid drills. Andy and Billy lured the ponies over to the rickety wood fence so we could climb up and throw ourselves onto their backs and ride. But not Shelby and Tall Paul. They just watched, laughing at us when we fell off, even Tall Paul laughed, a teensey sound. It was worth it just to hear that. We crossed paddocks, rode mules and big goats, hanging onto their scraggly manes, playing Hopalong Cassidy, Andy's favorite cowboy game.

It felt powerful to straddle an animal—to be up on his strong back, hugging his neck, in charge of him—made us forget everything, especially time. We wondered why humans always had to think about a past, present and future and animals only seemed to think of right now. We didn't exactly put this into words but it's what we were all wondering. I know I was. We had a sudden new feeling for animals—they were so far away from air-raid drills that they comforted us, their hot breath blew back in our faces and warmed us.

When it started to get dark we split up, and Andy and I headed for home, and the awful intensity of our dinner table, a place where more might be required of you than you had to give. I had come to dread it because it was a time of ridicule, and fighting too, as if that's all in the world we were about.

Andy was stuttering. Every night daddy asked him a question and when he tried to answer he'd stumble and repeat a word three or five times. Donnie joined in laughing

114

and mocking Andy. They gave him advice about how not to do it anymore, how not to st-st-st-stutter.

At first Andy smiled shyly because he was nice and didn't mind being the brunt of a joke. That's when Donnie and my father moved in for the kill. They made unmerciful fun of Andy, made him answer questions until his voice was a pitiful, broken thing and he blushed so red he looked like he might catch fire. They made him feel shame just for being himself and taking up space and air. I felt that way sometimes too. But poor little Hopalong Cassidy was barely nine years old. How would he ever convert this cruelty into something hopeful? I wished he'd fight them. I wanted to defend him, but I felt as powerless as he did against Donnie and my father when they got this way.

One night my mother, who had joined in sometimes just for the fun of it, got mad at them and suddenly took Andy's defense. She screamed, "That's enough! Shut up and leave him alone now."

Donnie called Andy "mama's Little b-b-b-baby" and got a slap from mama. She said Andy stuttered because his teacher was trying to change his left-handedness. But I knew mama was sort of letting the teacher get away with it too, because even she hoped he wouldn't be left-handed. It was different and mama didn't like anything that was different. She wanted us all to fit in.

I thought I knew why Andy was stuttering. It was the air-raid drills and the bomb shelters. He felt under attack; everything was going too fast. I tried to tell them. I said, "Listen, listen, I KNOW." But no one would listen to me. My mother only

115

wanted to change the subject. "Shish now, don't be a trouble-maker," she shook her head shishing me louder, "Let it be."

"Lou-Lou dumb-dumb Poo-Poo," said Donnie.

"What do you know, Mithsus Austin?" said my father, making his tongue go out on the s's the way I did sometimes. Everyone laughed. I'd developed a little lisp long ago on my first grade teachers name, and ever since he called me Mithsus Austin when he felt like teasing me.

After he got his laugh daddy waited for everyone to tell him how good the dinner was, because he had cooked it. But I was sulking, and my mother was all excited to talk about her case now, her favorite subject. Lately she'd been taking private-duty nursing cases and my father cooked dinner to help out. He cooked the fish on Friday nights too, usually red snapper, perch or shrimps, the only kinds of fish we'd all eat. He was a gourmet cook.

Mama was wearing her white uniform and was still on her case even though her shift was over and she was home. She talked to the table at large, like she was on stage—she did the voices of the Doctors, imitating every quirk and gesture, until she got us all laughing. Then she narrowed her eyes and said, very serious: "Well, I could see what the prognosis was, but that damn doctor wasn't telling the family. He didn't want to lose the case see? string it out as long as possible, he figured. There was nothing anyone could do to save the poor bastard anyway." She drained her glass and asked for another.

So far she hadn't touched her food. None of us was eating; we were listening to her story.

116

My father liked to cook unusual foods with lots of spices. What we had on our plates was fancy, although I could only identify some of it. There was this nutty-brown rice, meat that looked like a veal cutlet with mushrooms on top, broccoli, which I didn't like, and some kind of white carrots. He gave her another cocktail. She grabbed it and went on talking, all excited in this way she had that no one could escape, like she owned all your attention.

Daddy rolled his eyes, urging us, "Eat, eat, the food's getting cold." But nobody did. He started hitting the plate with his fork every time he came down for a bite, trying to interrupt mama, but she went right on talking.

"It was the same old story," she said, lighting up a cigarette, "I had to take orders from this dumb doctor and do all the work, and then he got all the glory. I'm sick of doctors!" And she blew out the smoke and slammed her drink down on the table, suddenly furious. Some of it slopped out on her plate of food.

We tensed, the table got loud-quiet, my father leapt up. "That's it!" he said, and picked up his plate and heaved it into the sink where it crashed to pieces.

"Oh, you're just jealous!" my mother growled, and flicked a grain of rice that was on her finger right in his face, "you don't want me to do anything."

"Oh, yeah? Well, you're a liar and a know-it-all," he said, and turned her plate over on the table, dumping all the food out.

About that time Donnie hit me with one of those white carrots and I fired back a mushroom. He aimed a fork full of broccoli at Andy, but he ducked, and it hit my mother instead. She screamed, "See what you've done to Donnie? You've spoiled him. He's just like you. He thinks he can do anything he wants!" and she reached over and slapped Donnie, who had just taken a mouthful of the veal and mushrooms and it sprayed out all over.

"Hey," he said, not even crying, "this veal tastes fishy." He made a face.

"That's because it's alligator," my father announced, and he stomped off to the bedroom to get lost in his newspaper.

We were all surprised into silence. I took a little taste of the alligator. But even if I liked it, I felt too sick to eat now. Andy slid all the way down in his seat so his chin rested on the edge of the formica table. His eyes darted and his lips moved silently as he counted the little orange and yellow boomerangs that floated in the aqua sea of formica. Numbers comforted him. Mama was crying in her Manhattan. Donnie went, "Ugh, I'm not eating alligator" and ran from the table.

That was the end of my father's gourmet meal. He had worked hours on it. All he wanted was a little praise. My mother didn't seem to know that. They had a cold war going on too. They both just wanted approval, her for working and him for cooking, but they wouldn't give it to each other.

It was more peaceful around the house when she didn't work. Then she could cook the dinner, her plain New England fare as usual, chops or hamburg, and potatoes always, and my father could tease her about it and complain, and she could say, "just shut up and eat, you're lucky you have something at all." Then they were both satisfied, in a way.

118

I sank down even with Andy, wondering if it was like this in other families.

18.

At least my hair was growing out and I didn't look exactly like Little Orphan Annie anymore. It was unusually chilly and windy after school so we stopped going to draw horses and went home instead and had coffee-milk with mama. When Donnie came home he started swinging his bat in front of the mirror in the living room, trying to perfect his form. This mirror was antique, convex—it swelled out and falsified things. It made your nose look like a nozzle. Daddy called it a Bulls Eye mirror, and whispered that it had once belonged to mama's father, like it was a secret.

Mama yelled at Donnie over and over, "Quit swinging that bat and get outside," but he stayed parked in front of the mirror. There was no mirror outside. If I tried to walk by him I got hit with the bat. So did Andy. This was automatic. He owned the mirror and all the space in front of it that he needed to swing the bat in—the hitmosphere. He enjoyed making us go outside and walk around the house and come in the back door to get by him. He was more important than we were in his mind and he had to make us see that too. He believed he was in training to be the greatest baseball player of all time.

I used to tell on him when he hit me, but I didn't bother anymore. My mother just said, without sounding like she really meant it, "Stop hitting her," and when she turned around Donnie clobbered me again for telling. Sometimes I thought of trying to hit him back, but he was bigger and had that bat. So I just snarled at him and thought my hateful thoughts, and tried to stay clear of him, out of the hitmosphere.

Andy and I called Donnie the Masked Man—it was his code name. We hid in my mother's closet and shined the flashlight on her clothes, up on her medicine jar, very quietly. If Donnie found us he made Andy practice with him. They'd stand about fifty feet away from each other on the front lawn and throw the ball to each other. Boys can toss a ball endlessly back n' forth. Donnie gradually speeded up, throwing it harder and harder until Andy missed. Then Donnie yelled at him and spit at the same time, as if he had a plug of tobacco in his mouth: "What's the matter with you? Can't you take it? You gotta push yourself a little. Try harder than that. Jesus, Andy, you're no good." And he'd keep drumming away until Andy was crying.

Andy didn't like baseball that much but for some reason he thought he had to play it and also take any grueling punishment Donnie dished out. It was almost to help Donnie, like he thought Donnie was really criticizing himself in order to improve his own form. When I watched them I sometimes thought Donnie was crazy and Andy knew it and was afraid, so he was just humoring Donnie.

Andy and I had to hide in the car to play "jus preten" with my dolls. We made up an ideal family where everyone was sweet and gentle. We knew what we were doing without talking much about it. Neither of us was fond of talking by

121

then. Even though all my dolls were girls, we pretended one of them was a boy; he was the father doll, a farmer, which is what Andy wanted to be when he grew up, or else a cowboy. You could make dolls be anything by order of your own imagination. All our dreams for the future were tied up in these dolls. We sang softly as we dressed them: "Down by the sea shore early in the morning, see the little fishing boats all in a row." Andy loved that song. If the Masked Man started prowling around outside near the car we ducked down and got on the floor. If he caught us, Andy would have to submit to baseball, as well as Donnie's ridicule. Why did boys always have to be so mean and play sports?

Every chilly, dark night that whole winter our family sat together listening to the radio, and watching it too, with our mouths open as if we were catching the sound in them. Sometimes we had Hershey Bars with almonds, or Forever Yours, with "The Lone Ranger," *return with us now to those thrilling days of yesteryear.* Donnie da-nummed all over the place on his hand horse.

At nine o'clock, Andy and I were sent to bed. We started sleeping in the same bed because it was so cold. Mr. and Mrs. North came on, and my parents had martinis with them and we could hear all the glasses clinking in the living room, real ones and radio ones. Donnie's favorite shows were "The Inner Sanctum" and "The Phantom." During these, Andy and I tried to plug up our ears we were so frightened. We fell asleep that way and had nightmares and wet the bed sometimes too.

One night I woke up with something hard poking against my butt and I froze. Andy must have been dreaming he was the jolly Jerry North and I was his Pamela. I prayed to God Andy wasn't going to be crazy too. I started saying the Hail Mary real loud and Andy woke up and stopped moving. Then he dropped back into sleep like a stone. Thank you, God, I said over and over in my mind until I fell asleep again too. In the morning I couldn't tell whether it had been a dream visiting or real. But after that, Andy and I didn't sleep together anymore. We didn't pal around as much, either.

At school I sank idly into the fifth grade reader which featured Dick, Jane, Sally, Spot, and Puff the Cat's neat, uneventful world and floated there, resting from a real world that had shown me anything could happen at any old time. I planned on riding the year out like that, with Shelby sitting behind me scratching my back.

But it wasn't meant to be. In the middle of November, on the very day I turned twelve, our regular teacher got sick and a substitute teacher was brought in. I came out of my slumber to face a blonde Amazon. At 5'-10" she loomed above us, a big broth of a woman, with a heartwarming smile. She was taller even than Shelby, who felt linked to someone at last, if only just by size.

"Hello, my name is Miss Packer, and I'll be your new teacher, at least for the rest of the year." She said, with a cheery lilt, strolling around the room so we could each take in an eyeful. We were dumbstruck. Platinum blonde curls framed a gentle face with peachy skin that had soft down on it and no powdery make-up, only a little red lipstick across lips that were clearly there to frame beautiful white teeth that were there to help her talk. Marie would call her a doll and a half. Everything about her seemed to have a good reason. Her eyes were blue, transparent, yet reflecting wisdom. She wore Leopard-frame glasses she took off when she looked at you, and put back on when she read. In parts, she might sound like a movie star but all together she was more cozy looking, like a librarian.

I found myself enraptured, sitting in the second desk right in front of her. I could hear every inflection of her soft, sensible voice giving instructions and creating word pictures matter-of-factly, using her hands expressively, her eyes sparkling. For the very first time in school, I was interested in learning, and here was someone who had something to teach.

She wore long cashmere coats with big droopy, cuffed sleeves. When we showed interest in her coats she had us look up cashmere in the dictionary: fine wool from the undercoat of the cashmere goat. Goats! However did they get the smell out? I wondered but didn't ask. She had a camel colored coat, a red, a royal blue, a black and a white one. Every day I wondered which one she'd wear. They must have come from wherever she came from because coats like that in Miami were as rare as rhubarb. She wore them like bathrobes, over little silky dresses that were as thin as night gowns. When everyone else had thrown off their sweaters she was still wearing her big coats, as if she was 20 degrees cooler than the rest of us, pushing up the fat sleeves as she wrote in chalk across the board all kinds of fascinating facts. When she finished writing, she took out a bottle of Jergen's

Lotion and squeezed some out—it smelled like almonds—rubbed her hands together, then wiped off the chalk with a couple of Kleenexes, the whole time pacing and talking in a language I was falling in love with.

She read to us from the newspaper, stories about new products, and events in the world, and once about the strike of the International Bridge and Structural Steel Workers Union, of which my father was a member. Sometimes at the dinner table daddy talked about scabs and finks, who he said were the sorriest bunch of people. I was surprised to find out scab and fink were real dictionary words and meant people who crossed union strike lines and went to work anyway. Miss Packer quizzed us: "Who invented barbed wire? Who is Philo T. Farnsworth? What is plywood?" No Dick and Jane stuff. We had to think. She told us rust was just electricity that goes real slow. Uleta must be electricity heaven. She gave us new words, like mall, media and ethnic, words that were going to be important some day, she said. And she wrote new words on the black board that hadn't even made the dictionary yet. I liked words because they were smart, and if I knew them I felt smart too. In my family I always had to try and prove I wasn't dumb.

Miss Packer made sense of the world. I loved her style and grace. She was like a beam of light, a sunbeam, come at last to show me how to be, how to live.

She read to us from Emily Dickinson, and we were all rapt with attention, even the boys: "Hope is the thing with feathers That perches in the soul And sings the tune without the words And never stops - at all."

125

In my little room at home, I looked out at the night sky, and I could not imagine an end to it. Plus I felt like I was being watched by something on the moon. I began to write my own poetry:

Sometimes in the night
I stare across my room
I come upon my window
And there I see the moon

Andy, two grades below, was still swimming in the drowsy world of Dick and Jane. He didn't care though, as long as he could do numbers. He loved arithmetic better than anything. When report cards came out after Christmas, I got E's in everything, except arithmetic. Mama said, "Why can't you get an E in arithmetic like Andy does?" But I couldn't. Numbers were pointless to me. I liked words, pictures.

Donnie, in the sixth grade, had become a master of, "the wheel that squeaks the loudest gets the grease." That's what I overheard mama tell daddy. And she said it was daddy's own fault. Donnie caused his teacher to have staggered recesses and he was constantly sparring with her. She said he was "a disruptive influence in the class." It was just grease to Donnie. Mama was summoned every week, for a "conference." Daddy calls what Donnie is having "histrionics," caused by his great boredom with school.

When everyone in school had to take home these little individual jars and bring back a "specimen" for the county nurse, Donnie saw a little way to get relief from his boredom. He took aside Charlie Whitfield, who was not too smart, grinned into his face, a friendly, sports-coach type grin, and said confidentially: "You know those bottles of specimen everyone has to take home and fill, Charlie? And bring back to the county nurse tomorrow? Urine, Charlie? Piss? That's your specimen—and from it those people down at the School Board can tell everything about you, and your family. They can tell everything you've done, good or bad, just from that specimen a your piss."

Charlie came from a family where there was inbreeding with a few idiots being the unfortunate result. Old man Whitfield had never been too smart—all he ever did was drink cheap wine and panhandle. Charlie was afraid he himself might be on some borderline, but maybe just a little bit smarter, although it was getting harder and harder to keep up. But Donnie had given him an edge. So Charlie filled his little jar with water from the Oleta River, like Donnie had suggested, instead of his own urine.

When Charlie's specimen was examined there was chaos in school. The county nurse took him home and God only knows what happened there. The University of Miami lab that examined his specimen found that it contained moccasin snake urine, assorted algae, and alligator products.

Donnie enjoyed it more than anyone. He had a wild and crazy laugh at times like this—the laugh of a real true prankster. Charlie didn't tell because boys have a code of not telling, no matter what. The way I saw it, Donnie was at a crossroad in his life where he had to choose between being a great baseball player or a criminal. I didn't know which way he'd go. It depended on what would get him the kind of attention he needed, the kind that you could always see him straining for. I saw that he was paving my way through school, though. Teachers asked me all the time, peevishly, if he was my brother. What could I do but say yes and try to appear studious, to provide some contrast, cast doubt in their minds that we were just alike. But in truth I was full of myself, too, and felt a new need to express something, I didn't know what. It was fierce like Donnie's need, only I kept it hidden better. Miss Packer was the only one who never mentioned my brother—she hadn't gotten him first. Instead, she looked at me as a singular person outside of any family, and seemed to think I had something to offer in the way of energy and talent, because she egged me on. She prodded me to draw pictures of what I saw. I could feel myself growing more avid.

That year January and February were so cold in Miami that it actually snowed a few flakes, although they immediately disappeared. "It almost snowed," is the way the Weather Bureau put it. The citrus trees froze and tourists stayed away in droves. Everyone complained about the economy and constantly consulted one of the main indices of tourist traffic: the garbage. Garbage men were spies. More people made more garbage, so down at City Hall when they wanted to know how many more people there were each day they asked the garbage collectors. Then they blabbed it all over the radio, and more people stayed away. Even I knew that people wouldn't come if they thought no one else was. In Miami, the main thing for sale was the weather.

I envied Miss Packer her big coats as I sat in my thin orlon sweater daydreaming about summertime. It was so cold that the corners of my eyes and the tops of my ears cracked. To distract myself I had a recurrent memory from a summer Sunday at Crandon Park Beach when I was nine that I enjoyed carousing around in. My father pretended to be a giant sea turtle in the warm shallow water, and I rode on his back while he stayed underwater holding his breath for what seemed like super human periods of time. He crawled around saving me from the waves, and when I was afraid he was staying under too long I pulled his head up and he gasped for air gratefully. He trusted me to save him in time. After that we stretched out on the sand and watched the flamingos. Their color might have been comical on any other animal or bird, but their form and the graceful way they moved gave an elegance to that gaudy pink color. I was enchanted by them.

And then in the shade of the palm trees my father told me about true balance. "You lie here on the ground, flat on your back, right under these trees," he demonstrated, "it will work with any trees anywhere, but these will do." He closed his eyes and I copied him. Then he said, "Now open your eyes and stare up into the tree tops at the sky for a long time—until you can imagine that the sky is the ground—make a picture in your mind. For every branch you see in the sky, there is an equivalent branch in the ground called a root. Now reverse it—imagine that the branches are roots and the roots are branches." After awhile I could do it. "Oh yeah!" I said, awed. And my father smiled and said: "Maybe we've been walking upside down all our lives, you ever think of that?"

129

I felt a great peacefulness descend upon us there, under the coconut palms. The light and ocean breezes made velvety passes across our still bodies, as we relaxed completely, our minds holding on a rhapsodic thought, full of grace, and I felt we were, for once, in harmony and balance with the whole universe. Afterward, riding down Collins Avenue on the way home, I studied the backs of my mother and father's heads and I thought that would be how I would always remember them; that even when I had a life of my own, they would still be ahead of me. I don't know where my brothers were that day but I was alone with my parents for once, lying on the back seat of the car, while high girlie voices piped from the radio,"...dream when you're feeling blue, dream that's the thing to do... just watch the smoke rings rise in the air... you'll find your share of happiness there...."

The bright neon signs from the motel marquees flashed across my face. I watched them through the window, gorgeous and hypnotic, the colors creating soft, favorable patterns in my mind as we passed, like a neon lullaby. I fell into a sweet half-sleep. From that day forward, neon light was organic to me, it was alive as well as beautiful.

Then the best part—pretending to be asleep when we got home so I'd get carried in—so agreeably played along with, gently lifted, and folded into my daddy's heart, a place that smelled of home to me, a flowery bed of ease. It felt like daddy was a giant, like Earl Wauldin, and I loved the small fragile feeling it gave me to be nestled in his arms. Shelby also loved this feeling. She told me she sometimes played possum so her daddy would carry her too.

Then I heard my mother say: "She's getting a little old for that isn't she?"

19.

The bell rang and jarred me awake. Imagine, a teacher that let you daydream like that, and sometimes even asked you what you dreamed about? Most people are only interested in their own dreams. Miss Packer called it woolgathering, and said dreaming was important, that something might even come of it someday. I'd vaguely heard her give a book report assignment. This was how she got us to read. She never told you what book to read, anything at all was okay, probably even the telephone book, but you had to write about it. So far, I'd done *The Hidden Staircase* by Nancy Drew and *Winnie the Pooh at Pooh Corner*, both mysteries.

Our bookcase at home contained some interesting books. I wondered what the Yates' would think of them. The Yates' came from another world to me, but for some reason I always thought of them when I went to the bookcase. And when I was playing in the Yates' front yard I thought of Zelda Fitzgerald who I had been reading about and seemed to live in our bookcase with her husband Scott who was a great romantic writer. I don't know why—They were from a whole nother world altogether, nothing at all like the Yates', but for some reason I blended them in my mind. The only book I ever saw at the Yates' house was the Bible. Some people only need one book their whole life.

At home, our wall of bookshelves had a big green couch pushed up against it so all the reachable books were from the couch up to the ceiling, and underneath was stacks of old magazines, and clippings daddy saved out of the newspaper. I could stand on the back of the couch and get at every book. On lazy winter afternoons with the sun streaming in the windows I'd go to the bookcase and slowly examine the books—letting the quiet reality of each one enter my head. Also there was the school library. I had checked out *Take a Call, Topsy* and after I read it I shoved it in a corner of our bookcase where it still was because I can't return it yet. I love it too much. It's about a great dancer. I checked out and returned the next day *Patty O'Neil on the Airways*. I didn't like it because it was trying to tell me to be a stewardess. In our bookcase there's a book called *How to Win Friends and Influence People* that has a photograph of a man wearing glasses on the cover that Donnie scribbled all over. He doesn't like anyone who wears glasses.

There is *God's Little Acre* by Erskine Caldwell which looks like a dark tale, and *The Barefoot Mailman*—books I have lined up to read as soon as I finish John Steinbeck's *Of Mice and Men*, which I am now reading and would do my report for Miss Packer on. Mama said I am too young for John Steinbeck, but I'm reading it anyway.

It's about Lenny, who loved to stroke little animals so much he squeezed them too hard and killed them. And about his friend George, who stood by Lenny anyway. Lenny reminded me of Shelby even though they are really opposites.

They're both big, but Lenny couldn't judge his own strength, whereas Shelby has an extra perception of hers. They both have a real soft center.

There are dirty books in the bookcase, too. On the top shelf where they are hard to reach are my mother's nurses training books, with "illustrated" diseases and terrible malformities, naked people with frightful conditions, and never anything I can find saying what had caused them. It's as if the causes are so disgraceful they are kept a secret. The photographs are in brilliant red color, and stark black and white. A series of pictures takes you through all the stages of a disease from start to finish. There are gross illustrations of the intestines and veins and other body innards, where the color blue is added in, like an exaggeration, all shocking and horrible. I will never be a nurse.

Sandy Yates big blonde sister Joyce married a soldier and a few months later he was sent to Korea where there was a war going on, leaving her pimply and crying and all swelled up. Whatever marriage held, she missed it something awful even though it didn't look very good on her. I took the book on obstetrics down and followed the progression of a pregnancy with transparent womb illustrations so you could see the changes in the baby as well as in the mother's body. There are abnormalities, waterheads and mongoloids, all photographed as ugly as possible—unfriendly photos—photos that cast aspersions, as my father might say, on the human animal. The style of the photography is coarse like the dirty pictures I've seen hidden under Badger's counter, along with a cigar box full of packs of rubbers and a half-pint of whiskey that smells like my mother's medicine.

Of Mice and Men pitched me in wonderment. I don't know why but John Steinbeck reads like my father's own voice. Did they know each other? Was John a boxer too, like my father had been? Did he ever get thrown in jail for disturbing-the-peace-and-fighting-in-public like my father had? And did he start writing in there behind bars? the way my father started making drawings, of Norma Shearer who looked just like my mother, Irene Dunn and Greta Garbo, Nelson Eddy and Jeannette McDonald, whoever they all were. He wrote their names on his drawings. I remembered him reaching up over the visor for his pack of Lucky Strikes, and throwing them out the window to the chain gang we passed when we came down through Georgia. It was something I often saw him do if we passed a gang of convicts working by the roadside.

Daddy's drawings survived the wild days of his youth that I'm not supposed to know about, but do because I overheard him and mama talking. Once I heard him say boxing was an art form too, and mama laughed at him. I love to go to his bureau and take the drawings out of hiding and study his penciled cross-hatchings, turn the pictures over in my hands, wondering where he got the odd pieces of cardboard they are drawn on. I breathe in their musty smell, and hold it as long as I can.

I dreamed about being an artist now and a dancer at the same time. I would get married and have beautiful, sweet children and a clean "harmony" house, all painted white. I'd learned not to tell my dreams, except to Marie and Miss

Packer. Especially not to my mother. My inclination to dream and draw and dance meant to her a foolhardy disregard for survival which she felt was her job to correct. Dreams were ecstasy to me though—they cleared my head of confusion and put me in a peaceful mood. I loved to nod off in a dream state and order up the world like I wanted it to be. But if my mother caught me, she said: "Hey you! snap out of it, come down to earth, will ya?" One Saturday she took me downtown to see "The Red Shoes." It was beyond beauty and art, beyond the drawing of pictures, oh beyond life itself—a whole nother world, one I idolized and feared at the same time. Mama and I sat together dazed, eating Necco Wafers. At the end when Norma Shearer throws herself in front of a train we were horror-struck. Mama cried and I was pitched into a whole sea of unfamiliar emotions. I saved all the white Necco Wafers and when we got home I got Andy to play holy communion with me. It helped some.

That same night my mother plodded around the kitchen, sipping Manhattans wistfully while she got supper. She kept looking at me like I was in some kind of peril. By taking me to "The Red Shoes" it seemed like she was trying to tell me: "You can't have it all, but if you're going to dream, here's the level to reach for." That's what I thought she meant, even though she didn't say it out loud; she was afraid to encourage me to dream. Movies were some kind of ultimate dream to her though, and I could see why.

The weather was still so bad, Andy and I came home after school every day. Most of the time, Donnie was out running wild and missed everything. Mama had begun telling us true stories about her childhood in Boston. I wished Shelby could have heard this. Mama talked about all the boy friends she had and how crazy about her they all were, Micky Calhoun and Jimmy Galvin always coming after her.

She said, "I should have married Jimmy Galvin, his family was so nice. . . stayed in Boston, but then I wouldn't have you kids," and she mashed me and Andy on the nose, and laughed and jumped up and started singing "Always, I'll be loving you always, with a love that's true, always, da da da de dum, Always," and we knew she was singing about our father. We liked best the stories about life in the balcony. From there she and her brothers and the other kids waged a kind of war on the world. Mama said: "In those days, live acts came on before they showed the movies and if the performers weren't funny the kids bombarded the stage with rotten tomatoes. Did I ever tell you I was a sweater girl in Boston, like Lana Turner? she was the first."

She pranced around the kitchen singing "It had to be you, wonderful you..." to the beat of her flapping apron. My eyes glazed over as I tried to imagine her world, especially the one in the balcony. She had given me the same advice over and over again. It was: "Always meet them in the balcony." To my "why?" she said, "Because it's dark and you can meet a few different ones and take your pick and you don't have to stay with none of them if you don't want to. But it's always good if you can get one sucker to pay your way in. Long as he's easy to get away from and all. And then if anyone tries to kiss you or anything, you know, get fresh, you say, 'What's in it for me?' And then you duck out. Always get them to chase after you—that's how it's done."

Andy listened, quiet, probably wondering if he was going to be a sucker someday.

Then she ended with a grave piece of advice, wagging her finger in my face: "Don't let anyone touch you. Don't ever disgrace me," followed by, "a word to the wise is sufficient." I could barely understand what all that meant. But it was something she always said whenever she shot her motherly advice bolt. Maybe I was too dumb or too young to understand, but I realized it was something important I'd grow into knowing someday.

Mama had a little drink, "to loosen her up," she said. And we had our favorite: coffee-milk, made with about three spoons full of coffee in a cup of milk. We made her tell us a certain story over and over again waiting for it to be different each time. Mama was a born liar. The story was about her three brothers in Boston shooting an old lady in the butt with a BB gun. The lady lived in the next building across from where they lived. They could all see her through the open window in her bathroom; that is, they could see her bare butt. Her head and shoulders were covered because the shade was drawn halfway down. So she couldn't see them either. She was always washing her big fat butt.

Mama said: "So one day my brothers beaned her in the butt with the BB gun and she went screaming and running down the hallway like she was being murdered,"

It's funny when she tells it because sometimes the cops come, and sometimes the lady catches up with mama's brothers and beats them up, while her pants fall down around her ankles. Different endings, like that. Mama will say anything to get a laugh. Andy rolls on the floor laughing.

Mama liked to talk about the dead, especially about Claire, her sister who had died of diphtheria, and how much she missed her and loved her. "I worshiped Claire. She was so beautiful... girls don't count in an Irish family though, only the boys matter," she said this so bitterly I winced. But I knew her brother's were sent to Harvard, and mama had to work her way through nursing school on her own. We were naturally interested in Claire's life and early death, but if we asked any questions, Mama clammed up, or snapped, "It's none of your business." The only way to learn anything was to keep quiet. Then she might tell a little more.

One day, while talking about Clair, mama lost her breath. She grabbed a paper bag and started breathing in it. When she got her breath back she turned stone-faced. She said we were lucky we never knew her father, and this peculiar treble came into her voice: "Oh, how I hated him, and I still do." Her eyes squinted and filled up with tears. Then she stopped. It was like she'd been testing us—how much can I tell them?

We had no grandparents—they were all dead by then.

Mama broke down and cried, and told us she had a history of horror that started a hundred years ago, when her blood relations had eaten cats and dogs and their own shoe leather to stay alive during the potato famine.

It was getting too sad, so she changed the subject. She put false excitement in her voice, and said: "Hey, remember the time the goat came up to the kitchen door?"

139

I laughed, and said, "It was a cow!"

And she said with a stern face, "No it wasn't dearie, it was a goat."

Andy yelled out, "It was a wolf!"

But if you're not in this family you might not think any of that is very funny.

20.

In spring I felt that old familiar joy that came with a seasonal change, only it was heightened by the severe winter we'd had. The seeds and eggs of Easter were more important to me because I'd learned that they meant resurrection. The seven deadly sins haunted me, along with the ten commandments. Sundays, getting ready for mass was a nightmare of sloth, anger, envy and pride, four out of the seven. We had to go every Sunday now because we were being primed for our First Holy Communion. Mama was exhausted from the effort of getting us all dressed and to church on time. She screamed herself hoarse. Once we got there, we were so mad at each other, and all our nerves so jangled that we sat scattered around the pews instead of together. I breathed in the incense to try and relax, to revive myself, and the priest cooled my burning ears humming latin I was too upset to care about understanding. After mass came the numbing of catechism—the nuns were trying to teach us devotion and piety. Donnie was scared of them, and hell, so he behaved for once.

We made our First Holy Communion on Easter Sunday, about twenty-five kids. All of us were a sacrificial offering to the resurrected Christ. We were dressed in new white clothes, even our shoes and socks were white, and all the girls wore white veils, like brides.

141

Afterwards my mother got giddy as we had refreshments and posed for pictures in front of our house. She was so relieved to have her duty over with. When it was my turn, I stood in the doorway holding my new white missal and rosary in the prayerful pose the nuns had taught us, and daddy snapped the picture.

My mother started cackling, "Look at her, some little holy angel you are, har. Quit looking so damn pious will ya, you're killing me, ha ha ha." She turned her drink over laughing. Donnie hooted along with her.

I didn't feel pious. I felt impure, and I wanted to be a nun all of a sudden.

"You want me to turn you over to the nuns?" she jeered.

"Ah leave her alone," my father said.

She came over to me. Her eyes narrowed and I thought I was going to get a slap, but instead she snatched the veil off my head. "Change your clothes now, miss pious puss."

Good thing I had legs and could get away from her, I thought. Then I asked the blessed virgin, who I hoped was forming me now, to help me not to have impure thoughts about my mother, and Donnie.

Even when summer came I kept on reading. At the end of the school year Miss Packer had given everyone a book. Mine was by Ralph W. Emerson. Every night after I washed my feet I took this book out from under my mattress where I kept it hidden from Donnie and read a passage. I thought about what I read until I fell asleep. Emerson was helping to form me too—he was helping me see how I might fit into life and how I might be useful in the world. One thing he said was,

"Character is higher than intellect." I think it means that what you do is more important than what you think or say. He also said, "He who hath put forth his total strength in fit actions has the richest return of wisdom." I could think about that for hours.

The strawberries were bountiful this summer because of the cold winter. It's called a bumper crop, which I think means the fruit has been bumped up by the weather to its highest and biggest harvest. We had more strawberries than we could eat or give away. They were all over the place, so we decided to sell them to passers-by.

Daddy built us a covered stand out by the road. It had a slanted shelf on which we displayed the berries we had packed into little wooden pint crates. He cut a huge strawberry about five feet tall, out of plywood, and Andy and I painted both sides to look exactly like a real strawberry. We shaded it, like we'd seen tomatoes on Del Monte cans done, from the top of the green cloaking stem all the way down to the red of the nadir, so it looked three-dimensional. We even put in the little yellow flecks you can see in a strawberry if you look real close.

"Details are divine," Daddy said, as he nailed the giant strawberry up on top of the stand so it was visible way off down the long, flat road, juicy and appetizing. Below the strawberry on a board he wrote in large green letters one word: FRESH. People stopped and bought the strawberries for twenty-five cents a pint, and we took turns sitting in the stand or ran out from the house at the sound of a horn. We all had plenty of spending money, especially Donnie, who didn't do much of the work but turned out to be the best salesman. He sold four pints for every one Andy and I sold.

We walked to a farm in Biscayne Gardens, about a mile up the road and picked tomatoes and strawberries alongside the migrants for fifty cents a bushel basket and came home with dollars in our pockets. Daddy said that we were all drinking from the wealth of poverty. Then he laughed real hard like it was his own private joke.

There was a new girl in town named Valarie Twombley who lived up near Biscayne Gardens, but east a few blocks, closer to the Yates'. Sandy took me and Shelby over there one day. We could lie down in the middle of the narrow tar road in front of Valarie's house for about an hour before a car would come. There was a mulberry tree in Valarie's yard, loaded down with berries, and whenever we went over there we climbed in the tree, and spent most of the day there, feasting on hot sweet purple mulberries until we got sick. Shelby just stood under the tree, reaching the berries with her long arms. We lay in the road for awhile, then ate mulberries again, until we were all blue in the face and hands, and doubled over with bellyaches.

The trick to eating mulberries was not to squash the caterpillars that lived and feasted in the tree. If you did, you might have to puke because the caterpillar's innards were chartreuse green. The combination of the purple mulberry and that chartreuse caused a nauseating compassion for the little creatures. When I found out they were transforming into butterflies I was aghast. It was the kind of information that stopped me cold. Why, I wondered, did magic always have to be so fragile? Why did something as beautiful as a butterfly first have to risk its life crawling amongst predators such as us? Whyever did all living things seem to have to go through trials? I wished God or my mind would just let me know.

Every day we went trespassing through citrus groves clipping greatfruit and lemons which we broke open, salted and ate whole. One of the Yates boys carried a pocket-full of salt. Oranges had become boring. But they were still my favorite. They made me think of my mother's story about getting her first orange in her stocking one Christmas when she was a kid, how thrilling and luxurious the orange was to her in the middle of a Boston snowstorm.

That summer we went all over Uleta in large packs, without having any idea it would be the last happy summer we'd spend like that together. Me and Shelby, Sandy, her brothers and Andy and Valarie and Tall Paul and Billy Brown, Rene and Baby Linda. Different kids kept popping up all summer long, and we traveled around together for miles, seeking small adventure. At the end of the day, we'd split up and find our way back home by some fluke of dead reckoning.

I don't know where Donnie was—probably playing baseball somewhere. I didn't miss him.

We swung on thick vines in the mango trees playing Tarzan and Jane. We sat in their redeeming shade sloshing our mouths on warm Turpentine mangoes, the most delicious mango in paradise, a wild mango not marketed because it was thought to be too small and stringy and because a sticky sap oozed out of it at the full stage of ripeness. Like guavas, they were not "clean" enough for the produce business. We sought them out and left the larger, marketable Hayden mango lying on the ground. Or we took them home to our parents—along with avocados. We didn't like avocados. Tall Paul called them alligator pears. There were so many mangos and avocados on the ground, you could walk on them, like stepping stones.

In the evenings we picked thorns of sandspurs out of our feet that had gotten lodged in the leathery flesh during the day, and cooled our feetskins in buckets of well water; that was heaven. We never considered wearing shoes, except when we had to—for church and school and when it got cold. Feet had to touch the ground, it was instinctual, like neon is organic.

We seem to have developed a native immunity to mosquitoes and other biting bugs that inhabited our world. We thought mosquitoes only bit fresh Yankees. Sometimes at sundown we chased the mosquito truck, throwing rocks at the cloud of insecticide.

Billy Brown, who was part Indian, said Poison ivy was conquered by eating one leaf. Forever after you would be immune to it. The Indians had been doing it for hundreds of years. Whenever we came upon a patch of poison ivy, whoever in the group was afraid of getting it was initiated on the spot. Billy rolled in it to demonstrate his immunity. Then a leaf was chosen and everyone watched as it was fearfully eaten and another immunity established. It was one of our favorite rituals. Once a very frail kid from up north whom we had initiated came down with poison ivy inside his mouth and throat and stomach and all the way out his anus. But most of the time it worked.

One day we started seeing stray goats around town, a sign Goatman had come again to strip us of our sins. We decided to go up to Ojus to see him and while we were there pinch a nice juicy-ripe pineapple. We did this about once a week. Pineapples were too rich to eat every day.

It was a long, sweltering walk up to Ojus and when we got there we called out to Goatman, who was parked back in the piney woods. He came out from under his wagon in a terrible mood, buttoning his pants. "What do you kids want?" he grumbled, his voice shooing us away. We just went on because we didn't want anything from him. I noticed another wiggling lump under that wagon, familiar somehow, but it was too covered up to tell who it was. We had just interrupted his social life is all.

We hightailed it across the street to where the pineapple patches began, and went on and on, covering about a hundred acres or more, and picked a row to flop in. The Pineapples grew low to the ground in long rows and between each row was a nice muddy irrigation ditch. We crouched down and crawled along on our bellies in the ditch; the mud felt cool and soothing in the jungle heat. All the girls had on short shorts and narrow little halter tops, except Shelby who always wore the full cover of a dress. The boys had on cut-offs and were bare-chested, browning in the sun.

The old man with a pellet gun who guarded the pineapples was a good acre away in his little shed, and we knew we could outrun him. He let a few shots rip as soon as

147

he saw us and then he leaned back in the shade of the shed watching, smoking cigarettes. We popped our heads up over the spiny tops of the pineapples like rabbits, trying to catch his eye, daring him to see us and shoot, also sensing that he was too nice in his dusty old khaki way to really do it. He got mad enough to spit, but he stayed close to his shady shed kicking the buzzing bugs, and pacing, until he got too hot and went inside to get him a Co-cola. We watched him good as he watched us.

In a minute, he came back out and yelled: "There's snakes in them ditches," to scare us off. But we laughed at him. We'd seen the snakes—they were harmless little green and black snakes, garters. The only snake we feared was the deadly coral, and everyone knew what they looked like as if it was a tattoo on your brain. They were small with bands of orange, black and yellow color that looked like Indian cloth. Those were a caution. They could kill you if they struck in the right place, got a main artery and pumped that venom through it. You would probably be dead in about five minutes or less. But most people survived even coral snake bites because they bit you on the fleshy parts of the hand or around the feet. Who knew why? One of nature's little mercies that you couldn't count on.

We took a long time selecting the biggest juicy-ripe pineapple we were going to eat because we wanted to savor the crawl, close to the cool earth—to wallow in the delicious mud until our bellies were cool as watermelons, until the smell of ripe pineapple filled up our heads and we couldn't wait any longer to taste one.

Then we made a selection, and took it away from there, to our chosen place, under the shade of a huge rubber tree. A pineapple is a prickly thing you approach carefully. Billy Brown cut the top off with his pocket knife, and sectioned it vertically into wedges for each one of us. We ate it like watermelon, burying our faces in the hot, sweet meat until we had sucked the rind dry and our cheeks were red and acid-burned, but we were serenely satisfied anyway. One pineapple was so rich it went a long way. That's why we weren't much of a threat to the watchman.

Afterward, sticky and muddy as new-hatched turtles, we threw ourselves in a cold rock pit and swam around for awhile in the chalky water, stirring it up until it got too foggy to see through and a sulphury smell roiled out.

Then we walked back up to Uleta, air-drying on the way, and stopped by Badgers Grocery, thirsty for cold drinks. Badger smelled like stale medicine, and he was looking at us cross-eyed and talking with the front of his lips. He told us to look at the notice on the bulletin board. It said:

Anyone who may be related to the above
please come forward and appear for
a marriage ceremony.

This was handwritten, and above it was tacked a printed announcement of a wedding, to be held at the Higher Ground Nazarene Chapel, uniting Delora Divine and her betrothed, Joseph Oroniakete, to be held on the twenty-second of July, that was about two weeks away, with a reception immediately following in the church-yard.

Someone had scribbled beside Delora Divine's name "The Delicious."

21.

The other news around town was they were dragging the Oleta River for a body again. Anytime someone was missing the first thing they did was drag that river. Old man Whitfield had been missing for days, and he used to fall asleep on its banks a lot. Alligators won't usually attack people—it's crocodiles over in Africa that attack. But they will get drunks and small dogs. Something about a laid-out drunk attracts them and a small yapping dog is a challenge. Also, Goatman lost baby goats to alligators.

Marie and I talked all this over while she sewed away on her Singer and did the blow-fish. We talked about the notice in Badgers and all about the wedding.

"Delora is getting married and she wants her father to give her away," Marie said, "I don't think that's asking too much. Nola won't tell her, so she's hoping her own father will know who he is and come forward. Otherwise, she's going to have to walk down that aisle alone."

Marie was making Delora's and Baby Linda's wedding dresses out of gobs of pink, dotted-swiss, misty light as marshmallows. It must be awful not to know who your father is, so I asked: "Is Baby Linda's father going to be there?"

"Lands no, but it's no secret who he is. He was a teen-age mistake Delora made but she didn't marry it. He's off in Korea now, don't care a hook or a damn about baby Linda. But this fella Delora is marrying, he does, loves that baby like it was his own. Best looking man I ever saw too. They're going to look like the king and queen of Florida up there on that altar."

Then Marie asked me if I'd gotten precious yet. At first I didn't understand what she meant.

"You know, your period, your monthly."

I shook my head lickety-split. Whyever did she want to know that?

Marie got me invited to the wedding, and I was so excited I could hardly wait. I had never been to a wedding before. I gave some of my strawberry money in towards a present, and we got Delora and Joseph a 42-piece set of dishes just like Marie's, called Fiesta Dinnerware. It had eight different bright colors so you could have a change everyday, plus one left over.

When the wedding day came, I was in my closet getting dressed to go when I heard Donnie scratching around in my room. He had been out in the yard burning the trash, so I thought he was just emptying my trash basket. I put on my emerald green dress, white socks and my Sunday shoes, black, patent-leather Mary-Janes. I put my hair, now grown to corrugated waves, up on the sides with barrettes, and I looked good and plain as a weed.

My mother and Donnie had been teasing me about this wedding. They wished they could go too. I heard them outside hooting and laughing about something. When I went out there, my mother said, "Well, well, well, here comes the Queen of Sheba now," and Donnie said, "That book she was reading is by an atheist pinko, so I got rid of it."

"That's a lie," I said, and ran back into my room and looked under the mattress. My Emerson book was gone. I came back outside and said real low, "Gimme the book, Donnie." It was getting late. He got me in a playful hammerlock and dragged me over to the trash barrel laughing. There was a little fire going in it. My mother Leaned out the doorway, and cackled, "You didn't need it anyway, Carrot Top."

I don't know what happened, but when I looked into that fire, something snapped and a surge of energy shot through me. I broke loose from Donnie. My head was hotter than the hinges on hell, and I was in a pressing darkness empty of thought, blinded. I picked up a bottle from the trash heap, whacked off the neck of it in one snap on the barrel rim, and went after Donnie, who was running away from me, laughing maniacally. I chased him around and around the house—I don't know how many times we circled it. Donnie, long-legged and skinny, could always outrun me. My arm was reared up, clutching the jagged bottle, my temper at an uncontrollable peak that scared me because I knew I was lost. I heard my own voice growl out the words, "I hate you" and it amazed me. If I had caught Donnie I would have ground the bottle into him and it would have been a masterstroke, payment for everything. But he ran into the house and locked himself in the bathroom. I threw the bottle as hard as I could at the house, and ran past my mother who raised her eyebrows and said, "Ut-oh, temper, temper, you're just like your father." She didn't know how close she came.

I ran down the street away from them, turned the corner and collapsed on the ground under the guava bushes, overcome with shame. The loss of my temper was the worst indignity I had ever felt. My life seemed like one big sticker patch after another, and I was ready to give up. I wanted to die right then, and I tried but nothing happened.

I was a mess, crying big gritty tears, sweating. My shoes were full of sand, my socks were dirty. I sat there and ate a couple of guavas, emptied the sand out of my shoes, pulled the beggar lice off my socks. My face dried, streaked with dirt and tears. I vowed then that I would be just like my father because I sure as hell wouldn't be like her or Donnie. I wanted to be tough and strong and fair, and never do anything like this to any daughter of mine. I ate a few more guavas and then He Carries The Sky came walking up. I thought I was dreaming.

I was cast back in time and saw my father and Blackie in their denim work-clothes and steel helmets, holding the black lunch box. I remembered them standing in the living room of our house when it still had open rafters. They had just come in from work and my father was showing Blackie his house, his children. My father jumped up to get candy from the man in the ceiling—that's what he called it—so we'd believe there was magic in the world. He stretched his arms, covered in long blue sleeves, way up high, and then he jumped, and candy came falling down from the ceiling. Blackie had laughed, watching our happiness.

Now he was standing before me dressed in a black suit, with shiny black shoes, his black hair combed back slick,

154

broadcasting the scent of Wildroot, and he said, "Girl, can you tell me how to get to the Higher Ground Nazarene Church? It's my wedding day." Now I knew I was a native Uletan. I was guide. I belonged. Oh what joy filled my ragbag of a heart. I wiped my face and stood up.

He had parked his car down the road so no one would mess with it, and gotten turned around. Now I led him on foot, taking a shortcut through the mango grove to the Higher Ground Chapel, same place they held Lentini's funeral. We were the last ones to arrive.

Inside the church four old men, four contenders, the "likely suspects," as Marie called them, stood with their backs against the wall, on display for everyone, fidgeting a little, like boys. Delora saw Blackie, and her face lit up. She was a vision in pink dotted swiss, the tiny dots white as thistledown and her straw hat ringed in fresh white gardenias. Her golden-tanned legs flexed in new six-inch Springulators. Baby Linda, dressed in the same dotted swiss, had her blonde hair fixed in an upsweep, anchored by gardenias and ribbons, all Marie's handiwork.

There was a heavy silence. It was Nola's moment. She stepped forward in her rosy-colored chiffon veils, to unveil the secret of the father of her daughter, till this day she had possessed alone. These men knew nothing—only she knew, and now she seemed to be biting into her secret one last sweet time before she gave it up.

The wedding guests were a hushed sea of up-turned faces. Who would she pick? There wasn't a sound as we all studied the men one by one. First there was Bicycle Bill, the tallest,

155

brown-eyed like Delora, and handsome underneath his sulk. The most likely, he was of the circus. Second was Goatman, the shortest, all cleaned up for once, his features hidden behind woolly face hair, his blue eyes hopeful looking. Third was old man Badger himself, still in his grocery store outfit of plain white shirt and khaki pants; but he had brought fifty pounds of cold cuts to the wedding feast. It was wrapped in white paper and lying in a near pew, adding the essence of bologna to the chapel's legendary other smells. And next to him stood number four; to everyone's relief it was old man Whitfield, whom the gators hadn't eaten yet. He was sober for once and dressed up in a gray three-piece suit a couple of sizes too big for him, his thumbs hooked in the vest pockets like he was the mayor of Uleta. I looked at these men who each thought they might be the bride's father, who wanted to be even, and I knew who Moonbeam's father was, I just knew it. I knew things now. I could read faces, see signals.

Nola stepped forward and from behind I recognized her familiar lumpiness. So I wasn't surprised when she took Goatman's arm and silently presented him to Delora, who leaned way down so he could whisper something in her ear. She looked doubtful, hesitated, turned, looked back over her shoulder at Bicycle Bill. She knew too. But she smiled, accepting, and gave a nod, so everyone took their places. The organ music began, but I heard trumpets. Delora walked down the aisle on Goatman's arm looking a little puzzled, probably wondering how she got so tall. No more a wonder than why she didn't have moles I suppose.

In the middle of the ceremony, Blackie picked up Baby Linda, who clung to her papoose doll, and he held her in his arms like he was marrying both of them. He might have picked up Mole Lady too, I thought. They said the "will-you-takes" as Marie called the vows, and then they tenderly kissed, turned, and faced us with big smiles—the three most beautiful people in Florida. The music started again. I recognized my favorite hymn: "Just a closer walk with thee, grant it Jesus if you please." And we all filed outside to the picnic area, to barbecue a goat.

As far as I know they lived happily ever after. All of them, especially Nola, who no longer had to hide under the covers in Goatman's wagon. Does one romance foretell another romance, on and on like that in a slick chain meant to keep us from dying out here on Earth?

Oh I hope so.

22.

When I went home, mama was crying. Donnie had set Andy on fire. "Watch Andy," she said to me, "watch him while I lay down for a minute. Oh god, I'm gonna have a nervous breakdown."

I sat on the edge of the tub by Andy, who was soaking in cool water in his underpants. He smelled like singed hair. His face was streaked with dried tears and soot and his shoulder and arm were fiery red, but he told me it didn't hurt anymore. I thought then how one person's wedding day could be another person's burning day, and I would never understand life no matter how hard I tried.

"What happened? Where's Donnie?" I asked Andy.

"He ran off. I found our old screen door with the duck still on it, you know, but it wadn't any good anymore. It was rotten and all warped." Andy ducked his self under the water and came up spitting.

"What's that got to do with anything, Andy?" I whined back.

"It's what ca ca ca caused all the trouble. I was showing it to mama, see, we were standing outside by the kitchen door looking at it. Mama was holding onto her new broom." He went under again.

"So what?" I said, pulling him up.

He sputtered, "Well, see, Donnie, he just come over there juggling these two fire sticks he made by, uh, tying rags soaked in kerosene around mama's old broom handle, he broken it in two pieces, and...uh..."

"Andy, get to the point. What happened?"

"Okay okay, He threw one of them at the screen door while I was holding it and, uh, the fire went right through it and, uh, it ca ca ca caught my shirt on fire."

"Why'd he do that?"

"He just wanted to see if the fire could go through screen, that's all."

"What'd you do?"

"I ran."

"Oh, Jesus."

"But mama tackled me and beat the fire out with her new broom. Then she went after Donnie with it and whacked him a few times before he got away. He he. It wadn't his fault, though."

When Andy got out of the tub, I helped mama pat his burns with pieces of aloe plant while he yelled. Mama said the sticky juice was the best thing there was for first-degree burns, which is what Andy had. There was nothing we could do about his singed curls. "It's lucky his whole head didn't catch on fire," she said.

Then daddy came home carrying a little black-and-white puppy, as if nothing at all had happened, like he was coming in from another world. He found her at Sunny Isles Beach where he was working overtime building motels. "She's a helluva good swimmer," he said, "that's why she's alive." He

159

winked and set her down and she scuttled right over to Andy, her tail doing a dance on her wiggling butt, to the tune of her pit-a-pat heartbeat. Andy petted her happily and she started licking him, licking the aloe off his shoulder and mama yelled, "Get that damn mutt away from him," and slapped at the pup, who ran under the couch. Mama was crying now, so daddy took hold of her and calmed her down and listened while she told on Donnie.

After that, we started meeting daddy at Sunny Isles after he got off work. There were about four good hours of daylight left, and we swam and cooled off in the surf, and had a picnic supper while the sun went down with a fierce dazzle over the Everglades. The salt water was healing to Andy's burned skin and the ocean calmed us all down. Except for the puppy, who we named Daisy. She liked to chase us into the surf, overly excited, but unsinkable, and making us all into better swimmers for trying to get away from her yipping bites. Daisy became our loyal watchdog, our protector, and if there was ever any danger she barked her head off to warn us. She taught me I could love again, too.

One Sunday we went to Dinner Key to swim and go clamming. Daddy still had the Dory boat, the Ellie-Nora, which hadn't blown away in the hurricane. We usually put in at Dinner Key and went out to little islands around there to dig clams to take home and steam in our backyard over a fire. He had traded our '39 Ford in for a big old Chrysler automatic that mama could drive, too. It weighed tons more.

The Chrysler was so heavy it started to slide, imperceptibly to us, but Daisy barked, alerting us, and we had time to scramble out before it slid right into the water, pulled by the weight of the boat. Daddy waded in and unhitched the boat and drove the car back up the ramp as water gushed out the back windows.

Mama stood on the bank screaming the whole time: "Watch out, oh, oh, oh, he's sinking, I'm gonna have a nervous breakdown..."

That's when I began disbelieving that mama was ever going to have a nervous breakdown. By warning us she was on the edge she kept herself from toppling over. She had her history too, but right then I stopped believing a nervous breakdown was part of it. I looked at her and saw she was a displaced person. She was an Olive Oyle to daddy's Pop-Eye and squealing came naturally to her.

After that, the car always smelled like a combination of seaweed and fluid drive oil. The nappy felt seats dried hard as tar. Moss grew on the floorboards. Daddy called it a compost heap and laughed wildly, and mama scowled.

They were opposites, my two parents, and the longer I knew them the harder they were to understand. Marriage must be a connection as high as heaven and as deep as hell. Whenever I thought of love, I automatically thought of my cousin Willy. But I was beginning to wonder if there was another kind of love, more gladdening even than cousin love.

And while my thinking went on in that direction, I noticed I was getting bosoms—little knots were untangling in my chest and swelling out, itching me too. Used to be, I only had to wash my feet, now my whole body demanded it more often. It was producing a wild scent. Even my head was more oily and I had

161

to wash my hair in Lustre Creme once a week. I didn't mind though because a beautiful blonde girl named Marilyn Monroe was pictured in the advertisements for Lustre Creme in *The Ladies Home Journal*, and there was some suggestion that I'd turn out like her if I used the shampoo too.

My face had a rash of red pimples on it. So did Donnie's. Seemed like there was something to overcome all the time. For about the hundredth time in my life, I wished I'd been born a boy. They had power from the gate. They seemed so much simpler in design, and they had more freedom to come and go as they liked, no questions asked. For instance, Donnie never even got in trouble for burning Andy. He just stayed out so late everyone was already asleep when he came home and the next day no one wanted to confront him.

23.

I didn't know exactly what was happening to me but it made me feel panicky and mad at the same time. Mama said it was just hormones, and for me to get over it. I knew we weren't allowed to get sick, and if we started to, mama would say "Get over it" in her Major General tone and we did. It was some kind of disgrace to get sick. But if we managed to come down with something and let it get the better of us, it would be accompanied by a feeling of shame, from which the only escape was to get well as quickly as possible.

Mama was a believer in mind over matter where her children were concerned, and sympathy only got in her way. Sometimes we got the curative power of aspirin, but always those three little words: "Get over it."

Except if one of us got really sick, which I had the gall to do that summer. It turned out my panicky feeling was not just hormones, whatever they are. One day I got so tired I couldn't keep my eyes open—in the middle of the day! Sharp pains shot up my legs, back and neck. My stomach went queasy. When I started to burn up I went to my mother. I tried to explain that I didn't mean to cause trouble, but I was only yowling like a sick puppy, nutty with delirium by then. All I wanted to do was lie down and sleep forever. I couldn't move. My neck was blown-up tight. Once, when I opened my eyes I could see I was on the green couch by the bookcase on

163

top of a white sheet. But everything else got blurred by the heat coming off my head, steaming up my eyes. Someone was putting a cool cloth on my forehead, mama? and then I was out again. Dreaming, far away, smokey, purgatorial dreams. The fourth commandment is chasing me on a white horse, drumming me: "honor thy father and thy mother," over and over. I see a blurred image of mama hovering over me, treating me equally for once, like I am equal to my brother's, at least in the good health she knows she has given us all. She's dressed in her nurse's uniform, wearing her cap from the Bayonne School of Nursing that she graduated from, white, banded in thin black ribbon—and she's telling us she has to go take a case now, to attend to people who really are sick, like we would never in a million years be, because she guarded our health herself.

A heavy hand weights my forehead. I hear voices, a doctor? he lifts my legs one at a time, pinches my toes so I flinch. A funny new word intrudes into my thick-walled sleep: *polio.* Somebody, mama? is bathing me in cool water. I hear her trilling Tor a lor a lora. That's good, I'm coming back I try to say. She is coaxing me to swallow a pill.

I fall asleep again and when I wake, mama is still there. This time the heat in my head is gone so I know I'm getting better; I am like a wave breaking. I try to sit up. So dizzy. I have to go bad.

"Wait a minute," mama held me down. She slid a cold pan under me and I peed for about an hour.

"Are you back among us dearie? Three days you've been out—you gave us all a scare. You could have died from that hundred-and-five fever. What a struggle I had just keeping you from going into convulsions."

"What's wrong with me?"

"It's glandular fever. Thank god it wasn't polio."

Mama told me about a new wonder drug that had helped her save me, a mycin. I imagined this Greek warrior sent inside my body by mama, battling the fever until it was vanquished.

She said she knew I was going to be all right when I started babbling, "I have pretty hair, don't I?" over and over, and she had reassured me, "Yes, you do, honey; yes, you have pretty hair. Don't you remember?"

I shook my head, blushing. She didn't seem very mad at me for getting sick.

After that, we were forbidden to swim in rockpits anymore—or we might get polio. Polio was a dreaded disease that paralyzed you, made you have to live in an iron lung machine that looked like a rocket with a mirror on it. Mama said I was just lucky.

So about a week later, towards the end of summer, I ventured out for the first time, still shaky, weak as a rained-on caterpillar, and fell in love at first sight.

On this day, hot as a Dutch cooker, Andy and I were roaming the back roads of Uleta, cutting through yards so we could avoid going down the street where the man hanged himself. We didn't like to go down that street, it was haunted; it reminded me of sorrow, of my murdered cat. I was always fighting off the highfalutin idea that if I'd known that man I could have stopped him from killing himself, and somehow

165

Blackie would still be alive too. I would have gone up to him and pointed out the harmony of the trees, and how if you just studied the trees they were enough to live for. Instead, he hung himself from one.

Me and Andy were looking for pink periwinkles with white centers, "whiteys"" we called them. Periwinkles usually had red centers except for the rare "whitey," and old Mrs. Pitts would pay a dime for every one we brought her. They grew among sticker patches and were a pain to find.

We ended up in a field knee-high in periwinkles, and pissy smelling weeds, with a lot of butterflies dive-bombing us. This year the wild Milkweed plants were big, drawing the Monarch butterfly, the prettiest one in the kingdom. We kept stumbling on stones sticking up out of the ground, and finally we sat down and looked close at one of them and read: HERE LIES, and the rest of it was slanting under the sand so we couldn't read it.

Then we realized we were surrounded by these stones, we were even sitting on one—they were jutting up all over. I wondered if they were emerging or submerging. Sometimes I wondered the same thing about myself and all the other people I knew. Stones and rocks always appeared to be alive in some way of their own to me. They were organic, like neon. Once I told daddy that the rocks at Sunny Isles Beach seemed to be growing. He laughed and said, "That's called erosion." If this was erosion, these tombstones were growing too. On another stone we could make out one word: INCONSOLABLE and a date: 1708.

166

"Pirates!" Andy announced, without the shadow of a doubt. He was a staunch champion of pirates. Every Halloween he turned into one in about five minutes. He had that costume down.

These must have been the early settlers. But why was this graveyard abandoned? Here was proof that the terrain was constantly shifting. One hurricane could have completely covered this graveyard with sand and nobody had bothered to dig it out. Who knows when? And now another shift was uncovering it. We had detoured around the street where the man hanged himself only to find a graveyard.

I was having a strange thought about how the dead lived anyway, on and on, when I saw a sun-bleached bone, it was a wrist bone, arching up, and I knew the hand and fingers were just beneath the sand. Oh my god the whole skeleton must be there. Andy saw it too and took off running, his red hair standing on end. I lit off after him, shivers of cold terror propelling us both—running so fast we planed above the stickers.

That's how we happened to come out on the road in front of Shirley Hanley's house; a flat, narrow black-top with room for one car, or two, if they each rode over on the sandy shoulder when they passed, a pebbly road, dogpatched with soft tar where it had worn, so you could carve in it all summer long, a road like all the others in Uleta—except this one would seal my fate.

We were sweating, Andy and I, our hearts pounding. We flopped in a patch of periwinkles, panting and laughing wildly like escapees, lucky to be alive.

167

Shirley Hanley was out in her play-yard across the road, hanging on the fence, watching us. She had half a finger missing on one hand from a lawn mower accident when she was four, so now her family treated her like a little princess, only they fenced her in.

In the fourth grade I had gone by Shirley's every morning before school. We were in the same class and her mother liked for me to walk with Shirley to the bus stop. Each morning, Mrs. Hanley ironed one of Shirley's starched dresses, ordered from the Sears Catalog , five new ones every year, no matter what. The dresses were starched, sprinkled and then rolled up and stacked in the Frigidaire, in-waiting to be ironed. The ironing board was always up, right there, next to the Frigidaire. Getting Shirley ready for school seemed to be the most important operation of the whole house. When I came in, Shirley would be eating her breakfast in the clean, steamy, white kitchen, the delicious smells of coffee, toast, oilcloth and starch all mingling.

Next, Mrs. Hanley bathed Shirley in a white-footed tub with Ivory soap and rushed around with hot towels, patting her dry while Shirley giggled. She leisurely put on her little white cotton underpants and camisole to match, all pressed and laid out, and then, Mrs. Hanley, the wardrobe mistress, held Shirley's freshly ironed dress over her head and gently slid it down, as if it was a silk wedding gown. She buttoned up the back and took about ten minutes tying a perfect bow, with the result that Shirley had that cherished look—her mother's regard showing through. I sat and watched this ritual, endlessly enchanted, my imagination stirring like I was playing dolls. I wondered what it felt like to be cared for like that, to be a big, live baby-doll.

Now Shirley was yelling for us to find her a whitey, as though it was easy. She was used to people doing for her, giving her whatever she wanted. Andy and I sat motionless, with just our eyes moving, like bug-eyes, straining to pick out a scarce mutation amongst hundreds of regular periwinkles. We ignored Shirley who was over there in her own world anyway, humming a dumb song.

About a hundred yards down the road, I saw a boy coming towards us, casting a tawny light. I held him in my field of vision, growing familiar with him as he drew closer, lazily, like a ship coming in from sea, and fierce too, like a wave building, before it rolls ashore and knocks you over.

When he was about ten feet away, I felt myself turning involuntarily in his direction, magnetized by his glow, golden as butterscotch. His hair was a quiet shade of blond, cut in a flat-top with fenders that stood up like velvet pile. His eyes were aqua-blue. As he came closer I could see the faintest skim of blonde down on his jaw, and his cheeks had a beet-colored iridescence in them. He grinned ironically, as though he had a secret, showing off even white teeth and laughing eyes, like he meant to win us over.

Sh-boom. My heart pounded. A fluttering began in my stomach. I blushed, as my cheeks caught fire. My mouth went dry as an empty jar. I forgot about whiteys and everything else, and hopped onto the sandy shoulder beside the road, which was hot enough to roast a goat on, but not hot as the inside of my own head. I squatted down, and

169

started digging my initials into the runny tar with a stick, trying to recover my missing brain. I leaned into it, breathing deeply of the exotic smell of hot tar, getting dizzy from it, and feeling the burn of my short-shorts riding up my crack.

He was standing right above me and my heart sped up and pounded so hard I was sure he could hear it. I crossed my arms over my heaving chest and rose up, intending to run, but I was stuck in place, like a stick in tar. So instead of running, somehow I got outside myself and hovered above in thin air, where I looked down and saw that I was just a skinny, red-headed ragamuffin tomboy, with a drum beating in her bumpy chest, with a freckled face flushed red as blood on fire. I squeezed my eyes shut to stop the picture. My breath was coming in little pants and I was unable to make a sound or word one. I couldn't even breathe.

He stood there casually. His bulk felt like a lost twin, like a new phantom limb I'd just grown that would change me forever. A feeling so strong engulfed me then, surmounting all that I had ever felt before combined, a thrill beyond my baby imagination, a sensation so new and large that the capacity to have it came as a stunning shock. I suddenly understood songs, my mother and father's fire, the truth of that wrist bone.

Andy, who to my surprise knew the boy, came to the rescue. "Hi lardass," he said, grinning big.

Grinning back with those white teeth, and shadow boxing Andy's chin, the boy countered: "Tim Murphy to you, skinny." Then he looked right at ME like I should recognize his name, he was so famous.

"This here's my sister," Andy said. I blushed anew at the sudden mention of me in his presence—even my hands blushed. I floated above like an overblown balloon ready to pop, suddenly conscious of my every move. OH NO, DON'T LOOK AT ME, I screamed inside, not making a sound. I looked away quickly, unable to bear his eyes, my stomach fluttering, fluttering.

Shirley started right in singing and giggling at the same time: "Fools fall in love just like wise men..." HOW DID SHE KNOW? Tim looked over at her, smiling, mildly interested. She beamed back, stumbling on the words of the song, "...when they ought to, should be, right back in school." She waved a white hanky like a surrender and kicked tiny pebbles across the road at him, provocatively, I thought. Where had she learned to flirt like that? Tim smiled, but didn't make a move.

I heard Andy telling about the abandoned pirates' graveyard we found, and that must be when I got back inside my body. And then Tim was gone, a dim outline way on down the road, and I didn't remember him going. I added a + T.M. to my own initials in the tar.

The rest of that day was like a rattling husk. I remember going over to old Mrs. Pitts' house, watching her ring the necks of some chickens that continued to run wildly around headless, jerking blood all over the yard. The first time I'd seen that I'd gotten queasy, but this time I didn't hardly register it. We sat on her fence watching, yet I was in another place, dazed and tingling, my bearings lost. I was hanging on the earth by a thread and I knew it.

Andy sensed something was wrong with me so he started telling me things to try and wake me up; like a Geek was somebody in a circus who bit the heads off chickens with his teeth. I just looked at him.

After Mrs. Pitts paid us for the two measly whiteys Andy found, I don't remember when, we cut through her yard on the way to Badgers where we were going to spend the twenty cents on R.C.'s and Butterfingers, Andy's favorites. Chicken shit squished luxuriously up between my toes; I noticed for the first time that it had a pleasant texture, warm and silky, and I didn't even care if I stepped in it. I had a whole new set of cares.

I kept looking over my shoulder for Tim. He was all I could think about. This was different from what I felt for Blackie so long ago, and my cousin Willy in the hurricane. All of a sudden I had something—I was filled up with it. What would I do now? As I mooned over my situation, it came to me that love was rigorous; it took a kind of courage I wasn't used to, and sacrifice. I began making bargains with God. I would need my right arm, but I was ardently willing to give my left arm for Tim, if only, oh God, please let me have him. I don't know what I wanted to do with him. A love nest came to mind, high up in a tree where we could be together, and somehow merge. The only boy I'd kissed up to that time was my cousin Willy.

Now with all my heart I wanted to kiss Tim Murphy.

24.

That night at the dinner table I asked for starch in my dresses.

"Starch! what?" my mother shrieked, almost dropping her Manhattan. "If you don't like the way I do your dresses, dearie, you can do them yourself."

"Okay, I will," I said.

Mama gave me the worst sucked-lemon look.

We had been to Byron's and I have two new outfits for school. One is a plaid skirt and white blouse, with a white orlon cardigan I'll never be able to keep clean. The other is an organdy dress, Jello yellow. I'll wear each outfit twice, but not in a row, then I will wash and starch them with whatever Mrs. Hanley uses on Shirley's dresses, and iron them and repeat the cycle, mixing in last year's clothes that still fit. I'll work on my appearance until I no longer look like a ragamuffin.

"You're a pill," mama said, laughing a wicked laugh.

Marie was having trouble with Gus and now as we sat at the table eating our supper we could hear them, if we strained to listen, shouting and arguing, into our silences. This must be why daddy didn't want houses built close to us.

"Hush—hush up," mama snapped, "Listen to them!" like she was more interested in their fight than in us. When it grew quiet I thought Marie must be crying.

173

The next morning I went over and she was sitting at her kitchen table with a purply eye, listening to "Burnt Toast and Coffee Time" on the radio. She loved Arthur Godfrey and Don McNeill. They were the kind of men she'd go good with—or someone like my father who might bake cakes and make persimmon jelly with her sometimes. Instead of Goofy Gus the Grouchy German. Mama belly-laughed and said I was a pip when I told her my name for Gus. It wasn't a good time to be German. Hitler wasn't dead enough yet.

Marie started crying and said she was getting a divorce from Gus. This would be her fourth divorce, and I could hear my mother squawk, "Again!" But I didn't really blame Marie. I decided divorce must be okay when you got to the end of your rope with someone, and you didn't go together too well to begin with. Marie was like a movie star to me—she could get away with the luxury of divorce.

She sobbed, "He doesn't want to touch me because of my skin, he's revolted, as if what I have is catching."

I said quickly, "Oh, Marie, he's just stupid." I thought that would distract her because it was a known fact that Gus was not too bright. It was something she could hang onto and then just forgive herself for not seeing it sooner.

"He doesn't give a Continental damn about me," she said, crying even harder.

After she was tired of crying, she wiped her eyes. I looked deeply into those twinkly blue eyes, there was a long silence, and then we both just burst out laughing for no reason I could think of.

Marie puffed her cheeks full of air and did a couple of blowfish. Then she said, "Any-hoo, I hope he gets hit with a jai alai ball." Gus worked at the Hialeah Fron Ton as a janitor. I knew just what she meant when she said that. My father told me once that jai alai balls travel at speeds up to 190 miles an hour and you die if one hits you.

That was the end of that long summer. I was in the sixth grade and not only did I get Miss Packer again, but Tim Murphy and Shelby Wauldin were both in my class. Suddenly I loved school.

Right away Miss Packer started taking us out on field trips. I couldn't think of anything I'd rather do than travel the roads in a bus, sitting beside Shelby, right behind Tim Murphy, studying the back of his head. Miss Packer told us she was combining history, geography, Indian culture, art and architecture. We did arithmetic, science and reading first thing in the morning, before we left. During morning recess, as I cleaned off the board and erasers, I peeked at her plan, written up in her beautiful hand and lying open on her desk. We were going to places all over Greater Miami, Miami Beach and the Everglades, whole other thrilling worlds.

Miss Packer strolled up and down the aisle giving a running commentary on everything we passed in our big yellow school bus, the "rolling school room," she called it. As we crossed a bridge over Biscayne Bay and entered the Island of Miami Beach, she surprised us by saying the island was entirely man-made. In the early 1900s, Carl Fisher and a band of developers, who called themselves "Architects of the Future" had dredged up sand from Biscayne Bay and piled it on a narrow strip, building it up wider and longer, and in turn making Biscayne Bay deep and cavernous in places, giving stone crabs a home. They did this until they had created an island, just like children playing in the sand on the beach. You had to cross a bridge from the mainland to get to it. So then there were jobs building more bridges, and more jobs building houses and hotels to stay in while you were there. And then came the boom years of the 1920s when gangsters came and Miami Beach was considered the most exciting place in the world. Until a devastating hurricane hit on September 17, 1926. The bust came after that, with the depression mama always complained about, and the economic crash of 1929. Miami had been rebuilding ever since, Miss Packer said.

Now in the winter of '53, Miami Beach had a rich, tempting atmosphere and it was swarming with people from up North, talking funny and wearing bathing suits even though it was way too cold. Little geometrical motels with competing neon signs had sprung up here and there on both sides of Collins Avenue, the main road. We glided toward the southern end, and Collins suddenly widened and curved to accommodate what Miss Packer said would be the largest, most beautiful hotel in the world when it was finished. There on the beach side, curving and rising like giant totems with arches was the steel skeleton of the Fontainebleau. As we passed I strained my eyes to pick out my father from about a thousand workers with hardhats. I thought I saw him and Blackie, way up on top, up there with a tree, of all things. Suddenly I was frightened. I started praying to God, right then, to protect them, so they wouldn't fall. It would be almost another year before the construction of the Fontainebleu was finished.

Now I was worried about my father. Everyone in Miami laughed at the Fountainbleau, called it a sand castle that was growing way too big, a pipe dream, somebody's crazy fantasy. Every day The Herald and The Daily News took another potshot at it. But it got more and more real every day, and more dangerous. Only the workers took it seriously. My father said it had more steel in it than the Empire State Building in New York City, and it wasn't going anywhere in a hurricane. I decided that I loved the Fountainbleau because it was so daring, but most of all because my father was working on it and my prayer to keep him safe required love and loyalty, the same as the men working on it had.

We went across the Venetian Causeway and South on U.S. 1 all the way to Red Road. We had already been to Villa Vizcaya, which we passed again. Miss Packer wanted to show us a far less famous, less grand, but in certain ways more important house. A lot of the world seemed to be about houses and buildings. Miss Packer called it real estate.

As we turned North on Red Road, she told us this used to be the edge of the Everglades, where the Seminole Indians hid from "the Devil," which is what they called Andrew Jackson. He tried to drive all the Indians out of Florida back in 1812 and kept on trying for nearly fifty years. But he had not succeeded, the Florida Seminoles are the unconquered, and have never signed a peace treaty with the U.S. There were still lots of Seminoles here, Miss Packer said, further

177

back in the 'glades, along the Miami River. She said we would visit them one day soon, but we couldn't expect them to trust us because white men had driven Indians on a "Trail of Tears" that was equal to anything the Nazis did to the Jews and Poles and Catholics, and had nearly made the North American Indian extinct. I hoped there was a hell for people like Andrew Jackson and Adolph Hitler, and I vowed never to follow anyone who wanted to gang up on another group of people.

We came to the important house on Coral Way, and as we all stood on the open porch that went all around it, Miss Packer painted a picture: "In the early 1900's this house was called "Guavonia" and all the land around it as far as you could see was a fruitful guava plantation. From this porch the Indian campfires could be seen glowing out in the 'glades. The owner of the plantation, Solomon Merrick, had come down from New England, and he had formed a good friendship with the Indians. Guavas were not very profitable in the marketplace, and nobody liked how they smelled when they were ripe. So the grapefruit replaced the guava, and the name of the plantation changed to Coral Gables, named after the gabled tile roof on the house. By that time, Solomon's son George had taken over and had bought more land, expanding the homestead to 3,000 acres. It was George Merrick who laid out a beautiful plan for a new city on this land in the 1920's, and this is it: Coral Gables!" Miss Packer swept her arm out over a whole bunch of houses that looked like little Spanish castles, built among huge sheltering trees. She told us the names of the trees: banyan, royal poinciana, jacaranda, gumbo limbo, coconut palm, mango, avocet and cocoplum. It looked like Paradise; I took a deep breath and swallowed paradise.

After we looked inside all the rooms of the spacious Guavonia, we toured the neighborhood. Merrick had designed all the building sites on curving, tree-lined streets and forty miles of inland waterways that he landscaped, like Venice canals, with Bridges of Sighs over them. Miss Packer showed us the place where he had quarried limestone for the buildings. He didn't just leave a giant ugly hole. He landscaped it with moss-covered rocks, royal palms and flowering bougainvillaea, built an arbor over it, and tapped a spring to continually fill it with clean, cool water. He named it the Venetian Pool, and opened it to the public. I couldn't wait to tell my father about all this. Maybe someday we could swim here, even if it was a far thirty miles from Uleta.

As our bus tootled over the Bridges of Sighs, Miss Packer sighed when the bus leapt a little, and we all did it too, and laughed at the fun. She said there was a way to develop land for people and this was it. The crisscrossing streets had low concrete markers with romantic Spanish names like Granada, Andalusia, Cordova, Sevilla, and the sidewalks were tinted pale pink. I had never seen such beauty.

I began to get an idea about where I was, outside of Uleta, and to understand that every place and person in the world had its own features, its own origin and history, and everything was all looped together in time.

25.

One day I came home from school to find a party going on in the kitchen. My mother had two new lady friends suddenly. She was all aglow, the queen of everything, reigning at her kitchen table. She fixed highballs for everyone with a fancy bottle that said Canadian Club on it. I looked over surprised to see my secret friend, Marie, sitting there with her faded-beauty look, now flushed a boozy red. The other lady was Dot Murphy, Tim's mother who happened to come from Boston too, like my mother, only more recently, and they'd just met by chance at the Greyhound Inn. Dot was talking about her ancestry, said she was half Irish and half French. Mama jumped in and said, "But your accent is pure Bostonian. As soon as I heard it I knew."

Mama was all excited. What a find for her. She didn't yet know I was in love with Dot's son, Tim. No one did.

I was fixing a peanut butter and jelly and a glass of milk when I heard my mother say, "Badger had a bun on." "What's a bun?" I asked, chomping on my sandwich. They all howled with laughter, like it was a private joke.

"Oh, there's a lot you don't know, dearie," my mother said. Then she hopped up and started dancing all over the place, holding her dress up over her knees saying she was the last of the red-hot mamas, in this fake deep voice. She shimmied around ungracefully but everyone laughed because she was funny too in an odd way that also embarrassed me. I did not laugh. Whatever she did, it was like I was doing it too or something, like I was responsible for it and I didn't want to be.

Dot Murphy started calling me Bedelia after that, I don't know why. "Where're you floating around to all the time Bedelia?" she'd ask me with the same smile Tim had, and I'd smile back at her and shrug my shoulders. She probably didn't think I had a scintilla of a chance with her son. Mama called me "Honeybunch," and Marie said I was getting a shape like the Venus de Milo. I don't know who that is. Rita Hayworth is who they compared me to next, but I knew they were only trying to make me feel good. She's a famous movie star with long flowing red hair.

They began regarding me with new interest, like they could see changes in me that had to do with being a lady, because that was their advice: "Be a lady, be a lady," The drunker they got, the more they said it: "Be a lady, be a lady, be a lady," whatever that was.

Now when they saw me coming they sang, "Gotta get your old tuxedo pressed, Lou-Lou's back in town," and I tried to laugh it up a little with them before I slipped outside to escape, running fast as I could, climbing up the first tree I came to, shaking off that lady stuff which gave me shivers round the hinds of my legs.

My ears perked up one day, when Dot Murphy started talking about Tim—how he walked in his sleep all the time, and how one night he walked into the kitchen, opened the ice box and pissed in it. Then he just shut the door and went back to bed. The ladies fell out laughing. Luckily she had seen him do it so she cleaned it right up. Otherwise, no one would have ever known the difference.

Sometimes they told birth stories and I hid in my closet and listened. Once I heard mama talking about Donnie's birth: "He was so big, he weighed over nine pounds, they had to use forceps on his big head, to get him out. He was never right after that." Then she cried and they all said not to worry, it wasn't her fault, Donnie was alright. It made me feel sick.

After the ladies went home, if I was lurking around, my mother warned me, "Now don't tell your father, Miss Goody Two-Shoes, just say Dot Murphy dropped by but don't tell him Marie was here."

One time I said, "But that's a lie."

"Just a little white one," she countered. "You like your father better than me, don't you?"

I didn't answer that. How could I?

"But why can't Marie be here?" I asked her.

"Because she's such a drinker," she said, breezing past me to go lie down and sleep it off before supper, her parting shot: "and don't spread around how old I am either."

26.

I completely forgot my mother's advice to always get boys to chase after me. I chased Tim Murphy so unmercifully around the school yard he got afraid of me, like I would devour him or something. He kept plying me with coconut patties, which he seemed to have an endless supply of, to keep me at arms length. He climbed up a tree and kicked at me, and he wouldn't come down until I backed way off. On the bus he jumped in a seat next to Shirley Hanley, so I couldn't sit beside him. I wouldn't have hurt him, there are such things as moral impossibilities. I just wanted to be near him. I couldn't understand what he was so afraid of, and why he didn't love me back.

One day Miss Packer took us out the Tamiami Trail to visit a real Seminole village, not a set-up tourist attraction. After we got out of the bus, we had to hike across a saw-grass prairie, then through a bamboo and cypress jungle for about a quarter of a mile, then cross the river in groups, by canoe, paddled by our bus driver and one of the chaperons, while two Indian boys pointed out the way and laughed at the paddling style of the white man. The wild conures up in the trees mocked us too,"gaw, gaw, gaw, gaw."

I let Tim go on and waited until the last group, which always included Shelby because she was so big. By now she'd grown about another foot. She was fully developed and looked like a grown woman twenty years old. She had to wear a brassiere as big as my mother's.

On the other side of the river, it grew darker as the sun got blocked out by the big old hardwood trees, mahogany, red maple, live oak and the gigantic palmettos that we were tromping through. And then there it was, a cool, swept-dirt clearing, smoky and mysterious, enclosed in a wide circle of papery-trunked gumbo-limbo trees. The Seminoles slowly appeared, walking out from under chickees and from around fires to see who had come into their village. It was winter and the campfires were the only source of heat. Old mothers stayed put around their fires working, cooking, dying cloth, and sewing. They sewed strips of cloth together that they had dyed, into bands, so they looked like coral snakeskins. Then they made blouses and skirts out of the cloth, and now, in the winter they wore many layers of these, all piled on so they looked like fat rainbows. They were tough and healthy, and in their big brown eyes was a look of betrayal—and also of curiosity, mainly about Shelby, whom the children surrounded and touched to see if she was solid and warm-blooded. She had on a red and brown striped dress, and they seemed to revere her, as though she was a live totem. They wondered at Miss Packer's blond enormity too, in her pastel pink cashmere coat, and even my redheadedness was a curiosity. Shelby whispered to me that she was part Indian, and I believed her—it was there in her sad brown eyes. In my heart I was Indian too.

Miss Packer was in a huddle with the old chief for awhile—he seemed to know we were coming—she gave him

184

books and pencils. Then she began explaining the design of the chickee as we solemnly followed her around, eavesdropping on family life going on inside. The chickee hut was a platform built four or five feet off the ground, supported by cypress tree limbs and covered with roofs made out of cabbage palms. There were no walls, allowing for the free circulation of air as well as our snooping eyes. My father didn't believe in doors within a family; the Seminoles didn't believe in walls or any privacy at all it seemed. They weren't even self-conscious, as we watched them bathing and nursing their babies. All the little children followed us around touching our skin and clothing, as interested in us as we were in them.

As we stared at the hammocks under the chickees that held the babies, back-and-forthing in the gentle breezes, Miss Packer painted a picture of village-life, of snakes and alligators and flood waters all converging on the camp, and being outsmarted by the Seminoles who were safely up in the air in their hammocks and chickees, out of reach.

There were no men in the camp, only a few young boys and the old chief. Miss Packer tried to find out from the women where the men had gone, but the women didn't want to understand her English. They spoke their own Creek language and looked away from her blondness. Miss Packer finally said, with a shrug, that the men must be off working somewhere, or hunting. That's when I knew my father made up that story about how Miami got its name. The way he told it, two Seminoles, a squaw and a brave, were riding down the river in a canoe and the brave said, "You are so pretty today," and the squaw said, "My-am-I?"

We presented the women with boxes of food we had collected from the whole school. There were mostly cans, and I wondered if they had a can opener. They seemed the most happy with two big bags of corn meal and some Hershey's cocoa. I saw they were going to mix them together. They presented us with red and black bead necklaces, the kind you could buy up at the Indian stands along the Tamiami Trail. They made them here and supplied the stands.

Little children started handing Shelby and me their hands, gently sliding them in ours with a smile, and walking alongside us faithfully. I took Shelby's hand and together with the children we formed a serpentine chain and played go in and out the window, to peals of giggles. I was beginning to like the smoky, ripe-fruity smell of the village, a comfortable smell once you got used to it. Every now and then, a whiff of wet dog fur assailed me, of kerosene, skunk, and rotting marine life—the forever Glades. Shelby and I were the last ones to leave. We wanted to stay there and live in that exotic outland, it was so peaceful, easy, and sweet.

The next week we went to the Fairchild Tropical Gardens, and Miss Packer told us there was going to be a scarcity of plants and trees someday because rain forests all over the world were being destroyed. That was hard to believe when we were surrounded by them—but I knew I couldn't live in a world without trees. I loved learning their names, the beautiful words they were known by. Miss Packer knew them all. Whyever weren't trees and flowers capitalized? when even the names of streets were.

We stood for awhile and watched the bamboo grow. It was a species that grew four feet a day. Shelby watched the bamboo grow with more interest than anyone, more than she'd ever shown in anything else before. It was like she'd found some inexpressible kinship with the bamboo.

And then, as we sidled along the pathway, there it was before us, the great talipot palm. Miss Packer talked softly, as if the tree could hear. It was a rare giant palm that bloomed only once in its lifetime and then died. She directed our eyes about forty feet up in the air to the top where the fruits of its first and only bloom were then ripening. She had brought us here for this event, I realized with admiration. I felt Shelby shudder beside me as we both stared up, listening to Miss Packer. The talipot grows like crazy for forty-seven years, flowers and then lives for one more year until the fruits mature, then it dies. It was the saddest thing I had ever heard of, but somehow it gave me new hope for death—the condition of being dead seemed to have some new substance or purpose to it. Shelby looked ennobled for the first time in her life.

A giant's life is short, I knew, and I liked to be by Shelby more than any other person in the world except my father. Now I wondered if she would flower before she died and how her life would unfold and if I'd even be there to see it. I wondered about my own life too, and if I'd ever get Tim to like me, in a thousand years.

27.

It was hot, sitting on the school bus next to Shelby, headed for home. My legs, even through my yellow dress were sticking to the seat. We squinted and dodged our heads but nothing shut out the sun's bright light for any long enough kind of time. In fact there was no sense of time at all in this June heat—just sweat. It made me feel angry, especially when I looked back at Tim sitting next to Shirley Hanley. There were two days of School left. It was like a stomachache now—you'd just like it to be over with—and take off the shoes, untie the sashes, get rid of the sashes. I'd outgrown them. All coverings felt burdensome now. Shelby was just sitting there beside me looking numb, but I knew it was her nature to move slowly and be tranquil no matter what. I admired her for it.

I don't know how it started, but I caught this really fat girl I didn't even know across the aisle staring at Shelby, and I started feeling sour towards her. She stared at me too, then at Shelby, who kept on looking straight ahead. She eyed Shelby up and down, gloating, and then looked out the window. She kept doing this, glaring and making faces. Finally I said, "What are you looking at?"

Donnie, who was in the seat behind watching this, said, "Yeah, fatso."

"Nothing," said Fatso. "What's it to you anyway?"

After about a minute of silence, Donnie nudged me on the back. I couldn't think of what to say next. I hated this girl suddenly, and I'd never had a feeling like this towards a stranger before. I knew it was partly the heat.

"Plenty," I said. But I was way too late responding and she didn't know what I was talking about.

"You talkin' to me?" she said, screwing up her face in a scowl. I could see she was just plain mean, like a boy could be.

"Yure fat," I said, like a quick slap. Then I laughed, and looked over at Shelby who was still looking straight ahead with no expression on her face as if she didn't want any part of this, and didn't even care.

"Watch it, freckle face," the girl said real loud, and I blushed, a reflex.

I thought at least I could outrun her so that emboldened me: "Go jump in a dirty rock-pit." I said, real smart-alecky.

By the time the bus stopped to let us off at the Youth Center in Uleta, we had traded a few more insults. She would like to have insulted Shelby instead of me, but she couldn't think of anything to say that would get her attention. Once she said, "What's wrong with her?" pointing at Shelby.

I glared back and said, "Nothing, stop pointing."

"You gonna make me?" she said.

"Yeah, maybe she will," Donnie piped behind me.

When we all stood up to get out, I saw that this girl was bigger than I thought. In fact she weighed about twice as much as I did. And I had been asking for it. Getting off the bus, the steps seemed too far apart and my knees started shaking. Donnie was already taking bets, taking long odds on

189

me. He thought fat people were uncoordinated. As I watched Shelby's back she walked on down the street slowly towards home. A circle formed around us with me and the fat girl in the middle. Everyone was yelling, trying to get us to face off and start the fight. The space was no man's land between us. No one dared get in it. I hadn't even put my books down yet. Once I did, it would start.

Suddenly I didn't want to fight, and I decided to walk away, but as soon as I turned, Donnie turned me right back, grabbed my books and said, "Get back in there. What are you, a chicken?" Then he shoved me toward the girl who was bigger than any two people there. Right away, she threw a shadow on me. I darted around to get out of it. I could see Tim Murphy and Shirley Hanley watching, Tall Paul, Andy, Billy and them, all my friends, watching, and I came out in gooseflesh. I was fighting, so even if I was a girl I was under boys code, no interference, finish your own fight. Even if they wanted to, Paul and Billy couldn't help me now.

Once she grabbed me it was all over. Her arm was like a steel clamp locking on my arm. I kicked at her and swung wildly with my other arm, but she grabbed it too and twisted it behind my back and knocked me down and sat on me, all in one fast motion. I couldn't believe the pain. If she moved an inch my arms would break. My back exploded and then I realized I had no breath and she was too heavy to lift to get one—I was going to die. I could hear her demanding, "Say uncle, say uncle."

Donnie leaned down into my face coaching me, "C'mon, Lou, lose it! Now! Lose your temper!"

I said with my last breath, in a little puff, "Uncle," but I felt the weight lifted off before the whole word was even out. I cracked open my watery eyes and breathed again, and saw Shelby lifting the girl straight up off me. Everyone was yelling. Donnie leaned into my face and yelled: "Why didn't you try harder? You could have beat her—you didn't have to say uncle so quick."

I pulled myself into a knee-chest position and tried to urge the pain out of my body. My pants were wet as though I was sitting in a puddle. I stank. I closed my eyes and burned with humiliation. My ears were blazing. Didg and Charlie Whitfield kicked dirt at me. Then everyone left me to my shame and ran over to where Shelby was holding Fatso a few feet up off the ground. They surrounded her chanting, cheering, egging Shelby on, but she just dangled the girl out at arm's length, and then placed her high up in the branches of a rubber tree. Of all things, she couldn't get down. I don't know how Shelby knew this, but the girl was so afraid up in the tree that she started crying. It was too high to jump, and she couldn't climb down. Without any change in her placid expression, Shelby said to the girl: "Just stay there, forever."

Everyone laughed uproariously. I had managed to stand up by then, and hobbled off down the road without looking back. I felt like a nothing, like a dead petunia. The tomboy act was over, it had worn me out. I was too big for my own britches and got the sand kicked out. I wanted to take on the world like a boy did, but something was stopping me, maybe my redheadedness. I couldn't be tough like boys and live by their code. I didn't want to anymore. Any girl heavier could just pin me down and the pain didn't seem worth anything like winning or glory or honor or any of those boy-strong-things. I was a coward. I would give up again, in a minute, I knew it. I had to be another kind of strong that came more natural to me, strong like a woman, and graceful too, like Miss Packer was. Lord, I needed grace. All the way home, the feeling of failure and self-loathing stayed with me like a possum you can't run off.

I took a long bath and sang, "How much is that doggie in the window" so I could yelp like a dog without attracting attention. When he came home from work, I told Daddy what happened, and he played the harmonica for me, warbling soulfully, healing me. "Sanguine," he whispered between songs, "be sanguine." It was one of his words, one that made us both feel good, made us be what it sounded like: cheerful, hopeful. He wanted me to let bad things pass quickly, and not turn out to be such a brooder. He played our favorite, "The Sidewalks of New York," fanning the harmonica with his right hand: "East side, west side, all around the town...." and I tapdanced to it, shuffle-ball changing until I beat the floorboards hollow.

At the supper table my mother looked at my face and said: "Are you constipated?" She was always monitoring everyone's bowels, of all things, especially if you were in a bad mood. The Masked Man and Andy didn't talk about the fight, just gave me dirty looks. They were disgusted with me for losing.

That night as the sun went down, we played Blind Man's Bluff in the moonlight in our front yard, as if nothing had happened. There was Tim and Andy, Donnie, Sandy Yates, me and Valarie Twombley. Luckily, Shirley Hanley wasn't allowed out after supper. We stirred around in a wide circle, and each of us took a turn being blindfolded, and spun around in the middle, and then pointed toward the group who on the count of three had to freeze in place. Blindly, we stretched out fingertips, brushed against arms, groped and grabbed, guessing who the person we caught was, just by touching, sniffing. All the senses could be used except sight. When it was Donnie's turn he seemed pulled toward Sandy as if by magnetism and Sandy went in his direction first when it was her turn. Then they took a long time touching and guessing. They were like my miniature magnetic scottie dogs. When it was my turn I couldn't find Tim anywhere.

At eight-forty-five, just as night was falling, Tim's father came by our house on his way home for supper, from his night job at Velda Dairy, and brought us ice cream bars and Fudge Sicles, we could take our pick. We feasted on the cold creamy chocolate, sitting on the ground, still warm from the day's sun. The ice cream cooled first our heads and then our bellies and the night sky grew starry and wide. Greater Miami must have the biggest sky on Earth I thought; the flatness of the land opened up the arc. I could lie back and look at the moon and always feel upside down.

We were all enthralled with this new game of touching each other to see who we were. Every few minutes I remembered the fight with that poor fat girl, and felt sick to my stomach. So I tried to forget about the awful fight, and home in on the tender feelings I had for Tim Murphy instead—funny new sensations in my deep-most parts that I liked, yet they made me feel odd and nervous.

I heard a song on the radio, coming out our wide open livingroom window: "Once I had a secret love... that lived within the heart of me...all too soon my secret love...became impatient to be free." I felt the words to be my own true feelings somehow duplicated.

After that, we played Blind Man's Bluff almost every night, our senses smoldering in the bright darkness, growing sanguine amidst the bursting summertime, and atingle with the certainty that Mr. Murphy would come by with the ice cream at exactly eight-forty-five, to cool down our wild rising passions.

28.

My mother's honky-tonk afternoons with Marie and Dot thinned out. Mostly mama had a little afternoon drink alone now, and once I walked in on her laying in bed talking to herself. Her hand froze under the sheet, "there's no law against talking to yourself, is there Miss High and Mighty?" she asked me, her eyes widening in outrage. Made me believe in doors for about the hundredth time.

With school out we were all free, but it wasn't like any summer before. This was a fidgety freedom. There were too many foreign feelings in my body. Was I the only one, or was everyone feeling this way? I couldn't tell by their faces, and nobody was talking about it.

My father scratched my back and read out loud from his newspaper to me every night about the Cold War. When the Olympics ended, the U.S. won seventy-six metals to Russia's seventy-one. It was almost like another war that was over and we'd won. The Red Russians were our enemy and they were growing way big like a giant, like a watermelon from an aberrant seed. People had even stopped wearing red; it was a suspicious color. Orange and mint green were real popular, avocado green was the new in-style color, but beige was the biggest color of the year, like Ike's uniforms.

My mother had a red wool bathrobe with white piping around the collar and cuffs. She had brought it with her from up North and every summer the moths ate a little more of it until by now it was full of holes—but in the winter she still wore it. When I looked at that robe, I always thought the holes were the Red Russians eating away.

Daddy knew I was having a scrappy thirteenth year so he gave me little tags of advice like, "Watch out now, fate is tetchy," and "never kick a skunk." He meant don't disturb anyone, go about your business, walk away from trouble. He said: "love is the sweetest joy, the wildest woe." Things like that, that were poetic and soothed the awful withering feelings in my heart. It was helpful, like when someone holds the jaws of a gator open for you so you can look down its throat.

We got a television set. Philo T. Farnsworth had invented it—a combination of a radio and a movie in one little box for the home. We already had the habit of watching the radio, even though there was nothing to see. So now we watched this new box and got a moving picture of a black and white world along with the sound. It took about five minutes for it to warm up. Then from the TV came people chanting, "We like Ike, we like Ike" all the time. It was like the catchiest thing in the world. He looked too clean to me, too neat with his crewcut and doll-like grin. I felt too scraggly to like Ike. Besides, we were democrats.

I wanted something so bad, but I couldn't ask my father for it. I had to ask my mother even though I was afraid to. Sure enough, she laughed at me. "A bra! What have you got to put in it? Ha-ha." It wasn't true. I had small boobs and a lot of other girls like Shirley and Valarie wore bras whether they needed them or not just so they'd show through their blouses. So I switched to wanting a door on my room—a little privacy for a change. Donnie and Andy were always walking by, trying to catch me getting dressed, and I thought Didge and Charlie Whitfield and maybe even Bicycle Bill were probably watching me through my curtainless windows. I was getting too big to dress in the closet.

I was brooding by the guava bushes one day when Shelby came along and led me over to this new kid, Lyle's backyard, where there were a bunch of other little kids I didn't know all sitting around in a circle under a banyan tree. Where had they come from? I didn't know Lyle very well either, because he was older, about sixteen, and he was talking dirty already. I'd overheard him a couple of times with Charlie Whitfield and Didge saying the worst word in the world that started with an F. Lyle parted his black hair and slicked it down—no crewcut for him.

We sat in the circle too, and I relaxed while Shelby braided my hair which had grown long again. I twirled on the sweaty little wisps of loose hair around my face and dozed off. The other kids in the circle were all giving Lyle their full attention.

Shelby said, "He's talking evil." I opened my eyes but I couldn't hear him as he moved around, sort of confidentially whispering things to little pairs of ears and then there was twittering and frightened looks, sometimes in our direction.

After he'd done the whole circle we were last. He stepped right up close in front of us, unzipped, and took it out of his pants, like it was a snake he was holding in his hand. Everyone stared wide-eyed. Someone screamed. I got to my feet, gasping. Lyle came toward me mumbling through a deep-six grin. He grabbed my hand and put it on the prow of his hard clammy snake. I felt a shock of terror streak through my body. I jerked my hand away.

The next thing I knew I was running out of the woods and down that guava-lined street with my mouth wide open in the wind, choking off my breath so I couldn't get the scream out. I was running as fast as I could, fear propelling me, so fast I was planing. I kept trying to scream but no sound came out. I looked back, and Lyle was coming right behind me. Then I turned the corner and was in the homestretch, the screams coming now: "Maaaa-mamma!" He slowed down as I reached the steps of The Sea Breeze and Daisy came out from under the house and started barking at him loud as a truck horn.

"Home free," I began to chant through a voice that had mercifully returned, "home free, home free, home free," and I got inside the house and collapsed.

"Whats a matter? whats a matter?" mama screached, shaking me. After I calmed down and told her what happened, she was mad. She got what she called her Norman Irish up. She marched me right back over to Lyle's house. I hated this so much.

But when Lyle started denying everything, and his mother said it was just my imagination, and Lyle said I had egged him on, I screamed, "You're a lousy liar."

Then Lyle's mother said, "Well, obviously a person of your ilk shouldn't be accusing my son."

My mother flew at her, "Why you son-of-a-bitch! Who do you think you are? You're ruining this kid by letting him get away with this. You'll be sorry someday for making a little pervert out of him." She was boiling. We left out of there, mama still cussing a blue streak. I don't know what did it, but I think it was the ilk thing.

I wondered what ilk meant and if there were other people in the world that thought they were better than us, because of something called ilk, and if I'd ever come up against it again.

I got the chills and mama put a blanket over me and said it was just hormones, I wasn't sick, and what Lyle did had nothing to do with sex or love. I was shocked when she said sex. She'd never said that word before. And she hardly ever said the word love, either. I almost fell asleep thinking about love. I felt my mother's hand on my forehead a few times checking my temperature. We didn't say "I love you" in my family, but I felt it then, about my mama. We were all too shy of our feelings, and besides those three words were somebody else's invention in Hollywood, too feeble to serve the fierce feelings we had.

I lay on the green couch looking up at the ceiling and for some reason it came to me that my father's trick of getting candy from the man in the ceiling was him acting out his love. I'd never thought about it while I was scarfing up the candy, but now I realized what I'd known all along—that the candy was really up his sleeve, he'd palmed it. He was the man in the ceiling. I thought about him even though it was my mother who had taken up for me. I don't know why. The only other person I knew who loved her father as much as I did mine was Shelby. I was sure she got away from Lyle because, for one thing, she was bigger than him—she was bigger than any of the boys– so no one bothered her. I smiled to myself now, remembering how she'd treed that fat girl for me, and she hadn't been able to get down.

There was something vulnerable about being a girl. I suspected it was the womb I'd seen in the medical books, and in this pamphlet they passed out at school called "Basic Biological Facts," put out by Kotex. The womb must be what everyone was protecting.

I was dozing when of all things I heard Shelby talking to my mother in the kitchen. I had always kept Shelby away because of my mother's diagnostic impulse. She couldn't help it—it was second nature to her to tell people what was wrong with them, or guess, or try to find out—to talk about embarrassing personal facts right out loud.

I strained my ears to hear Shelby's soft murmurings. Sometimes I could hardly hear her when she was standing right next to me. She was just being agreeable. Knowing wasn't important to her like it was to me. She already knew all she needed to know and had taken it in easily, like a glass of chocolate milk. She was a real true Sunbeam. I felt like a greenhorn puppy next to Shelby's vast wisdom, not much of which spewed out her mouth. It was all in her body's movements, in the way she accepted and in her generous indulgence of every single moment. I smiled lying there thinking about Shelby and my mother face to face. I didn't have the energy to do anything else. I heard my mother's excited voice every now and then. Once I heard the words "early menopause," whatever that was. But at no time did she come in where I was and take down the medical books with the pictures of bloody insides in them as I had always feared she might do when she saw Shelby.

They got chummy out there in the kitchen. Shelby was asking after my health probably, so she could decide what to do with Lyle. Once my mother started in talking, Shelby fell into her good-listener posture; she was the best. I hoped mama would tell her a good story at least. Then I just couldn't hold out any longer and I fell asleep. Before I did, I smelled chicken soup. Shelby had a good influence on my mother just like she did on everyone.

Of course I dreamed about snakes.

29.

Instead of a bra or a door, I got a bike. It was blue, second-hand, cost seven dollars. It was in pretty good condition once I shined it up. So I didn't walk anymore. I pedaled out in an ever widening radius, observing life getting thicker and thicker in rubbery old Uleta.

My luscious landscapes were going, and not with the wind either. Developers were moving in, taking trees to make plywood and putting housing developments up in their place. Five beautiful mango trees for one ugly house. The fruit of the land was disappearing fast. There was a bulldozer out leveling the pineapple fields, ripping through the vigorous plants. There was a glut of pineapple on the market and people needed houses instead. I went back every day and watched—in no time at all concrete block houses, identical but painted different easter egg colors of pink, blue, yellow, green and Eisenhower beige, sprung up. The houses sat in straight, flat rows just like the pineapple plants had, inviting their own self-styled doom I thought. Wherever would the people come from who would live in all of them? New prey for Lyle.

One day the ponies and horses were gone from Croft's Ranch. The next day a bulldozer leveled it, took out all the trees and fences. They were building a shopping mall over land that had had a previous life. Always and forever

202

something valuable would be under that mall, and none of the new people would know about it.

Where was Goatman this year? I rode all over looking for him. And then one day I saw his goats grazing behind the Higher Ground Nazarine, back in Mole lady's darkness.

One Saturday afternoon I rode over to Sandy Yates'. Right across from her house they were bulldozing our cow pasture to build more tract houses. Where were all these people coming from? my mind screamed. All of a sudden, something harum-scarum seemed to be happening around Uleta. Where was the planning like Mr. Merrick had done in Coral Gables? Now it seemed like Miss Packer had been warning us that this was coming.

Sandy and I went down the street to where her uncle had a combination house and service station. She'd begun hanging around there lately. Her hair was fixed in a real neat pony tail, high on the crown of her head, her face was freshly washed, and she had her big sister's lipstick on, Strike-Me-Pink. The very color of flamingos.

The yard was packed with old beat-up cars, parked under the shade trees, some just for parts and other newer models up on ramps with guys down underneath them standing in greasy pits and reaching up inside the cars. They talked about cars in languid voices. You could tell they lived to fix motors and to know them in some intimate way. They crawled up underneath them or leaned way down inside the jaws of the open hoods totally absorbed, detached from anything else that might be going on in the world. There was a big, black '49 Plymouth, and a greyish-green Hudson

Hornet getting lubes and oil changes. Packards and Chevys and Studebakers were lined up like black n' white checkers.

"See that '49 Merc over there? She'll outrun any of these others," one guy said, and nobody argued with him. Cars were important to guys, and I tried to see why.

If there were women in the house behind the station, they never came out. After awhile the younger guys began disappearing one by one and when they came back they were all cleaned up. Saturday night was the high point of their week. It was the one night they de-greased themselves, put on clean white T-shirts with a fresh pack of Lucky Strikes rolled up in one sleeve, and creased, pastel-colored, gabardine pants with a little skinny belt, hair shining, slicked back into a ducktail with Wild Root Hair Tonic. You could see they were about nineteen or twenty, a man to me.

I was a skinny little cracker who up until that moment felt comforted by my homeliness. I listened and watched, holding on to the handlebars of my bike. Sandy was over sitting in a new maroon Oldsmobile with one of them. Music blared out the windows: "Maybelline, you done started back doin' the things you used to do..."

I could smell Wild Root, cigarettes and Juicy Fruit gum all mingling together on the three men who leaned up against a car looking me up and down. It seemed to waft over with their voices: "You're gonna be pretty good looking when you grow up, honey. Look me up in about five years, will you, sugar?"

I shivered automatically and knew I wasn't adequate, and doubted I ever would be. My breasts were just little mounds, but as far as I knew these were the first men to notice that I

204

was growing up. Total strangers. I got on my bike and pedaled home as fast as I could. I didn't even say goodbye to Sandy. I wished I could go over to Marie's, but she and Gravy were living at Skeeter's now, and I wasn't allowed to ride that far away. Skeeter was divorced now too.

Did divorces run in families?

The rest of that summer, I turned into a loner, wandering around Uleta on my blue bike. I watched the developers taking all the land, butchering the grapefruit trees like they had no value and building uniform boxy houses on the flattened out ground. There was even talk of leveling the ancient Spanish Monastery and the Greynolds Park Fort—the land they were on was too valuable. I prayed hard for that not to happen. It seemed like all anyone talked about anymore was money. Selling land and building houses to make money. Money controlled everything.

I wished I had a sister. Everyone else had a sister. Girls seemed to come in pairs in other families. Valarie's big sister taught her things. If I had a sister I'd teach her art. One person teaching another is what life was about; one person showing another how to live. I missed Shelby but there was no way she could keep up with this bike even taking giant steps. She was busy with her father, the great Earl Wauldin, working on their new act. Besides, what I was seeing was too ugly to show Shelby or anyone, and I couldn't stop it happening. It made me want to kiss my beloved Uleta good-bye, float right out of it like I did my body when I ate guavas.

I climbed into my favorite rubber tree—they hadn't gotten that yet, and sat for long stretches of time, chewing on weeds and thinking. Above me in the highest branches, chartreuse parakeets, wild escapees, screeched eeeh-eeeh. Sometimes if I saw a person coming down the road, I got on my bike and faded. I didn't want to talk to anyone. Once a harmless black snake wound his way over to the limb I was sitting on, and while in the past I always got away from snakes, for some reason I didn't move this time and we stared at each other in a face-off, until the snake gave up and slinked away. Earl Wauldin passed underneath my branches one day and didn't even see me. But I saw him, his shoelaces were untied, and I saw an awful loneliness in his mammoth back as he plodded away, down the road. Loneliness belonged to me too. Just because I was still a child I wasn't expected to feel it yet, but I did. I was sitting up in that tree trying to keep myself company because there was no one I wanted to be with. Not even my truelove Tim Murphy, who always ran the other way anyhow. I had to live with that lurching in my stomach every time I saw him. And all he did when he saw me was laugh this sort of worldly-wise laugh he'd developed while he was in a sanatorium getting over TB when he was a little kid. He had a barrel chest I would be very happy to feel the full weight of, but all he did was run from me and laugh. I gave up chasing him around. Besides, he hadn't even become intimate with a car yet.

Twice a week I went up to the Youth Center and drew pictures of fruit, vegetables and hibiscus flowers, which the art teacher set up for us on a tabletop. She walked around glancing at our drawings and talking about herself. She told us she was a naturalist and a vegetarian. I could lose myself in the drawing, listening to her steady voice, and I didn't have to talk if I didn't feel like it. I could just sit and stew in the juices of a whole bunch of new feelings I couldn't understand, but were swelling my chest with untellable emotion, which I tried to let out through my drawing hand.

One day the art teacher walked me home so she could talk to my mother. I was too shy to try to stop her even though I knew it was a mistake. At the door she told my mother, "Your little girl has talent. I give private painting lessons at my house every Saturday morning, and I'd like her to come over. It's just for an hour."

"How much does this cost?" my mother asked suspiciously, not even inviting her in.

"It's only a dollar, for the hour, and I supply everything." the art teacher said, smiling down at me. She was beautiful but I knew my mother didn't think so. For one thing, she didn't wear a brassiere; you could tell because her titties were hanging so low, and she had a deep bronzy tan and no strap marks, like she might be that way all over from sunbathing naked. She had long straight hair just hanging loose and free and a swishy skirt, and Jesus sandals on her feet.

After she left, my mother called her a bohemian and said she didn't want me influenced by anyone like that. But I already was. I wanted to study the art teacher's mysterious style and be just like her, and someday if I ever got big titties I'd let them jiggle loose too, like she did.

My mother took a sip of her medicine, lit a cigarette, puffed on it like she was mad, and said, "Art lessons, puh!

207

You haven't been through a Depression, dearie; if you had you might know the value of a dollar."

She looked at a drawing I'd brought home. "What the devil's that supposed to be?"

I wasn't a bit surprised. I knew my mother didn't like art. Art was something my father and I could do and she felt left out of. She would never let us be artists if she could stop us, only she acted like she was saving us from some dangerous fate—as if art could bring about our ruin.

The art teacher dropped her price to fifty cents, but I still couldn't go, so she finally told me I could take lessons for nothing, just to come on. I went over to her house one Saturday, where she kept cats among other things, like a huge basket of peacock feathers, clay bowls with fish and flowers floating in them together, and big ole box turtles that walked the floors. There was even a picture of Reddy Kilowatt hanging alongside some other paintings on the wall. Turns out she was the designer of Reddy. I saw then that somebody has to draw something for the first time, and then everybody gets used to it and thinks it's always been there like a natural thing. I went back once more, and then I started feeling like a criminal sneaking over to that braless bohemian's art cave, so I didn't go anymore. It unexpectedly felt funny doing something my mother was so dead set against, like art was some kind of disgrace. Mama didn't think artists were achievers at all.

My life seemed assembled with no room for art in it, not then, but I knew that someday I'd get around to it and I'd make it be my center, and somehow art would set my chained self free.

30.

The seventh grade homeroom teacher didn't like daydreaming and wore a wig that was pulled so far forward she had about a one-inch forehead, making you suspicious of her brain power. Besides, she and all the other teachers kept on waking me up all day. Oh, how I longed for Miss Packer. I needed rest and had just about all I could hold of knowledge for awhile. I was grouchy as a bark, busy worrying something to death and everything else was at a standstill because of it. All my girl friends had started. They wore bras and knew how to hang around talking and laughing with boys—while I only watched. They had their own private language. They'd say, "Oh, I fell off the roof," or "I got my friend," or "I'm ridin' the white horse," everything in code like that, frosted with a sugary pride that turned my stomach. None of them called it precious, like Marie did. I knew it was all about blood—that I had to bleed in order to get on with life—but I didn't mind. It was even a little exciting. I just wished I'd start too so I could belong to the future. I was in a stagnant present and everything seemed to be changing fast except me. Bark Bark.

Valarie Twombley's breasts began to grow. I mean really grow. It was like that year we had the bumper crop of strawberries. By Halloween, she looked like Lana Turner except she was only fourteen. She came to the house to get me to go trick or treating, and my father's face lit up like the top of the Columbus Hotel. I had on what mama called my glad rags. I was always a gypsy for Halloween, and every year my costume got better because I added new touches. This year I sewed spangles around the hem of this full skirt Marie had given me a long time ago that hung low on my hips. The spangles were bottle caps, Nehi, Orange Crest, RC's. I had tons of old beads on and rings and earrings that hung down to my shoulders, so I made a lot of racket, which was to keep the boogers away. Valerie was a swan ballerina—she had on her sisters white strapless tutu, with silver sequins, and feathers hugging her ears.

Andy is a pirate as usual, Donnie's a tramp, Sandy Yates is a pin-up girl; she's got on her bathing suit and a sarong, like Dorothy LaMour. Tim's a bullfighter, and it's pitch dark but his red satin cape flashes, capturing my eyes. There are ghouls and vampires among us, maybe Whitfields and Platts. We meet up with kids who have white sheets over them with eyes cut out and I don't know who they are, but one of them is tall like Lyle, and it's not Shelby because she won't go out trick or treating. For a change I stick close to my brothers. It's our favorite holiday, a chance to raid Uleta and bay at the moon like wild dogs. We go marauding around in large packs, but only two or three of us go up to a door at the same time, because you get more candy that way, and sometimes loose change. It always rains on Halloween and sure enough a chilly mist started right up.

This year we swarm all over the new housing projects; all the houses are so close together it's easy to get a lot of candy in a short time. The horde of us walk all the way to Ojus and beyond, screaming "TRICK OR TREAT," plundering, breathless, grabby hunters. "Hotdiggety," Andy says if he gets a WHOLE candy bar. Mostly we get penny candy. If a person doesn't answer their door we soap their windows, tramp through their yards and go on to the next, giddy with our wild ways. Deep into the drizzly night we roam farther and farther, defying the bogey men and werewolves, and losing different kids as they got tired, soaked or scared, broke off and went on home.

Around midnight, just the three of us are left, Andy, Donnie and me, and we straggle home too, dragging our damp pillow cases, so full we can hardly heft them any longer. The tail of my skirt is wet, the spangles heavy with mud. My bare footskins are cold and sore.

We are all worn flat out and freezing, and mama screams at us for staying out so late. Then she rifles in our booty for the kind of candy she likes, Mary-Janes, Mounds or Non-pareils. We're proud of our hauls—we had put the ask on enough candy to last until Christmastime.

At school we lined up in two lines, boys on one side, girls on the other, and waited for half a day to get a shot in the arm of the new vaccine that would save us from the dreaded crippling of Polio. Inside the lunchroom, we had to take off our dresses and shoes, and get weighed and measured for the right dose, and get our sizes recorded. That's when I noticed Sandy Yates breasts had grown bigger too, like Valarie's. She had on a white bra. I just hoped it was catching. My own were about the size of guavas.

Valarie Twombley must have seen them bulging through my undershirt because the next day she gave me a pink cotton brassiere that she had outgrown already. It had stitching going all around in circles on stiff triple-A cups. I lied and told her I got "my friend." I probably never would have either except for the bike wreck. It happened on one of those corduroy roads that were all over Uleta, the kind you don't talk or chew gum on when you ride or you'll bite your tongue. I didn't feel too good that day anyway. My head was hot and throbbing and I'd been in a slump for about a year. I was only trying to get home. I stood up and pedaled faster. That's when the wheel hit a rock and spun out, throwing me off balance. I went a-flying but still hung onto the bike, dragging it along the gravel with me for about twenty feet, until we ground to a stop.

I lay spread-eagle for awhile, not moving, deciding whether I was dead or alive. There was a great falling feeling in me that continued on, a sensation of dropping in my hips, like something inside me had released a bag of marbles in wet sand. I felt a wave of nausea, then pain. I was tangled up in the bike and my knees were encrusted with stones glued in place with my own sticky blood. My arms were the worst— from the wrists to the elbows, they were scraped to a bloody pulp. I felt like taking a nap right there on the road. Eventually a car would run me over, finish me off.

Daisy, who had followed like a goat, started barking and licking my wounds, so I came awake thinking of Didge and Charlie Whitfield, those spit-healing bastards, and then I thought of Lyle, which caused me to have a shot of adrenalin

I stood up on. I stumbled home leaning on the bike for support. I was sweating and crying, and it felt like I had wet my pants. And then when I got home, I undressed and saw the blood. What a mess. But I was one of them now—I belonged. Now I'd be a full woman too, and someday part of the grand creation cycle. I couldn't believe it.

When I asked my mother for "Modess Because" she cackled, "When I was a girl we had to use rags, haw-haw."

Hurt my feelings—rags for something Marie called precious.

Then she said: "You know what genitalia is don't you? Stay away from it now. A word to the wise is sufficient."

That night I plopped on the floor in front of the television set. Mama had wrapped my arms and knees in gauze and tape, and my whole body ached. We watched The Ozzie and Harriet Show. I thought, is this what other families are like? It was embarrassing. If this was what a normal family looked like and acted like, we weren't even close.

I find it's not easy being a woman. First there are jangles in my head and I don't want anyone to see me or bother with me because I feel on the verge of crying all the time, or getting mad. I'm in a lonely tunnel with a diluted little sorrow that belongs only to me, and although I know I can talk it over with Marie or Shelby, I don't feel like it. My pants are stuffed with white cotton padding called a "Kotex", and I don't feel like climbing trees anymore.

I stare out the window of the school bus at the familiar sites on the way to North Miami Junior high—it's goodby Fulford Elementary, goodby childhood, goodby paradise. I have to be a lady now, a dangerous woman, there's no turning back.

First, the bus passes my own house sitting in the middle of five acres of scrubby land. But all around it where the developers have been, the Easter egg colored houses are rising up. We turn on to Seventh Avenue and pass the old white stucco house where the Trafficanti's, a gangster and his wife were double murdered a few years ago. Their blood was all over the inside of the house and on the grass in the yard, pints and pints of it, but they were never found. A mob hit, it was called—no bodies for a reason. The house sits empty all these years later. Former tenants have looked for blood stains missed by the cleaners and found them. Then they move out. In a blink the house turns blood red. Next comes Pflueger's Taxidermists, where they drain the blood out of dead animals and stuff them with straw and mount them so they are life-like replicas of their former selves. I shiver—all this is spooky to me. Even the archery fields which come next—I imagine people missing the target and spearing each other. There is blood on the grass. Whyever was blood red I wondered? What if it was chartreuse green like caterpillars?

We cross the bridge into the unspoiled lushness of Biscayne Gardens, where Skeeter and Marie live. Biscayne Gardens could disappear for good, like it does each time we pass it. The developers are nearby. We go over the railroad tracks, the smell of creosote mixes with my own fiery smell of blood and ammonia. The trailer parks under the banyan trees seemed permanent once, but now I know they are not. Nothing is. Even the B.P.O.E., where they have Saturday

215

night barbecues, will disappear, for a price. Everything in the world is about blood and money and real estate.

In seven days it's over and I am my old self again. The first thing I do is climb a tree and spraddle my legs, which are tense from being held together for a week. I think the best thing I have heard it called is "the curse."

Donnie was having hormone problems too, I guess, because he'd become a kleptomaniac—stealing clothes and records in the new shopping mall in North Miami Beach, which is what they renamed a whole section of old Uleta, which is really Crofts Ranch. He showed me the loot and acted like they built the stores just for him to help himself in. He laughed when he never got caught. "Too bad you don't have anything worth stealing," he teased. "I'm tellin'," I said. But I didn't.

Two weeks before Christmas I came home to find part of the living room ceiling lying on the floor. Chalky rocks of dust were scattered everywhere and a thin haze of white dust had settled over all. Shopping bags with presents in them were lying in the rubble. My mother paced around the room biting her lip and holding her forehead squealing, "Look at this mess—who's going to clean this mess up?"

Andy and Donnie were sitting on the couch side by side while our father knelt before them on one knee, demanding to know: "Which one of you did this?" Neither one said anything, so he kept repeating the question, over and over. "Tell me or I'll punish both of you."

Donnie nudged Andy. "Tell him," he said.

"Whadda you mean?" Andy shot back, blushing.

216

"It's okay. If you'll just confess, I won't punish you," daddy said looking straight at Andy. Andy looked down at his feet and didn't say anything.

On the floor I could see paperbags with parts of games and toys sticking out of them. My parents' hiding place for Christmas presents had been uncovered.

"Okay," my father said. "Andy, you go wait in Lou's room. Donnie, go sit in your room. I have to figure this out." Then he and mama went out to the kitchen to argue.

"Just because he blushes doesn't mean he did it," I heard my mother say.

"Oh, you always stick up for the little baby," my father shot back. "I'm gonna go outside and sneak up and watch them through the windows. Then I'll be able to see who the guilty one is."

In a few minutes he came back in the kitchen door huffing, "I think Andy did it," he announced. "He kept trying to brush something off his knees, trying to get rid of the dust I bet, the evidence. Donnie didn't do anything. He just sat there waiting."

I ran outside and looked in my bedroom window. Andy sat brushing his knees, a nervous habit he had, and crying softly. Mama and daddy came into the room solemn and quiet like jurors. They didn't see me outside watching. Daddy took Andy's hands and looked at his fingernails. I didn't know what that could mean since Andy's nails were always caked. He had hands exactly like daddy's, and he used them just as much too. "Admit you did it and I won't punish you," my father said, handing Andy's fingernails up to my mother to see. She just shook her head doubtfully and didn't say a word. My father rolled Andy over and spanked him, and then sent him to bed without any supper. It wasn't a hard spanking—Andy's cheeks probably didn't even burn—but it was humiliating.

Usually Donnie got blamed for everything. You get a reputation in a family, and it was like Donnie had dibs on all the bad stuff—anything went wrong Donnie was the first person they looked at. When daddy had to dig up the septic tank they said it was Donnie's fault. Made me feel sorry for Donnie even if they were only joking. But you could never show Donnie your sympathy; he'd turn on you, make you out to be a sucker.

Now I had the feeling Andy had been railroaded. Because if he had done it he would have admitted it. He just had a way of always looking guilty. It was simpler to blame him, because to blame Donnie was to take on all his other misdeeds as well, which were really mounting up lately. My father was afraid to do that—afraid of getting swamped, afraid he would get too mad and lose his temper.

The next day I was gliding past the Greyhound Inn on my way home from school when my eye caught the reflection of the back of a couple of heads familiar to me. I went on home and when I got there Donnie and his friend Brian were looking up at the hole in the ceiling and laughing about it. "The old man thought Andy did it," Donnie crowed.

I looked at Brian,"The Bat," that was his baseball name because he was even skinnier than Donnie. I doubted he weighed even a hundred pounds and he was taller than

218

Donnie, too. Donnie's baseball name was "The Whip" because of how fast he could swing the bat, I guess. I saw how they had done it. "The Whip" had given "The Bat" a hand up through the opening—only, once he got into the attic he forgot to walk on the rafters and stepped in between where it was just plasterboard and came crashing through, light as he was. Andy probably hadn't even been there.

My mother came in the door then, her arms loaded down with grocery bags. Brian rushed over to help her. She liked Brian better than any other kid, and she was always on her good behavior with him, like she was Harriet Nelson or something.

"Mrs. O'Neill, my mother said I have to tell you it was me fell through your ceiling and I'm awful sorry about it. I'll pay to fix it up, though." Brian said this fast while she was distracted by the groceries. Then he turned his bandaged elbow over and looked at it to get her sympathy. "Shucks, we were just fooling around."

"Hey wait," Donnie said. "Wait a little minute here. It wadn't me. I didn't do anything."

"You were just there, huh Donnie?" my mother said, burping unexpectedly.

Donnie fanned the air. "Well, heck yeah, but I didn't tell Andy to take the blame."

"No, you just let him." She glared into Donnie's face.

"Geeze, Brian, why'd you have to go and tell?" Donnie whined.

"Shoot," said The Bat, "no serious damage done anyway. Nothing I can't fix up if your pop wants me to." Then he brushed off his bandage and walked toward the kitchen door. "Let's go throw a few, Donnie, gotta keep this arm in shape," and he tipped his baseball cap to mama, "Ma'am."

Donnie scampered after him, grateful for a chance to escape. That day they chewed a lot of tobacco and spit after they caught and before they threw, pretending to be Pee Wee Reese or Virgil "Fireball" Trucks or some other hero on a baseball card they got out of the Wheaties box.

At the dinner table, Donnie was green and holding his stomach. He couldn't even eat. He acted like he was taking his punishment already, self-imposed before it could be dished out to him. Nobody knew he had been chewing as much tobacco in one day as Yogi Berra chewed in a month.

My mother, very slowly, like she was afraid of something, told about Brian's confession, and his offer to repair the damage.

Daddy went through the roof. His white skin turned hot pink. He slammed his fists on the table so all the food and dishes jumped up in the air, and he hollered, "There isn't going to be any Christmas this year!"

He glared at Andy, who wouldn't look back at him or say one thing. Daddy was mad at Andy for not sticking up for himself, for taking blame that wasn't his. Then daddy seemed to deflate, his two big arms dropped down to his side, he huddled over his dinner and started eating slowly, holding the fork as if it were heavy, and he was just worn out. He looked over at Donnie disgusted with him for being so tricky and dishonest and letting Andy take the rap. Donnie just sat blank as a bog, fermenting. Mostly, daddy was mad at himself

220

for being in too big a hurry to drum up evidence against Andy and punish him. Now it seemed like something he could never take back.

I wanted to change the subject—just erase everything fast. The table was silent and gloomy for what seemed like a year as we ate our lamb chops, boiled potatoes and peas. The lamb tasted lamby so I slathered it with more mint jelly and then I was stunned to hear my own chirpy voice say: "I saw you and Marie at the Greyhound Inn today, mama." God, I knew that was something I wasn't supposed to tell. Her face made a hush grimace, that vanished when my father looked over at her.

"That was Marie maybe, not me. You were mistaken, dearie," she said sharply. Then she glared at my father, daring him to pursue it. But he was too tired, thank God.

"What's for dessert?" I asked, to distract them.

"Fig baaars," mama answered, exaggerating her Boston accent.

Everyone groaned.

"Where the hell's the apple pie?" daddy said.

31.

I decided accuracy and truth were the most important things in the world to try for. It was about houses, blood, money, real estate and even cars, but it was also about accuracy. The truth was the only way to keep track—otherwise I could see how a life could get swallowed up in lies.

The Greyhound Inn was a bitter place to me now. I suspected it was the owner who had poisoned Blackie so long ago, yet it seemed like yesterday. I didn't like seeing my mother in there pining away, taking pleasure in being sad, or even laughing. There was no longer any allure in its yeasty smell or bluesy music or in the nasty way people acted in there. So everyday I passed it by and never went in, even when I saw my mother and Marie in there cutting up. I went on home and had the house to myself for an hour or two, until my mother stumbled in to take a nap before she fixed dinner, which had become to her like an ordeal she faced every night.

We had Christmas as usual. My father liked it too much himself to keep the promise of his threat. Donnie was the only one who wasn't a bit surprised by any of the gifts, and he even had the nerve to be disappointed.

In January, Donnie started stealing hubcaps, skipping school and running wild. For weeks I didn't see him much except at dinner, and then one day I caught him diddling

Annie Whitfield up in the bleachers at the Youth Center. It was a Sunday and no one was there except Annie and Donnie and Didg Platt and Charlie Whitfield. They were all up there taking turns playing with Annie, who had her underpants down around her ankles and a cow's contentment on her face. They were making up words like poon-tang, whatever that meant, and holding up their glistening fingers laughing. Annie wasn't known for anything besides how dumb she was. I got out of there, but not before Donnie saw me. He caught up with me on the road and begged me not to tell, being nice for a change. Who was I gonna tell that to? What was he doing with those people anyway? They all scared me to death.

Sometimes when I stayed out too late and had to walk home in the dark I encountered Whitfields and Platts in the shadows of trees and palmetto bushes on the way. I thought I felt their hands and arms brushing me, reaching out to grab me and I'd run as fast as I could, past the deep darknesses, a sound caught in my throat like a scream running backwards—a sucking in of a scream, a rrrrrrur, like when I ran from Lyle that time. You might say they weren't really there, but I always knew they might be, they could be if they wanted to. And now Donnie was in with them too. I felt so disgusted.

Everything Donnie did backfired and made him look bad, so daddy ignored him even more. "He's recalcitrant," daddy said, and went right on reading his newspaper as if putting a word on Donnie took care of it.

Our father was modern and scientific. He thought big. He liked facts, new inventions like formica, and television. He said nuclear fission was the most important discovery since the beginning of time and would change the whole world. Little feats of ego embarrassed him and deliberate wickedness made him angry. He was afraid of his own anger because he knew he had a bad temper. The depth of his love could probably be felt in the depth of his anger but I never wanted to test that. Donnie and my mother seemed to want to, though, all the time.

And there was something else. My father had been a middle-weight boxing champion in New Jersey when he was twenty years old, under an assumed name because his mother Louise, who I was named after, didn't want him to box. He considered his fists to be dangerous weapons; he hardly ever made a fist. I had seen the newspaper clippings about him in with his jail drawings and some pictures of him all dressed in white, even his shoes, teeing off at some golf links with the white Cadillac convertible parked in the background that Louise had given him before she lost all her money in the crash. I knew his past life from these yellowed documents hidden in the dresser, even though daddy would never talk about it. I loved to go look at them on a rainy day— spread them all out on the bed and measure them against who he was now and how far he had come. He had worked on the Empire State Building in New York City, the Columbus Hotel in downtown Miami, lots of bridges, and now The Fountainbleu. Every night I prayed to the heavens to keep him safe from falling.

He had never hit me once, not even a smack on the butt when I was fresh. His paws were gentlemanly to me. I knew he couldn't use them in anger very easily—that it would take the loss of his temper, and more, for him to close his hands into fists.

Every day Donnie, a/k/a the Whip, the Masked Man, did another bad thing. He'd got himself on a roll, building up a giant pile of villainous deeds that no one could ignore anymore: stealing, disrespect for teachers, skipping school, lying, bullying, fighting.

"Do something," my mother nagged my father every night, "stop him, he's belligerent."

I read the note his teacher sent home to mama: "Donnie is a troubled child with an overactive mind and no self-control. Quiet him down or take him out of school."

Then he got suspended from school for pissing off the roof of the lunchroom. He was in a contest up there with Didg Platt to see who could piss the farthest. It was during recess, so most of the school was outside watching.

My father ground his teeth as he read the newspaper. He drew plans for adding another room onto the house, to distract himself. Then he started hammering. His anger had been gathering for a long time, but he had been holding it back. What Donnie was doing was an affront to him and a terrible waste. Donnie had always been especially bright and full of something rich and strong. He had talent, along with his bad streak. Daddy wanted to be proud of him. But now Donnie was turning his talent into acid—he was corroding his life, and our whole family's with it. The father must stop the son ultimately, or be a wimp forever. That's what it seemed like it was coming down to. My mother said she couldn't spank Donnie anymore—he was too big. She was tired of screaming at him. Instead, she whined and complained to daddy, constantly nagging him to DO something.

The Devil was in Donnie, it was plain to see, and she expected daddy to try and beat it out once and for all, if only to fulfill the requirements of fatherhood. There didn't seem to be any other way. Mama kept at daddy, until one night he exploded.

I watched my fathers arms, the muscles bulging, his fists like angry faces, coming down on Donnie's body as he darted around the room, screaming in peril, trying to dodge the punches. Then daddy caught Donnie, held him down, both their faces blazing. Oh God, it was awful. Not so much the pain of the blows, which I could almost feel too, but the loss that it was, of control, of grace, of everything holy. The loss of our father's temper was like the end of the world.

Mama screamed, "George, George, Stop, stop! Holy mother-of-god you're killing him!"

And finally George did stop, his fury discharged, his self-respect sapped—his very personhood threatened by the raging beast, Temper. He had gone against his own best instincts, and now he would pay for it. I watched him punishing himself for days afterwards, and felt his vow form like a crust: that he would never hit Donnie again. Donnie would have to leave first. He had been a man who loved reason, a peaceful, gentle man. If only he could treat Donnie the way he did me, gentle him into behaving, tickle his back, teach him new words.

After that, there was an onus on Donnie, who pretended to be penitent. I didn't see how I could ever trust him or even be his sister anymore. He'd caused our father to suffer like the damned, driven him over the edge into hell. Donnie might do any old thing—he scared me worse than the A-bomb. And even though he had a dislocated shoulder, I didn't feel very sorry for him. I couldn't forgive him for what he'd done to Daddy, and what he was doing to our family.

I wished he didn't need so much, and that he could accept what he got. But he couldn't. Even when you were nice to him, after awhile he turned on you and tried to chisel you some way or another. It wasn't really your love he wanted, what he wanted was kingly worship. He couldn't stand for your attention to drift away from him for one second. He had to control the whole show, as if there weren't a couple of billion other people in the world at all, there was just him.

They should have put Donnie in one of those isolation booths I'd seen on television, on the $64,000 Dollar Question, where he wouldn't be able to hear or see the outside world, and just study him, study his act of communication, put wires on his brain and record him for science. Tap his energy in some positive way before he turned it completely against himself and the world, and started robbing banks or something worse. About Donnie I felt pure-dee sick.

32.

Not more than a week later, I came home and found Donnie and my father in the backyard laughing and palling around, while Andy sat on a stool between them with a towel around his shoulders and a new mohawk hair cut. Andy's red curls were lying on the ground in a heap, his shaved head with a thick red path up the middle, drooped over; he was looking down at his hands, folded in his lap like a prisoner's, like they were handcuffed. For about the millionth time I saw that Andy had hands just like our father. How could my papa's beautiful hands have done this to Andy? His ears were fiery red and raw looking, and I knew it was the deep-felt blush of humiliation. It hurt me just to look. I was so disgusted I felt like stealing something.

Donnie and my father were dancing around, snapping the clippers and scissors like castanets and yoicking about how this mohawk was going to toughen Andy up, make him a man. They were having a high old time. Daisy barked and stood by Andy, showing teeth. Donnie started demonstrating how to fistfight, which Andy was going to need to know in order to defend himself from all the boys who were going to try to beat him up because of his mohawk.

They were trying to change Andy, to brute him. I couldn't believe my father would do this. Donnie had to be behind it. He must have told about Andy playing dolls with me a long time ago, must have worked Daddy up and got him thinking that Andy was going to be a sissy unless he did something about it. But why wasn't Andy angry? Where was his spirit? He just sat there like a crushed bug.

What I thought was: I have to get out of this family. It was a hopeless thought because I doubted that you could really ever leave a family, no matter what. All you could do was wander farther and farther away, and you'd always be stuck with the love and hate and everything else you felt—you'd take it right along with you. My mother was right about one thing—I was destined to like strangers better than my own family, like she always accused me.

Something in their sickening gaiety told me that Andy was a scapegoat. Lying in the curls on the ground was forgiveness, my father's and Donnie's, for each other and for their sorry selves.

I went on into the kitchen, slamming the door hard. Mama jumped. She'd been sitting there by the window watching them, and weeping. But now she ran into her bedroom; I guess she didn't want me to see her all broken up about Andy's hair. My mouth felt like rabbit fur. I was galled by how little control I had over what was going on in my own family. I went over to the food cabinet looking for something to drink. There was a tall bottle with a big red apple on the label that looked refreshing. Ah, apple juice. I took a huge, thirsty swig, filling my canteen jowls. Right away I gagged— what I had already swallowed bubbled right back up my throat and I erupted like a hot volcano, hucking vinegar out of my whole face—it even felt like it was coming out my eyes, nose and ears. I turned and aimed it just in time, out the window, right through the screen, and on top of the heads of the three most important men in my life.

"Hey! Ugh!" they all yelled at once, "where'd that come from?"

But I was on the floor, doubled over trying to get my breath and couldn't answer. I crawled into the bathroom.

After I drank gallons of water and hung over the tub soaking my head for about an hour, I didn't care about one damn thing anymore. I had the pleasant sensation, while it lasted, that nothing at all mattered anyway. Drinking vinegar will do that for you. I laughed loud and freely like some wild maniac and no one could shut me up, though they all tried.

33.

Shelby wants me to take it on the lam with her. Run away and join the circus. She knows I am that fed up with my family and the hitmosphere because I've told her everything. She doesn't say anything about them—just offers me a way out, like it's a vacation.

In a week, on Saturday, the circus people will go to Sarasota for practice camp. It is six hours away by bus. My need is to go as far as I can on foot. But Shelby says, "What's another hour or two when you're running away from home? You can rest and do acrobats." It sounded good and permanent. She looked all the way down at her feet.

I eat some guavas, daydream. I get out there hovering up above myself leaving the burden of the decision back on the ground in biology. The birds are loud up here. Mating Cardinals sound like castanets.

The days go by like passing formations of blackbirds— closer to the time when I have to decide. And then something blissful intercedes: Summer. School let out on Thursday, and freedom beckoned. The outlook changed, and I chickened out. I told Shelby I wasn't ready.

Andy's torment was interrupted, too. Now he didn't have to go to school every day prepared to defend himself, my father's and Donnie's prep-for-life rack. The mohawk hadn't made Andy any tougher; it made him shyer. He planned to stay around the house all summer while it grew out. My father promised to take him sea fishing in the Ellie-Nora.

I liked Andy how he was, gentle, yet strong too, easy-natured enough to let people play with him, and yet not let them change him too much. He just grinned when they failed, as if it was all in jest and not real life they were acting out. He always let everyone off easy and hardly ever got mad, even when he had a right to. I'd never seen him lose his temper. Sometimes it worried me.

Shelby would be back before the summer was over. I would miss her. Luckily I had been spending a lot of time with Sandy Yates, the calmest sea of a girl, the most agreeable person I knew, besides Shelby and Andy. We played with makeup and jewelry in her big sister's dark bedroom in front of one of those pigeon hole dressers that had big curvy consoles on either side of the mirror. The consoles had drawers full of fascinating jewelry, scarves and cosmetics—a treasure trove that smelt of a future life.

On Friday night Sandy Yates spent the night. It was the first time she'd ever spent the night at our house, and I was nervous about what might happen. I was afraid Sandy would be shocked by the way everyone fought and cursed. All I could do was hope it didn't happen this time.

In my tiny room, there was a double bed, a dresser, and a chair all bunched up against the walls so you only had room to stand in one little spot in the middle, or sit down on the bed. It had that huge closet though, where I brooded, and usually got dressed, in dark seclusion. I wanted a real door on my bedroom instead of a flimsy curtain, but my mother said I was lucky to have a room at all. She always said I was lucky to have what I had whenever I wanted something else, and if she couldn't think of anything she'd say I was lucky to be alive.

My parents were going out to the Greyhound Inn to celebrate. At last, the Fountainbleu was finished. So there was only Donnie to worry about.

Just when I was having daydreams of throwing him in the Oleta River to the 'gators he got nice. He was fun even, a little frisky, and anxious to please. He was almost as shy as Andy because he was in love with Sandy Yates. Only nobody was supposed to know that. After a short game of Blind Man's Bluff—we didn't have enough kids for it—we played Monopoly and he wasn't even bullheaded about winning like he usually was. We made fudge and strolled around outside in the moonlight while the fudge cooled, circling the house, lingering under trees, talking low, giggling, brushing against the wet leaves, collecting lightening bugs in a jar. We all drifted off to bed around midnight.

It must have been two o'clock in the morning when we were awakened by shouting. It was my mother and father coming in, being tumultuous with each other the way they did when they had too much to drink. Only this time it was the worst I ever heard. My mother was crying and laughing at the same time and calling my father a son-of-a-bitch at the top of her lungs. I could hear him pleading with her to quit. Then she started accusing him of flirting with Marie, of encouraging her, and he kept on denying it and pleading with her, "Come to bed now Ellie, just come to bed." But she raved on about Marie: "She stole her own sister's husband, and now she's coming after mine." Then she went on about how she should have married Jimmy Galvin from Boston, that old story, and my father got mad and started shouting over her voice. He said she was "cracked" and called her a crazy jealous liar and then a name I had never heard before, but it sounded bad, "You slut! Get over here." Then he must have pushed her onto the bed because she screamed, and then whimpered, "please" and "wait".

"Just sleep it off!" He was indignant, I could tell by his voice. He started saying something about "knocked up," that my mother was never going to forgive him for knocking her up, whatever that was. She was never going to let him forget it, or anything else. Even though he didn't lose his temper, he said fire-eating stuff I knew he couldn't mean. It was like he was a different person from the one I knew.

My heart was breaking. There were flames in my brain. I could feel Sandy awake beside me, and humiliation filling the room like hot steam. I was glad it was dark. I hoped she wasn't as afraid as I was, of them, and of what might happen next. It felt like whatever slight balance we had as a family had careened out of control.

At first, I pretended I was sleeping, but I was too alert for that, bracing myself for the worst. I knew Donnie and Andy probably were, too. Donnie must have been even more embarrassed than I was. Sandy was the first girl he was making an effort for, the first girl he put his bat down for. He smelled like Wild Root Hair Tonic for her. He had made a fairly good impression, until our parents came home and spoiled everything.

But the worst had already happened. After that, there was breathing so loud we could hear it, but no more shouting. Then I heard my father snoring. Sandy was too polite to say a word. I felt covered up in hot disgrace, and I quickly willed myself to sleep to escape. To hear someone's private fight, all that yelling, makes you think they hate each other, that they don't belong together. But I found out that isn't true.

In the morning they both seemed happier than ever. My father made pineapple pancakes for us, like he did on special mornings, whistling while he stirred the batter as if nothing had happened, cracking jokes with Donnie, who was giving him dirty looks behind his back making Sandy giggle. After breakfast Sandy and I stayed in the kitchen to help my mother do the dishes. My mother liked to be with "just the girls" in the kitchen. She could give us advice and say things she thought were funny and deep.

She turned to me and Sandy and said, "Men! They're all alike." But her complicity was lost on me, and I looked at Sandy wondering if she understood. Sandy just smiled tranquilly. My mother said Sandy had good poise. Now she looked at me nitpicky: "When did you get so grim and serious?" she asked, as if she didn't know.

The man in question was my father and so far he'd been the only constant in the Universe besides the speed of light, and that was in dispute. He could soothe away any pain I had. His hands were magic. He wrote sentences on my back and gave me facts. Sometimes I could only make out one word but he didn't care; he'd let me fall asleep. My mother's touch was not on me anymore, unless it was to slap my face, to "straighten me out," as she called it. Instead, she taught: To live is to fight, never lose your nerve. She was always trying to get me "on her side" against my father, for whatever reason I wildly searched my imagination to find but never could.

Now she said bitterly, "Oh, you always stick up for your father." She laughed and nudged Sandy as if she had won Sandy over to her side. I didn't believe that. And I didn't believe what mama said about Marie either. I knew Marie's sorrow, and I thought her kinship with her sister was more important than any man could ever be.

After Sandy went home, daddy tried to apologize to me for the fight. He called whiskey ignernt oil. "You drink enough of it, you just get ignernt," he said, joking around. But it didn't help. I didn't know the person he was with my mother. He read the newspaper to me, all the puffed up praise about the Fountainbleu. Now that it was finished and gorgeous, everyone decided they liked it and were proud of it. He laughed about that, trying to get me to join in but I couldn't.

I felt nauseous and vowed never to have anyone over to that house again. It was too explosive around there; anything might happen. The threat of embarrassment plagued me. It was violent and unpredictable out in the world too, so what did I want? A little respect, for one thing—consideration, some order and harmony. I was looking for all that in the button jar that was my life, in my wild and jungly Uleta, fast disappearing, and it was too much to ask for.

So I changed my mind. Still in the doleful dumps from the night before, I took the four dollars and fifty cents hidden in my closet, and quit that house. Without very strong intention, I sidled away. As I went I had the thought that I was leaving home for good. When all else failed, there was always the road.

Only as I walked along did I begin to believe in what I was doing, and then I started running. I could feel the rend of disjoining from my family burning in my stomach. It was probably an act of high treason or at least against the law, or the EYES of the church. I didn't care. I was running away from my corroding family, the Greyhound Inn, the tree butchers, the snakes, the cotton saddle of the curse, from this whole wacky paradise. Stored-up anger choked off my tears. I wouldn't let myself cry; instead I seethed and burned the whole way up to Uleta.

The circus bus hadn't left yet. It was still parked beside the Youth Center with its motor idling. I ran to the bus and leaped on. Shelby was in the very back, laid out across the whole seat, her elbows behind her head. When she saw me, she raised up and scooted over. No one seemed to notice me or ask any questions. It was like they accepted me as another castaway, or some orphan, which is what I felt like. I started crying. I belonged only to Shelby now, to the vagabond life of the circus.

"Where's your stuff?" Shelby asked, looking me over with her rich, compassionate eyes, noticing my bare feet. All I had on was shorts and a blouse.

"I didn't bring anything," I sobbed, and covered my face in my hands so she wouldn't see how ugly I felt. I crumpled in a heap beside her.

We waved good-bye out the window to Rene and Baby Linda as the bus pulled out.

34.

In a couple of hours, we stopped in Immokalee for lunch. I had fallen asleep in Shelby's lap while she plaited my pony tail. We had driven across the Everglades on a desolate road called Alligator Alley and I missed the whole thing. We went inside and sat in a big round booth with the other circus people. Shelby told them my name and that I was a new acrobat. I didn't know anyone but Shelby. I still felt so bad I didn't smile or say much. They all tried to cheer me up, to jolly me into thinking my real, exciting life was just beginning. So I should feel free to be just as uninhibited as they all were. But I was a locked-up person. I was a criminal. I had beaten Donnie to it.

Suddenly I started laughing. It was as though I was just picking up from where I left off after hucking the vinegar. I felt like a reckless person, loose and unknown even to myself. But I knew what laughing to keep from crying meant now, and that I had turned another corner of life. The bearded lady nudged me, so I'd snap out of it, I guess. I couldn't tell how old she was, somewhere between sixteen and forty, and she smelled like my dog Daisy. She winked and put her hand on my thigh. I felt a cold shudder run up my spine and I moved over closer to Shelby so the bearded lady's hand slid off.

We drove through more Everglades, across a river at Fort Myers and another even wider river at Punta Gorda. I was all the way on the other side of the state and probably not even missed yet. When we got to Venice, I began to see the white-capped waters of the Gulf of Mexico blossoming out the window.

The first thing we did when we got to the circus camp in Sarasota was go to the cafeteria to eat supper. Shelby was starving. She had a huge appetite and needed to eat almost all the time to keep up her large body. I was glad because I didn't mind eating a lot. I had hungers too. The cafeteria was a lot like the S & W in downtown Miami, and I picked out my old favorite foods from when I was a kid: macaroni and cheese, lime Jello, a glass of milk, trying to soothe my mangled insides.

After supper we went and checked out sheets and pillows and towels, and found the barracks where we would sleep. The barracks buildings were set up in back of a big museum called, "The Ringling," which by this time was dark and closed. In the open courtyard we saw stone statues standing in the darkness like frozen ghosts, looking out into a field beyond at a giant tent. Shelby called it the Bigtop. Lights blazed from inside the Bigtop, and we could hear the sounds of roustabouts setting up the trapeze and the ropes and ladders for all the different acts.

Most of the girls had claimed their beds before they went to supper and left their things on them. So we couldn't find two empty beds side by side and had to settle for two with another one in between. Shelby let me use her toothbrush until I could get one of my own. I washed my feet good and then my face and hands. We went to bed in our clothes. Shelby had a suitcase, and I was sure she had nightgowns but not one that would fit me, so she didn't change either. She folded herself up in between the iron bedposts of the short cot the best she could and then she didn't move anymore.

I figured by this time I was missing. I lay in the darkness and imagined my father out looking for me. My mother would stay home sipping her medicine and probably pace back n' forth, squealing like Olive Oyle. My brothers would huddle in their room laughing, glad I was gone. I had taken my whole family right along with me, just as I thought. It was hot in the barracks, and I thrashed around until I sunk into the blankness of sleep.

In the dark middle of the night, I woke up smelling something oily like wet dog hair. Someone was snuggling down in my covers trying to wrap around me. I let out a scream. Shelby was up and lifting the bearded lady off me in one motion. She dropped her in her own bed between us and told her to leave me alone FOR GOOD AND FOREVER. The bearded lady giggled and said, "Okay, okay, okay," in a hoarse voice that sounded like a billy goat's.

All the rest of that night I tried to keep at least one eye open, so in the morning I was bone-tired from only halfway sleeping.

Shelby was anxious to show me around and get me in the training class for acrobats. My shorts and blouse were rumpled and stale, but I smoothed them down the best I could and used Shelby's toothbrush again while she changed her dress. Eventually I would have to find some other clothes.

Shelby plaited my mussed up pony tail all over again to get my hair out of the way for acrobats.

After breakfast, Shelby took me to the museum, which was open now, light blazing from it. It had a smooth, turpentine and beeswaxy smell, like when you first walked into a hardware store, and a hushed sound, like outer space. Along all the white walls hung huge pictures of a quality such as I had never seen in the world before. In some of them, I recognized a watery, airy kind of beauty like my daydreams. In others, there were just defiant splashes of color, like anger. One had neat boxes of different colors bouncing off each other and one had the nerve to be solid black. It was as if these pictures had been created in some other world by humans in some advanced state, maybe bohemians, but not by any regular people. As I stood before them, my heart started to fill up with color and wildness. I could almost chew on the rich sensation surging up in my chest.

A sign called it "Abstract Expressionism," but these words like the pictures were foreign to me. There were tons of yellowed marble statues of people from olden days standing around—they smelled moldy and didn't feed me like the huge colorful pictures of nothing did. I thought there must be some way I could make pictures like these too. But Shelby pulled me out of the museum and over to the bigtop where I'd have to learn how to earn my living as an acrobat first.

By mid-afternoon, I was sweaty, dirty, and exhausted from the training. I was so tired I kept falling off the barrel and my bare legs were crusted with sawdust. There were no real horses to practice with, only this barrel that went flying around the circle that you had to jump on and off and do flips and handstands on.

When the class broke for supper, the trainer told me to stay behind so he could give me extra help. The other girls grinned and winked at me, and I felt ashamed for being the worst one in the class.

The bigtop emptied out until there were just the two of us, and he started commanding me to jump on and off the barrel faster and faster, until I was out of breath. Then he stopped the contraption and helped me down, placing both his big hands around my waist. Instead of letting go, he told me to do a backbend right then. So I folded back at the waist and, while I was down there, I felt something hard poke against me and then he pulled me up and my face met his and he grinned and slobbered on me with his big fat wet lips. I grunted and squealed for him to let go, and he did, but as soon as I was standing free he leaned in and bit my titty right through my blouse.

I shrieked and started running like a cut cat. I didn't know if he was behind me or not. I hollered out, "Shelllby, Shelllby," but she was nowhere around there. Nobody was. They were all in the cafeteria having supper. I was so confused I wasn't sure which direction it was, so I hid behind the biggest statues in the museum garden, shivering and trying to FADE while the trainer prowled closer, calling out my name. I could see him moving slowly and using his ears. I tried to stay still, but my breathing was loud and ragged—I was on the verge of sobbing.

When he turned a corner, I ducked inside the museum and ran into the ladies room to hide. I washed my face and hands over and over again. I felt so dirty—not ordinary dirty, which you could wash off, but another spooky kind that gave me cold chills and wouldn't wash off, like when Lyle made me touch him. I broke down then and really cried. I let it all go. Sometimes you have to cry to live.

I put the lid down and sat on the cold toilet with my feet up and my arms wrapped around my legs, so no one would know I was in there. I buried my head down in my knees and sobbed. Oh, where are you, daddy, my champion? Please, please come after me.

For some reason I could hear my mother's voice in my head singing: "Tor a lor a lora, hush now, don't you cry, tor a lor a lora, 'tis an Irish lullaby." Funny how you can be so disgusted with someone and still hear them singing sweetly to you like they'd done years before, when you were just a kid. I sang it over and over for awhile in the dark and felt some better. Radio music started drifting across the courtyard faintly. It was the William Tell Overture—"The Lone Ranger" was on. I tried to think of good times and people I liked, to cheer myself up. I mounted my little hand-horse and da-nummed across my knees picking up my favorite cousin Willie on the trail, and then Miss Packer who waved us on in her big sleevy coat, and then Tim, my first love, grinning, offering us coconut patties all around. I was so hungry. And there was my father, standing like a bulwark against the mean world, pineapple pancakes lined up on his arms. I closed my eyes.

The next time I opened them, I was curled up on the cool tile floor, it was dark, and I didn't know how much time had passed. I tiptoed out of the bathroom, and in the moon's light I could see the museum was empty and closed. I tried all the doors but they were locked up tight. There was no way to get out unless I started yelling, or heaved something through the glass; but then the trainer might get me.

I walked up close to the paintings, inhaling them, inspecting them in the moon's dim glow. In the darkness I couldn't see the beauty—it had been turned out, like it was in the light itself and the way it mixed with the colors of paint. But I could make out shapes and jumbled lines that matched my own feelings.

I was not only missing and homeless now, but separated from Shelby and out of a job. I couldn't go back to acrobat class, so what would I do for a living? Maybe make art like this, if I had the paints and canvas. Thinking it over I was sure I could learn, but it seemed like a hard row to hoe and a long way off. I wondered how I would survive until then. I knew that art fed my heart, but I couldn't eat it and I was hungry—and hopelessly locked inside a museum.

I began to feel giddy, flaying my arms and twirling around in circles. I tore the plaits out of my hair and let it hang in wavy crimps, letting it fly as I zig-zagged through all the rooms, catching glimpses of myself reflected in the glass covering some of the pictures, a wild-haired runaway, dancing free. I was in a garden where beauty grew on walls, pure and raw and unmistakable. It was fearless and nervy stuff. Why did my mother hate it so? I sailed by the pictures, filling up on them, and feeling happy for the first time in months. I was so far away from her that I felt no guilt and nothing holding me back. Art was the purpose of life, I was sure of it now.

Then I heard the rasp of a key turning in a lock and my heart caromed. I ducked behind a sculpture stand and froze. The lights blazed on. I heard voices. Her voice, the first voice I ever heard in the world. It was mama—my own prevaricating mama—come to get me. I peered out and they saw me. There was Shelby, my Sunbeam. She had to duck down to come through the doorway, at least two heads above the museum guard who rattled his keys impatiently. I couldn't believe it was my mother standing there, not even yelling, not saying a word now, just gazing at me with tenderness like I was a wild animal she didn't want to startle.

I walked over close to her and saw tears well up in her eyes and cascade down over her powdery cheeks. "Thank God," she said. She knelt down and took me by my skinny shoulders, swept the hair out of my eyes. She was touching me fondly. She held me to her and I sank into her bosom gratefully, the dance-sweat evaporating on my body in a new set of relief chills.

When she stood up, she took my hand, looked around suspiciously at the paintings like they were bombs, and we were all in danger from art. She was not a very accurate person—she believed what she wanted to believe, instead of what was true. But she had come to rescue me.

I said I fell asleep and got locked in. I didn't tell about the trainer right then because I didn't want to spoil her good mood. While we were saying good-bye to Shelby and the guard, mama was as nice as Harriet Nelson, calm and smiling. She'd learned from television. But as soon as we got in the car, she started in on me.

"You look like the wrath-a-God," she croaked, jarring me out of my unmolested satisfaction and the sweet relief of my rescue and escape from danger's very doorstep. "Why in God's name did you run away like that? without telling anyone? You're lucky Rene saw you get on that bus or I never would have known where to look. I was worried sick. How could you do this to me?"

She had no way of knowing all that had happened to me, and I sure wasn't going to tell her now and make things even worse. So I sat there, still as the grain on wood, and got a belly-full. She drove sixty miles an hour, yelling at me. At one point she raised her hand; I thought to smack me and I flinched. "Wipe that smirk off your face," she ordered, withdrawing her hand. What smirk? Maybe it was better to get hit and have it over with.

"You're just a girl," she kept saying, drilling it in because I was so dense I had missed the meaning of that, which was limitations, captivity, and other sour grapes I had to learn to swallow. It was a man's world, she said, and how dare I think otherwise. "You're lucky you weren't killed, or worse. You're only fourteen years old. What's going to become of you?"

I was looking down and saw that she had on her nursing shoes, scrubbed with that pocky white shoe polish she never bothered to buff up. That's when I understood that she didn't know what she had in me, and it scared her. I would have to

247

hide myself better. The wind whispered through the cracked window, and I strained to hear the call of love.

She kept it up all the way to Lake Okeechobee, where we finally stopped to eat. She was taking us home a different way than how we had come on the bus. I was impressed that she could drive this far, that she knew the way. I told myself as I slunk down in the seaweedy-smelling seat beside her, that she must be screaming at me because she loved me and cared what happened to me, even if she didn't know who I was. I desperately searched my mind for something to say that would calm her down, that would distract her.

Then, prompted by an inspiration, I said: "Hey ma, remember the time the cow came up to the kitchen door and mooed? remember?"

But it seemed so long ago now, back when I was a girlchild, and I could no longer fight the tears that welled up in my eyes and streamed down my face.

"Oh, don't start crying like a big baby, now," she said, handing me a crumpled up tissue.

35.

When I had been home a day or two from my adventure, it seemed like I'd never been away at all. Nothing looked or felt different, as I expected it would—like the trip had only been a dream, and now I was awake again.

Every night after supper we started watching Television. It made us all feel calm and dazed, like sitting in a rubber tree did. TV eased the intensity of our family. My father said it was like opium: "Turn the opium on, tune the picture, fix that antenna, adjust the vertical, now the horizontal. . ." he'd command us impatiently from his chair, while he rustled his newspaper, which he read at the same time and then threw on the floor.

I noticed that time was changing. TV took possession of an evening's timefullness, broke it into half-hour chunks and gobbled them up, so it was time to go to bed before you'd had a chance to do anything else. We didn't even have time to play Blind Man's Bluff anymore.

I started feeling something surging in my bloodstream like a race. Suddenly everyone, in the summer of 1954, seemed in some kind of new big hurry. The beat was on. When I thought about it, I realized it hadn't happened suddenly but had been building gradually, all along, just like the developers. This energy I could feel inside me in an unbroken chorus was rooting in MUSIC. The airwaves were cranking up by the day, new songs spreading across the country like wildfire. They were on the radio, on everyone's lips, in the way people walked and swayed and thought about things. And with TV we began to watch ourselves.

One day when I was standing in my bike outside the Youth Center, I heard a song coming from the jukebox. It made me want to move and not ever stop, to laugh, to dance again. I dropped the bike and went inside. Kids were dancing all over the place. The ping-pong tables had been folded up to clear the floor. Kids who weren't dancing sat in the bleachers bopping. I peered into the jukebox to see what new number was playing. It was The Cadillacs: "Oh, they often call me Speedo but my real name is Mr. Earl..." It had a beat that urged my withering heart to answer. Everyone was moving a part of their body to this beat—feet, hips, shoulders and heads jerked involuntarily all over the room.

After I'd stopped chasing Tim and we didn't play Blind Man's Bluff anymore, I sort of lost track of him, but now here he was again thrilling my heart, unwittingly. He was standing across the room with a new guy named Chuck, whom I'd seen on the school bus. I walked closer and tried to see who they were watching in the crowd of girls out on the dance floor. It was Valarie Twombley.

When the song ended Valarie came up to me and said, "Hi, Louise. Wanna fast dance?" I'd never done it before. Most of the boys didn't dance yet either. They were waiting to learn. They were too cool to ask someone to teach them. We danced to "Shake, Rattle and Roll" and then sort of half-time to "Sixty-Minute Man." Dancing always came easy to me, so I just copied what Valarie was doing. Rene, who I hadn't seen since I'd been back, danced by and shouted she was sorry for telling my mother where I was, and I shouted back, "that's okay," instead of thank-you.

It was hard to slide on the concrete floor without any shoes on, and that day was probably the last time I went barefooted. In fact, that day probably marked the end of something and the beginning of something else, but I didn't know what then. All I knew was that in addition to wearing shoes I needed a swishy skirt and I had to start walking differently, and keep my legs slap together, if my body was to perform like Valarie's, which seemed to be the chosen way. Her big sister taught her everything.

Also, that day, when I got home from the Youth Center, mama had been to Byrons. But instead of pajamas, I was surprised to find two new bras, size 32-A, folded neatly, lying on my bed.

36.

I started going over to Valarie Twombley's on Sunday afternoons, after Mass. The Twombleys had come from Mississippi. Their house always smelled like fried chicken and chocolate pie. After church they had their big meal of the day and then all the leftover food would stay on the table with a cloth covering it until suppertime when they'd just knock back the cloth and whoever was around would eat again. The kitchen itself was a jumble of dirty pots and pans and used dishes it would take hours to sort out and clean, all covered over with a thin dusting of flour. There was no room to clean it up for one thing. For another, no one seemed interested. Everyone in the household had retired to their bedrooms. Mr. and Mrs. Twombley were behind a closed door which no one was allowed to open or even knock on. Valarie said they had a standing Sunday afternoon appointment in that room. All you could hear in the dark hallway outside was a radio playing loud hillbilly music.

Down the hallway from there, in the back of the house was Valarie's room, which she shared with her big sister and whoever else was spending the night. It was a huge room, strewn with clothes and make-up, and they had a shower-bath of their own that Valarie's sister spent a lot of time in, washing herself and listening to music on the radio.

Loud music played everywhere. Especially a new kind of music with a beat like African jungle drums. A lot of adults didn't like it—the beat stirred something creaturely in them they thought they'd already stifled, and they were embarrassed. The new music was called rock 'n roll and there was even one song that declared with confidence that it was here to stay, as if something with that much substance could ever dry up and blow away.

Behind the kitchen was a big add-on, meant to be divided into several rooms. The studs were up but it had never been finished with walls. Grandpa Twombley had his quarters here in a room right next to Valarie's little brother Ritchie, only there was no separating wall up so they each sat on their own beds, pretending not to see the other, and talked across the studs whenever they felt like it. There was a bathroom plumbed and studded in but with no walls either, just a door. All around the rooms there were nails in the studs with clothing hanging from them. The clothing sort of made little curtains of privacy. I remembered how much fun it was living this way before my father put up walls in the Sea Breeze.

Ritchie hung his toys on nails: trucks, toy guns, baseball gloves. Grandpa hung suspenders, walking sticks he'd carved and called snake sticks, old Civil War rifles, and small muslin pouches of tobacco. Otherwise, it was a big, open-air room, bright from all the windows that went three-quarters of the way around, and perfumed with the scent of fresh lumber, cordite, and Grandpa's Prince Albert.

I liked to hang around in that room and listen to Grandpa Twombly. I could relax and never felt like fading. They had what they called a front room, which was the living room, the only place in the house that was cleaned up and arranged, like a set for a play. Once, Grandpa took us in there and showed us how the room had been organized around their "color" television console. He said it was the "first color TV," as if he believed other designs would be coming out soon. The screen had a piece of cellophane taped on, which had diagonal bars of color in it—red, yellow, blue and green—like a transparent rainbow repeated over and over. The colors flashed across everything, even people's faces and blurred the picture a little. We all stared at it, accepting the impossibility of transmitting real, natural color over the airwaves. A black and white picture was miracle enough.

There was a door going outside from Grandpa's add-on, near our favorite mulberry tree. Beyond the tree Grandpa had a garden he tended year-round. "No such thing as a day off in Florida if yer a farmer," he'd say, and get his snake stick and a quart jar full of ice cubes and sweet tea and go out to his patch and stay there most of the day, weeding, running off goats and fighting the bugs. But not on Sundays. On Sundays he held court in his room and we hung in between the studs and listened to him. He told us things we never would have known any other way—the dicey kind of information that you can only get from old people, not from school. And he always made it all into a story. Mostly the stories were about Mississippi. He said it was a tragic place where for every one-hundred miles of poor black people there were two miles of rich white people. It was hard to be white in Mississippi without feeling guilty. It gave you the blues real bad. Especially in the rain. "You ever see wet cotton fields for miles and miles?" he asked us, "it's a sorry sight."

Grandpa said he knew the Presley's in his hometown of Tupelo. There were lots of them, cousins and brothers and all. And they were Welch like he was and most everybody else in Tupelo was. One of them, Vernon, had a son named Elvis; he was a new singer everybody was talking about.

He showed us pictures of Wales in a book. There were huge rocks, called stonehenges, standing straight up in fields, in peculiar formations he said "no one understood, nor knew how they got there in the first place either, thousands of years ago." He looked up the Presley name and showed us it was Welch, and had originated in the Presly Hills in Wales, the same place the standing stones came from. By and by, someone had added an extra e in the name.

Grandpa said Elvis had the old spirit of the rocks in him and that was why he was such a good singer. "And that's a fact," he said, "you all can look it up in the Library of Congress someday under Elvis's name if you don't believe me." He squinted his eyes and said on the sly: "The spirit was in them rocks and got inside the people and then some of the people left and went to Tupelo, Mississippi and took it right along with 'em. Probably Elvis didn't even know he was from Wales like the stonehenges, and everybody else just thought he was from Memphis." He fell back on his bed hee-hawing. If we didn't laugh, he gave us a wary look like we were just too dumb to understand how funny it all was.

Elvis Presley had cut a record, he told us, and a friend of his had sent it from Memphis which was about a hundred miles from Tupelo, but didn't have any gum trees like Tupelo had, and he never should have left it and all his friends just to come here and battle bugs, but anywho, here's how real true rock 'n roll music sounds if we cared to know. And he played "That's All Right Mama" for us. Then he played the other side of the little forty-five, "Blue Moon of Kentucky." I wondered if Kentucky was up there near Tupelo and Memphis, and if it had chewing gum trees too.

The music was sweet and exciting, and coded too, like it was a secret being revealed by Elvis alone. After that, we started hearing Elvis on the radio all the time and seeing pictures of him. He was a hunk.

37.

Late in the summer the circus came to town. Shelby was back and Uleta was zesty again. Marie got Andy a job taking care of the animals and he was getting us in free. I had never been to a real circus before. Andy showed us the ropes, things like walking around these giant puddles of briny water that were really elephant urine and too warm to cool your feet in anyway. Other kids went sloshing right through them with a look of surprise at how hot and smelly the water was. Mostly I was careful to avoid these puddles because I have shoes on all the time now, and look like I might be going to a dance.

"Don't look so serious," my mother said as we walked along. "Let your hair down, have a good time. That's what a circus is for."

But for me it was something else and not even how I dreamed it. There were too many flies, and it was dirtier, more confusing and excessive. The calliope music was gaudy, the steam whistles sounded harsh and mocking. There was an angry shit smell like chicken houses, mixing with the sugar scorching smell of cotton candy, peanuts, popcorn, mustard and kerosene: a smell-fest way worse than skunk.

Everything seemed designed to raise a false excitement at a time when I was trying to keep real excitement under control. We walked past some of Goatman's trained goats, locked up in a cage, and zebras, llamas, lions and tigers—

everything in captivity—then we saw the bearded lady in a cage too, where she belonged. I wanted to find Shelby and was afraid to at the same time. I knew she would be in some kind of captivity also, with the "TALL, DARK AND HANDSOME EARL WAULDIN," living curiosities.

"Hey, isn't that your friend over there?" My mother had spotted them. My heart pounded and I suddenly felt bashful. "C'mon, let's go see," mama said, and took my arm and pulled me across the crowd of people walking past. There was another crowd in front of Shelby and Earl who were both standing in huge hinged cases that looked like upright coffins, decorated in an Egyptian motif I kind of liked. A brass plate at the base of Shelby's was inscribed: THE COFFIN OF NEBET-IOTES 2050-1950 B.C., THE DAUGHTER MOST FAVORED BY HER FATHER. It was a copy of a real Egyptian mummy case designed to arouse interest in them. Shelby gave me a soft brown eye and continued to smile wanly at the staring, pointing, jeering crowd.

She was wearing a long green antique dress that had once belonged to Annie Swan, a famous giantess, now dead, and elevator shoes. I had seen all their clothes items closeup. Earl had on a brown suit, a white shirt, white tie, and a pair of size 27 shoes, with cork risers in them. Tall was never tall enough when you were a giant.

The barker said, "Ladeeez and gentlemen... see this giant eight-and-a-half-foot man walk around inside the big top...and right beside him, his lovely daughter, already over six feet tall, and only fourteen years old! Step right up ladeeez and gentlemen. Tickets on sale now... for an extravagant show of animals performing feats of almost human intelligence, lions and tigers and living curiosities!"

My mother moved up closer to Shelby and hollered, "Hey, how's the weather up there?" Then she giggled like she was the cleverest thing in the world. Shelby smiled down at her, not answering the question she has been asked at least a thousand times in her life. Then Earl and Shelby stepped through the black velvet curtain behind their cases and were replaced by "Unzie," the aborigine albino and "Lucia," the smallest woman that ever lived, twenty-four-inches tall, weighing twenty-five pounds. These acts had replaced the Three-Legged Man, and Mole Lady when she retired.

Daddy had no interest in the circus and had stayed home. Just like church. Donnie was over at the game booths trying to win a panda bear. Something about aiming at a target deeply bored me. Mama and I followed Andy inside the big top for the show. Marie would be performing on the trapeze. It was a benefit for some disease that she supposedly had. The ringmaster appeared, bowing and cracking his whip while the calliope filled the tent with melodramatic sound. Animals tumbled into the center ring and ran frantically around in a circle kicking up sawdust until they evoked the image of Little Black Sambo's tiger melting into butter, at least in my mind.

"Hi ya, hi ya, hi ya," the ringmaster shouted. "Welcome to The Barnum and Bailey Circus. Greatest Show on Earth!"

Girls jumped on and off horses doing acrobats and jangling on the horses' backs like they were hot to the touch, while the music whipped up to a rollicking frenzy. This would have been my act, only I'd do it real slow like a ballet and not

259

get the horses all sweated up and agitated. I wondered if anyone would want to watch that.

Then I saw the trainer standing in the wings, and I shrunk down and shivered automatically. Mama said, "What's a matter with you? snap out of it, will ya dearie?"

I couldn't tell her, so I drifted off for a long time, getting lost in the clown's act. Andy sat beside me chuckling in that shy way he had that always made me feel good too. The mohawk was all grown out now. It hadn't made Andy any tougher. I remembered something from the Nazarenes that God always tempered the wind to the shorn lamb. I couldn't see how the mohawk had changed Andy at all. It was like a wound that had healed that's all. Maybe there were scars underneath. I hoped not.

Something about one of the clowns was familiar. Then I saw his bicycle loaded down with junk, except his factotum sign was gone and in its place was a sign that said: B.B. Knickerbocker. He was wearing a red and yellow clown suit, only instead of bloomers he had on knickers with camp boots. He had a big red and white smile painted across his usual woe-begone frown and his brown eyes were widely circled in bright blue with silver spangles glittering in it, so he looked cheerful if you didn't know better- recognizable too- there were moonbeams in his eyes. He had a gun that shot backwards and he kept shooting himself and falling down over and over again, and the crowd around him roared. He was so frisky even I laughed, forgetting it was Bicycle Bill, the greatest sulker I had ever known.

Then the ring was cleared and spotlights flashed up in the dark ceiling caverns of the tent, on the highwire. I could see Marie perched up there in a box with the other performers, her eyes twinkling in the lights like Brenda Starr's. Then I heard the barker introducing her:

"This amazing fifty-year-old woman has a rare disease called lupus, ladies and gentlemen. She's up there anyway performing for us today, to benefit others with that disease. Folks, let's give a big hand to the Amazing Marie." The spotlight brightened and held on Marie who waved and smiled. I couldn't see a net in the darkness below her.

I blushed and felt bad-tempered as I watched Marie cavorting up there—being caught and thrown back, like a flopping fish. She was limber and seemed to still have her good timing. My mother was so impressed she didn't say anything, didn't even dispute Marie's disease. I began to see Marie as this funny little woman acting out her vainglorious destiny for all she was worth. Flying through the air she invited you to admire her, feel sorry for her, laugh at her, whatever you wanted to do. She gave you the choice. She put herself out there for you, generously. I could feel that old shadow of death inside the tent, stalking Marie and she was totally unguarded as usual. I looked hard for the net but still couldn't see one. I felt a strong desire to get her out of there but it was way too late. She was like a natural resource squandering itself. I could see Shelby and Earl standing in the wings in semi-darkness, watching Marie, with the spotlight blasting up on her like the eye of fate. Skeeter was

261

there too, holding Marie's little chihuahua, Gravy, stroking him gently, so he wouldn't bark and distract her.

Back and forth Marie swung in rhythm to the music, clapping hands over wrists with her catcher, drawing the awed applause of the crowd over and over. Finally she did a double flip in the air, missed the catcher and plunged down like a rock—into a net, now lit up so you could see it. Everyone went "Oooooh," and "Ahhh" at the same time, like they did when Lentini's leg raised the lid of his coffin. But she was okay. It was a fake fall I realized, part of the routine. She somersaulted over the edge of the net, threw her arms in the air, grinning ear to ear, accepting the ringing applause like the pro she was. Gravy was yawping wildly now, and Marie ran over, took him from Skeeter, and showered him with blow-fish kisses.

I stood like everyone else, clapping, cheering, whistling. Marie's performance left me burning to be an acrobat. When the applause died down, mama pronounced: "Well the circus is still no place for a girl."

When I got home I snuck the medical books down from the top shelf and looked up lupus. There were two kinds. Did she have systemic lupus or discoid? Was there renal involvement? Anemia? How did she remain so strong? It was the body against itself, and the sun was Marie's enemy. Why was she always out in it then, and why did she live in Florida, which hung the sun? I didn't think even she knew the answers. She denied it all, denied that old devil death too, out-maneuvered him by always staying in motion.

Marie was trying to "get her another somebody," as she put it. She said she always came out of retirement when she wanted a new husband. Her best feature was her legs, and how better to show them off than on a trapeze, with the added advantage of distance? She said some men were hypnotized by a pair of flying legs—"It's like they wrap around their eyes and brains some way, capturing them."

When I thought back on the circus, something seemed to be missing besides Mole Lady, The Great Lentini, and the boy with green hair. Then I realized it was Mrs. Wauldin, baby Linda and Rene. They had been nowhere in sight, as if they were a separate and different part of Earl and Shelby's life. Their family was not of a piece either. Was anybody's?

38.

On Sunday nights now, Sandy Yates and I usually spent the night over at Valarie's. Her big sister, Joyce, who was nineteen, was helping us with our clothes and make-up. When you saw her from behind, Joyce was tall and long-legged like Delora Devine, with long, shiny brown hair. But when she turned around you were disappointed that she wasn't beautiful at all like Delora was. Joyce's face was pitted from pimples and she used a lot of powder to fill in the holes. Her lips were too thin so she drew them on bigger with a red lip-pencil, and her nose, well it was like Pinnochios. Still, she was engaged.

I wished I had a sister, an ally, someone I could share the world with forever. I wished I could at least see Shelby more. She was the closest I had ever come to a sister. Sometimes I worried about her when she wasn't in school. But she was going to be a famous circus tall lady anyway and didn't need school for that. More and more, I felt I was missing someone, until after awhile I'd have to think real hard to realize it was just big ole Shelby.

Valarie's sister plucked my eyebrows into a sharp thin arch and then penciled them auburn because they were so blonde you couldn't see them otherwise. She brushed my flaming red hair, as she called it, and said I should try to be more like Rhonda Fleming who was a movie star with the same kind of hair. She put it up in a pony tail, almost on the top of my head, and said it would look real good in a short ducktail like Valarie's, and she'd be glad to cut it for me if I wanted one. But I liked having a ponytail to swish around when I danced. And besides, I didn't want to do anything to my hair that might draw the wrath of my mother again. My hair was important to her.

Joyce showed us all how to put make-up on and how to add little sexy touches to our clothes, like putting our collars up and wearing wide, black, cinch belts with full skirts and lots of crinolines and dainty ankle bracelets. She tied cords of black velvet with white, bunny-fur tassels on the ends, around our bird-like necks, and put her Evening In Paris perfume on our pulse points. She taught us a new exercise that would help us develop. As we lifted our arms and swung them forward, and then out to the side, we chanted: "We must, we must, we must increase our bust..." over and over, at least twenty times.

When she was done fooling with us she always disappeared into the shower and played the radio in there for a long time. Valarie said her big sister liked to lie under the stream of water, instead of standing up. She liked how it felt beating down on her. Valarie and Sandy giggled about it, as though it was some kind of secret thing I was too young for.

PART THREE

THE SPIRIT IN THE ROCKS

39.

The dinner table. Where it all happened in my family. We were having pork chops, potatoes and peas. Again. A variation on hamburg, potatoes and spinach. My father usually came to the table in his pajamas; he never wore a shirt and tie like Ozzie Nelson, that's for sure. On Friday nights he made cocktails for himself and my mother and they chattered, moving around in the kitchen. He'd have a dry martini, she'd have a sweet manhattan. He'd hand over his paycheck and they'd laugh and tease each other for awhile. This was their routine.

Monday through Thursday, when he came in from work he changed right away into his pajamas, and lay down on the couch exhausted, reading the Miami Herald until dinnertime. I used to wash his feet, Willie Boo on the left, Joe Toad on the right, and rub them with Jergens hand lotion. The heavy boots he wore all day long steamed his feet, made them burn and ache and stink. But I got familiar with the smell, warm, leathery and sweet like the inside of a barn. After I did his feet, he used to write on my back. It was sort of a trade-off. But we didn't do this ritual anymore, ever since I'd run away and my childlife ended in the same stroke.

For some reason everyone was unusually subdued at this dinner table. It was not Friday and yet my parents were having cocktails. Mama seemed to be pouting over by the stove, everything on the table, but she still wasn't sitting down. It was like that time long ago when she had to go into the hospital for an operation on her female parts. My stomach flipped. Daddy had to call her over twice to sit down. It was way too quiet, this table. Something was up.

We began to eat, then once we hit a comfortable stride, daddy started talking: "There's something your mama and I have to tell you." He held his hand up and patted the air so we wouldn't be scared. "It's a good thing..." he said quickly. He was his old sanguine self, but my mother looked doubtfully at him and seemed fearful, suspicious even. She took a sip of her manhattan and a deep breath.

Then daddy said, gleaming: "You're gonna have a new baby sister or brother."

"You mean...?"

"Ax any questions you want." He always said "ax" for ask to be funny. Now it sounded too cute. He quaffed a sip of his martini, making a slurping sound like he was trying to make us all laugh. His big blue eyes sparkled. Then he burped and said "Shirley," the way he always did, instead of "Excuse me," like a normal person.

Questions? It was slowly hitting us. A baby? My brothers were silent, like empty tunnels. As if on cue, we all blushed, even Donnie. How could this happen to us? Everyone would know what our parents did to make this baby. It felt like something had crawled all over me. I looked at my mother with a mixture of awe and shame. She looked back at me, embarrassed, as if she was the young and foolish one and I was the adult, about to judge her. Then I saw that they wanted us to be happy about this new baby. They sat there, looking pretty good for their ages, awaiting our approval, needing for us to yelp like puppies with pleasure. But the most we could manage was a rumble of disbelief.

"really?"

"you're kidding."

"you mean...?"

"when?"

Then I think I said it was a miracle. I did. It was.

Donnie and Andy stared at my mother with their mouths open. They were afraid to look at our father, who was eating his dinner now with a little strut in his bites.

"Early February," mama said, not looking at us.

In the next few days, as I adjusted to the news, I couldn't take my eyes off mama. She laid up in the bed most of the time, her eyes wide open, thinking, talking, then agreeing with herself. She was jittery and feeling old—she was forty. "Late in life, late in life, late in life," did a repetitious bump and grind in her mind, and she kept saying it out loud like a chant. It was what Dot Murphy said when she heard the news: "Isn't this a little late in life to be having a baby?"

You could see mama felt too tired to do this again. We had worn her out already, made her a nervous wreck, brought her to the brink. Hadn't she told us that often enough?

What are people going to think? she wondered out loud, all atither with nervous worrying, as if the condition she was in wasn't a natural one—like a superstition had gotten inside her, instead of a baby.

One day she suddenly announced, as though she was addressing a vast public instead of just us: "No matter what, it's a baby, a real human being inside me, and by God, I'm gonna have it. To hell with the abortionists." Dot Murphy had suggested that option, warning mama about mongoloidism at her age. Marie had offered to take care of the baby once it was born, no matter what it was. She would nurture it like a little hibiscus bush, and teach it things. Only mama would probably be too jealous to let her.

It was a doctor she decided to listen to finally. This was a surprise, knowing how she hated doctors. Her doctor told her she was healthy enough to carry a full-term baby, and to make it a little easier on herself and the baby by not gaining too much weight. She was determined to follow his advice. At last a doctor who knew something, who could offer an intelligent diagnosis. She plunged her faith in him. She stopped going to the Greyhound Inn and stuck to Friday night cocktails with my father. The jar on her closet shelf disappeared.

By the time she began to show, my sheepishness had faded. I was more ashamed of being ashamed and the only way out of that corner was, strangely enough, to embrace the pregnancy for all I was worth. I stayed close to home watching mamma, hardly noticing when that long summer finally ended and school started.

I began to daydream in school about who the baby was and what it would look like. I recalled the time table of fetal development I had seen in my mother's medical books, and saw in my mind the arm and leg buds lengthening. I knew it

271

was a girl—my own sister come at last. As the embryo took shape and her features formed, I visualized her. She would have dark, black Irish hair, big green eyes framed in dark brows and long lashes, sort of like my favorite doll Dorothy. Her skin would be pink and white and fair, but the kind that tanned if she went out in the sun, instead of freckled. She would look like Debra Padgett and Elizabeth Taylor combined, be sweet as a baby kitten—I felt her sweetness glow in my chest. She would have everything a girl needed. I would take care of her and gently but firmly guide her so she would never be mixed-up like mama said I was.

She stirred ambition in my father. He was thinking of going into business for himself, so, every night after he read the *Herald* he studied books about compounds and chemistry and taught himself formulas. He told me: "If you want to be first in the Yellow Pages you have to name your company Acme because everything is in alphabetical order."

It was like that at school too, always starting with the A's. Why couldn't they ever start at Z and go back? Why not start at O and I'd be first for once? O'Neill? Here. Do you have a brother named Donnie? Yes. Well, I hope you are not as much trouble as your brother is. Blush.

But I'm going to have a sister now too.

Louise O'Neill. Who was I? Who were all these other people? Everyone in school looked the same now. When had people started to smooth out so much? I couldn't see any differences. There were none with three legs or moles or any other distinctions anymore. What ilk was I in? When did everything get so beige? The world didn't seem as varietal and interesting as it once had. Instead, people all wanted to be the same—everything seemed to be about conforming and being normal, whatever that was.

Daddy read to me about a new ruling that had come down from the Court in Topeka, Kansas that said the laws enforcing segregated schools were unconstitutional, and ordered all the schools to desegregate with deliberate speed. That meant the colored kids would be coming to our school now, and we could go to theirs. I was excited. I couldn't wait. I had acquired a taste for the exotic, for otherness, and I craved it now that everything was the same.

Donnie had been calming down since the news of the baby. He was drinking high-protein milkshakes and lifting weights to build up his skinny body. In high school, there was a different teacher for each subject so I got a full dose of all Donnie's teachers after he was through with them. They were all curious because he had been so quiet and hadn't been in any trouble for a few months and they asked me was anything wrong with Donnie. They missed his big maw, I guess. Everyone knew he had something, they just didn't know what or when it was going to break the surface and end this irksome waiting.

He appeared to be channeling all of his energy into baseball. Every day he practiced, alone usually, unless he found someone to throw the ball to him; otherwise he just shanked it around by himself, endlessly swinging the bat and dreaming—maybe about the baby—but the baby seemed to clarify this other dream he had going. I didn't think it was about Sandy Yates, who he seemed to have forgotten.

At the beginning of the school year Donnie got himself thrown off the baseball team for mouthing off at the coach and being a wise guy. Donnie claimed he was too good to play high school baseball anyway, it was bush league. But everyone thought he was just bragging. Instead of going to pieces about not being on the team, Donnie began hatching a new, secret plan all his own. You could see him outside talking to himself about it as he practiced.

My father started adding on to the Sea Breeze again. The new baby would need a room of its own he said. He had added onto our house so much that it sprawled like a white-legged Yankee. Still, just seeing The Sea Breeze always made me unsteel my heart. It didn't look like any of the other houses in Uleta. They were all alike, boxes in straight rows, with the occasional circular cul de sac street to break the pattern, or else a street just stopped, until some other developer cut through and continued the row. Plywood got more and more popular and available—it was the sour fruit crop of all the trees they were mangling, my father said, the very absence of design. Television aerials started sticking up from the roofs of houses like metal trees. They reminded me of the tree the iron workers had put on top of the Fountainbleu Hotel that stayed until it was finished—the tree for good luck so no one would fall. And no one had.

Sometime in the past few weeks Andy had stopped stuttering. It was the baby. This baby was changing things already, even before she was born.

40.

Mama fussed at me for wearing make-up and thinking too much about clothes. "Who do you think you are, the Queen of Sheba?" she asked me sharply, when she caught me looking in the bulls-eye mirror one Sunday. I didn't know who that was, the Queen of Sheba. She didn't like my plucked eyebrows either. "C'mon down to earth, will ya," she said, just be yourself, be natural." What was natural? I thought she meant to be like her—she didn't wear hardly any make-up. I didn't want to be like my mother. People were trying to be normal instead of natural. I had the need to feel normal, to fool people into thinking I lived in a normal home with a normal family. Natural must be everything human that people were trying to escape from.

Even my mother was always trying to appear normal. She had become obsessed with appearances and neatness since becoming pregnant. She liked things tidied up, but she was still messy in ways no one could see, like with the truth. If someone dropped by she went into a panic trying to pick up the newspapers before the "company" could see them lying on the floor where my father tossed each section after he was through reading it. "Quick, straighten up," she gasped, "somebody's coming. Act normal, now." As if what we were doing in that house as a family wasn't normal. And as though we were being invaded by someone we were obliged to impress.

275

It made me feel funny the way she was. I wanted to be unrelated to her—my own mother. If we were being loud she'd hiss, "The neighbors, the neighbors will hear you, shush now." She never cared about the neighbors before— they were too far away anyhow. Sometimes when she said that, I went over to the window and screamed out, at the top of my lungs, until I started giggling and she had to, also. "Oh, stop, stop," she'd say. "You're killing me." And she'd get red, hold her big belly and laugh so uncontrollably she wet her pants. It was the only way I could bring the woman out of it.

I knew she felt threatened by the bulldozers and earthmovers, the same way she was by wild animals. But the builders hadn't gotten that close to our house yet. The nearest development was still out of earshot even though you could see it rising up on the flat land.

She would not laugh if she knew what went on at the Sunday night Youth Fellowship Meeting at the Twombley's church, the First Christian, downtown near Edison High School. I was doing all this dressing up just to go with Sandy and Valarie, and Valarie's parents who drove us. Not that it had anything to do with religion. I was naturally interested in religion, but I was more interested in learning about boys and how to act around them.

Up to this time I had only been slightly aware of the value of material things. But now I could see how important they were, how everything stood for something else whenever people were together. Like, for example, a motorcycle and a black leather jacket meant the boy who had them was wild and free. But you wouldn't walk up and say, "Hey, your freedom is neat." You'd say, "Your jacket is neat," because you weren't supposed to mention the real meanings, it wasn't cool. You were supposed to glaze over them. It was square to be interested in ideas when the world was so full of meaningful material things. I had to be careful because I was afraid I'd say the wrong thing all the time.

I was getting to be a good actress though. I flounced around in my full, midnight-blue taffeta skirt Marie had made me, with a scratchy crinoline slip underneath, and imitated what everyone else was doing. Even though I knew my integrity and very identity were threatened, I still copied. I didn't care. A part of me cherished this boot-legged identity with Sandy and Valarie more than anything else. I was making myself up with their help. Rock 'n roll stirred my blood and made me believe life was as exciting as I always hoped it would be.

On Sunday nights outside the First Christian Church in the dark parking lot, boys with suave, shining ducktails sprawled on their motorcycles, waiting, smoking Lucky strikes, dressed black and leathery despite the heat, their look similar: defiant, one eye happy, the other sad, the look of Cool. Cool was the way to be. Pretend you don't care or know what other people think of you. Get so recoiled and involved inside your own head that you aren't aware of anyone else, or care if anyone's watching you. Play it cool. Hide, withdraw, but stay alert and be timely. Everyone called them hoods, and while they waited for us to come out of church, these neat hoods practiced their cool.

Inside we hurried through the hymns and discussion of the Bible, peeking out the window to count the gathering throng. Motorcycle sounds made us lift the volume of our singing voices to the heavens, trying to cover them up.

When it was time for communion, we passed a tray of bite-sized squares of white bread and another tray right after it with little individual vessels of Welch's grape juice that clinked into slots. We each took a tiny square of bread, the body of Christ, and then a little swig of grape juice, the blood. And we felt pure and good. There was no confession and no one called it Eucharist like the Catholics did. It was just symbolic—not "the real presence." Still, I wouldn't tell my mother about taking communion at First Christian. It was probably some kind of sin even though it gave me a wonderful, cleaned-out feeling to commit it.

Finally, when it was break time, we smuggled cupcakes and punch out to the hoods, and pranced around all nervous and giggly, afraid to stand too still, or too close, to these dangerous glossy-haired boys. And cute.

They played their own hymns for us on a portable radio. When Hank Ballard and the Midnighters started singing, "I Just Love Your Sexy Ways," I thought I would pass out from the thrill of it. Hearing a song for the first time was like discovering a new rapturous place on your body, and then looking all over for it the next time.

I felt a sweet bestirring in my panties, like something unfolding, and my whole body swooned, heat temporarily blocking my thinking. I assumed all the other girls were feeling this way too—I mean, that's what we were out there for, wasn't it?

This bunch of boys went to Edison High School in the daytime and at night they hung around drive-in restaurants, various parking lots, and Sunday Night Youth Fellowship meetings, where they watched dainty little swaybacked Christian girls unfold in the parking lot and probably didn't even know that's what they were seeing, they were so cool. When a hood looked at me a certain way, I melted and felt like a new girl, beautiful almost—transformed.

We acted like we were inventing sex; we dressed for it, sang and danced about it: "Shake baby, shake shake shake, till yer Mama and Daddy comes home, shake, shake, sha-a-ake, I just love your sexy ways. Wiggle wiggle wiggle wiggle wiggle, till your hips get tired and weak, ooooh, wiggle wiggle wiggle wiggle wiggle till you fall out on your feet. Wiggle wiggle wig-ig-le, I just love your sexy ways. Upside down, all around, just any ole way... on the wall, in the hall, c'mon baby, do it baby, move baby move move move..." We were going faster than the speed of light, a newly tapped wildness erupting inside us.

41.

I had learned a new word to describe how fancy and loose everything was: fabulous. There were dances springing up all over. On Wednesday nights there was one in Biscayne Gardens, Friday night was the Youth Center dance, and there was one every Saturday night in Little River, but this was a "dangerous" dance I was not ready for yet. You had to go by car, for one thing, and there were gangs. Mama didn't think I was ready for any of them yet, even though I was fifteen now. I wanted the power and freedom my brothers had, they could go anywhere, but mama said I wanted too much. She let me go to the Youth Fellowship meeting only because Valarie's parents drove us there. She didn't know about the communion, or the boys out in the parking lot.

"You're just a girl, you could get hurt out in the world parading around," she fussed one night, while I was getting ready for a dance.

"Oh, woman," I moaned and made a face in the mirror. I had begun calling her "Woman" since she started showing good. She slapped me angrily on the arm when she saw the face. "Don't make faces at me, Miss High and Mighty."

I teared up, and tried to ignore her. I leaned into the mirror to apply mascara, and she saw her Coty face powder on the dresser, which I had borrowed from her to cover up my freckles. "And stay out of my drawers, too. You think I don't need anything anymore, don't you? Well, I can still show you a thing or two, dearie." She put her hands on her swollen hips and glared at my make-up job. "Tsk, tsk, tsk, well, now doesn't that look freaky?" It was her new word: freaky. She used it to express the stone cold soul of nature's failures.

Make-up offended mama. She wore only powder and lipstick. She rubbed a little of the lipstick into her cheeks for rouge, touched her tongue to her finger and polished her eyebrows and lids with spit. I'd seen her do it a hundred times. She liked looking like a plain Irish washerwoman.

"I can't be bothered with all that make-up crap," she said. But it sounded vain to me, as if she considered herself perfect without it.

I looked in the mirror at my long, blackened eyelashes that were all clotted together now because she was making me nervous. I wished I could start over.

She padded around my room, flipping things with her nosy hand, and I held my breath. She wanted to hurl something at me, I could feel it. She was like a grouchy hen, clutching her belly, her hen-fruit, and I was afraid of her. She said: "You're such a dreamer."

"Thank you, I try." I snipped.

She slapped my face hard for that, and then waddled away to answer the door. I tried to cover the red marks from her hand with more powder. The tears caused the mascara to run, so I smeared it all off in a hurry, turned out the light, and took a few breaths, trying to breathe normally.

Valarie and Sandy had come to get me for the dance. The woman always gave in as long as everybody else was going also. She liked to conform.

"Well, now, don't you two look nice!" I heard her chime, like she was imitating Harriet Nelson.

After that torturous night, I started getting dressed inside my closet, hunting up something to wear in the pitch dark, and then walking over to Valarie's or Sandy's to put the make-up on. Then we'd all go to the dance together.

When I wasn't dancing I studied the room to see if there was a boy tall enough for Shelby but there never was. Cecil Holt was the only boy in Uleta bigger than Shelby, but he was too mean with his ugly old forklift. My recurring daydream now was to take Shelby to a dance. A certain song always triggered it:

Let the little girl dance
She wants to give it a try
So let the little girl by
She's been a little wallflower on
the shelf standing by herself
Now she's got the nerve to take a chance
So let the little girl dance

When I told Shelby my dream she said, "I can't dance anyway, my bones are too dern brittle, so stop looking for somebody." Then she said she would come to a dance just to watch me. She was with Tall Paul a lot these days, but if they had any deep feelings for each other they were hiding them from view. Still, the silent way they had of not moving much around each other made them seem close some way, but I might have been imagining things.

The music had come gradually, beginning with a beat that matched your own hearts. By now the airwaves had filled out and grown huge, like some human-hearted organism, and the songs were coming faster than we could learn them. At dances I went all out, my ponytail just a-flying. The floor was awallow in clouds of churning crinolines, flurries of feet fast dancing. Yet for me, Shelby, my Sunbeam was always missing.

Once she did come to the dance up at the Youth Center to watch, but more and more I was losing touch with her. Her loneliness had deepened until she was way off somewhere I couldn't reach anymore. She stayed out of school with broken bones and I didn't like to go to her house because Mrs. Wauldin would try to engage me in what she called "pleading the blood for Shelby," which was some desperate kind of praying that scared me to death. I don't know why people can't talk to God simply, like talking to the sky.

In school Mr. Delong the art teacher gave us an assignment that would set me to thinking for at least the next ten years. It was: What is the difference between art and science? The more I thought about it, the less different they were. The process of selection, science, was very close to the process of imagination, art. I decided it was a trick question I would try out at the dinner table.

In class I drew a picture of a woman who looked like she lived in Renaissance times. She had an old-world hairdo, of tight strangely severe rolls, and was wearing a velvet dress with a large white ruff at her neck. I used India ink and water colors. I didn't know where her image came from, but there was something familiar about her. I tossed the picture and started a new one. This time it was almost the same woman but the ruff turned into a necklet of brown fur on the shoulders, with a pair of feet at one end and a little animal face with shiny black button eyes at the other. Then I recognized the woman. It was Nola without her moles. I knew then that nothing in nature was unbeautiful, not Nola, not even a dead animal. Drawing was like dreaming. You never knew what was coming up next.

Mr. Delong fished my drawing out of the trash and told the class not to throw anything away anymore, to keep all work and study our own progress with it. Then he hung the picture up on the wall and I blushed extravagantly. He gave me a book to read called *Brave New World*, by Aldous Huxley.

My mother was at the end of her second trimester. I drew my sister's eyebrows, eyelashes, the whorling skin ridges forming on her palms that would be her fingerprints. Mr. Delong called this picture abstract art because he didn't recognize what it was—only I knew. The bronchial tree was branching out in my next drawing, as it does in the sixth month, actively, wondrously.

After art class, I felt relaxed and joyful. I took the abstract art home and showed it proudly to my mother. "Phew, get that out of here. That's awful!" she said, as if it smelled. Then Donnie grabbed *Brave New World* and they tossed it back and forth between them, rifling it in my face when I tried to intercept it. This was the worst thing I knew of, when Donnie and my mother both ganged up against me.

"Aldous Huxley is an atheist," Donnie said, trying to rile my mother.

"You are so mixed up," she said to me, "it's because you read too much. You're not getting this book back, so just forget about it."

I felt so much rage I didn't know what to do. Why did her opinions have such power? I walked out and kicked stones and rolled around on the grass, getting filthy dirty, seething, and dreaming of a time when I would be free of that woman's judgment and my mortal enemy Donnie would be far away from here. After about an hour I went back home and looked for the book, but it was nowhere to be found, and for a change, nobody was home. I went into the big bathroom. My clothes were wrecked and my skin itched. I undressed and looked at myself in the mirror. My breasts looked like pale peaches and I had a fuzz of pubic hair, RED. I took a long shower, lying down and letting the water beat down on me in a steady stream. I opened my legs and then I understood. I wouldn't want anyone to see me doing this, but it felt so good. It was like something joyful coming together inside my wilderness.

Afterwards, I checked the shelf in my mother's closet for the whiskey jar and was relieved when it wasn't there. Every day when I got in from school I did this. I kept watch on my mother's eyes too, but they were wide open and warmish brown, even when she was crabby.

That night at the dinner table I dropped the bomb: "What's the difference between art and science?"

"That's easy," Donnie said. "Art is bullshit!" They all laughed except my father. He just looked blankly at Donnie.

"Trivial," my mother said, "art is trivial compared to science, especially medical science."

"Yeah, it's too trivial," I said bitterly. "That's what's wrong with the world."

"Don't be so fresh," my mother snapped.

But I went on anyway, emboldened by Mr. Delong, or maybe my own obstinate red-headedness: "If things were run by artists there would be no more wars, no starving people either."

"Haw! Where'd you learn that? If the world was run by artists everything would go right down the drain. Don't believe everything you read, dearie. Hurry up and eat now. Let's get this meal over with."

"Yeah, you dumb atheist," said Donnie.

"That's enough." said my mother.

After awhile, my father, who was still angry about nuclear fission, said, "Science holds the secret of destructive energy and art holds the secret of constructive energy. That's one difference."

"Well, I don't see what's so constructive about art?" my mother argued, "it's just a lot of hooey if you ask me."

Tears suddenly flooded my eyes and I ran from the table. "What's wrong with HER?" my mother squawked.

I couldn't feel more different from that woman if I tried, yet my biggest fear was of being just like her. I saw that art

286

and I were targets of her own self-hatred, and I hated her for it. But how could I feel that way about my mother without feeling bad about myself? If she only knew the joy it gave me to draw a picture.

She would never win this, as long as I refused to get it into my head that I had less understanding than she had, less sense. That was my only salvation—or I could die and change into her. It was painful to be where I was, opposing my own mother, and feeling that my very selfhood was locked up and she had control of the key.

I stayed in my room the rest of that night and had a good cry. Just a real good cry.

42.

The bigger mama got, the meaner. We were under siege. Every morning she yelled: "Get dressed, eat, get out!" so we wouldn't miss the bus. She couldn't wait for us to leave so she could go back to bed. I wished she wouldn't even get up. The bus stop was at the corner near our house, and I could hear her yelling and calling Donnie names as I waited with the other kids for the bus to come. It was humiliating and no use pretending I didn't know her. Sometimes if I was too slow it was me she was screeching at. Combined with my old white cardigan which had little ballies on it, I felt grungy and uncool.

Every night I asked God to let me have Tim Murphy. I had a better idea what to do with him now. I'd dance with him for one thing, wrap my arms around his neck and hold him close, then I'd kiss him. I added a prayer which had words from one of my favorite slow songs to dance to: "Heavenly Father up above, please protect the boy I love; Keep him always safe and sound, no matter when or where he's bound; then dear God help him to see that I love him and he loves me..." I usually fell asleep singing this low.

Tim was turning into a hood. He was slicking his hair back in side wings and smoking cigarettes, acting like James Dean and Marlon Brando. Only he was blonde, and had no motorcycle or leather jacket. He was more like a beach hood. All the boys that were beach hoods either already had or dreamed of having a convertible, and they hung around the beach getting great tans. Only, I knew Tim's secret: He was afraid of cars. He would never drive one. He shied away when everyone else was learning to drive, and always rode in someone else's car. I loved him more than ever and I would never tell his secret to anyone, not even him.

At dances, I wished he'd come over to talk, or ask me to dance, but he didn't dance either. He wouldn't even try. He just watched, smiling that sly smile he had. Dancing was my life now. I was a sworn companion to the beat. All of the other boys had learned how to dance except Tim. I liked being held and rocked slowly as the lyrics filled my head with thoughts of Tim who slumped against the jukebox playing it cool: "Talk to me, talk to me, hold me close, whisper low, please say the part I love just one more time..." Once in a while he took his comb out and slicked back the sides of his hair, then ruffled the middle with his fingers.

I liked dirty dancing too, slithering around the floor doing a lot of hand and arm and hip moves to the wicked "Work with me, Annie, don't be 'shamed, work with me Ahahneeee, let's get it while the gettin' is good, so good, so good a um, aum, a um uh uhm." Adults hated this song. By the end of a dance, everyone was dancing full-out to Shake, Rattle and Roll until we dropped, sweating, exhausted and parched. It took icy cold Co-colas to revive us.

One night Tim casually walked over, real cool, and asked me if I wanted a ride home in Chuck's car. Sh-boom, life could be a dream, sweetheart. Chuck drove his father's '51 green Hudson Hornet, and that night he asked Valarie and we doubled. Tim was good at being a backseat wit, while Chuck drove around and found somewhere to park for awhile before we went on home. After all the breathless dancing it was exhilarating to make out in the back seat with the guy I loved. My mother's Arpege perfume mingled with my sweat and Tim's Wild Root hair oil, enveloping us in a steamy cloud of musk. We kissed over and over and rubbed our bodies together harder and tighter until we got so hot I thought I would die. Then I woke up to what was happening and stopped him. Also,"SH-BOOM" saved us. When it came on the radio, we all stopped and sang along. It was our theme song:

> Life could be a dream, sh-boom
> If I could take you up in paradise up above
> And I could tell you
> You're the only one that I love.
> Life could be a dream, sweetheart.
> Hello, hello again, sh-boom,
> Here's hoping we meet again...

"Oh oh oh YES I'm The Great Pretender," also had the power to stop us. I was afraid to go the whole way. Tim got mad, because he was way ahead of me, and called me a tease. But how could I be that when I didn't really know what I was holding back?

After that, he went in the car with other girls, too, loyal as a fly, and then he tried me again to see if I was ready, but I never was. I had only to look at my mother to see what might happen. The swelling up that would take place was scary— that's what stopped me. And also I thought of what she told me and Andy once: that her father had threatened to disown her if she ever disgraced him. I could see that all passionate love was compromised right from the beginning by the fact that the female had a womb and all the responsibility for protecting it. The male could implant it and go scot-free. It was another example of a boys' power over me that I had grown to resent.

I felt with my mind as well as my heart, but I was a little ashamed of this. It was cool to be impulsive, sexy and spontaneous, and I thought too much, Tim said. Another thing I thought about, but was too proud to say, was that the guy I went the whole way with would have to want me in particular, not just sex with any old girl. Anyway, I suspected Tim had a crush on Shirley Hanley. She wasn't allowed to go to dances. My beloved sleepwalker was just looking for tail, as I had heard old man Badger put it. That hurt my uncool feelings.

One night, we all went to the drive-in to see a special preview of "East of Eden." It was an old John Steinbeck story I remembered from our bookcase. The movie starred James Dean, an actor we idolized, a guy giving everything he had. Magazines were full of pictures of him, in all the moodiness he dared to show.

Chuck and Valarie brought cigarettes and quart bottles of Budweiser we passed around while we waited for the movie to start, taking slugs of the beer until we got woozy and loose. Tim and Chuck talked back and forth to each other over the seats, as though me and Valarie weren't even there.

"Hey, man, did you see the Mr. B that guy had?"

"Yeah, I wanna get one like that. The risers, man, did you see those risers?"

"And that skinny belt. They are so cool. I want a square-back too."

The seats of the car were cozy, fuzzy-warm, smelled of motor oil and smoke, so high we could only see the tops of heads over them. Valarie's dirty blonde duck-tail was my focal point; then it slid down on the front seat and disappeared, and Chuck's slid down too. Al Hibbler singing "Unchained Melody" came over the drive-in speakers capturing us. Tim and I started making out too, and the car shimmered with heat and music: "First the tide...rushes in...plants a kiss...on the shore...then rolls out to sea, and the sea is very still...once more..." We were all horizontal now, kissing rubbing grinding, underneath a blanket of sky spangled with starlight just for us. Tim pleaded in a whisper: Just lay on top of me...go ahead...please...just try it once...get on top...oh please, c'mon." I knew that he wanted me to feel his hardness and he thought if I did, I wouldn't be able to resist him.

I straddled him in my aqua pedal-pushers, my white sleeveless blouse with the collar up, mostly unbuttoned now. My ponytail flipped across his face and he buried his head in it, nuzzling my hot perfumy neck and groaning for me to move on him, yes, more, more, while he tugged at my bra. I bruised myself against his rock hardness, the moist mix of pain and pleasure coursing, my breasts wobbling against his chest bone, then barely grazing the skin, softly, slowly. Our breathing grew desperate. The car was hot as a barbecue. I started to forget who I was—it felt like I was melting into Tim in one big hot-pot of pleasure.

I heard a pebble drop on the roof and looked up. Donnie was peering through the back window at us. Where had he come from? He gave me a suspicious look, as though I was a she-wolf predator and Tim was my victim. Then he hurled words at us like stones: "You little bastards, cut that out or I'm telling."

We all jumped up, yanking our clothes together, still thrumming with the vibrations of Unchained Melody. But our moods were shattered. For the umpteenth time in my life, I ground my teeth and grumbled: I hate you, Donnie.

43.

The Masked Man was blackmailing me. At first I only had to iron his shirts, but now every time I saw him he made a new demand. "Make me a grilled cheese, will you Lou?"

When Donnie caught me with Tim, that's what I felt like— cheese, melting and sizzling between their hot looks. Now Donnie's eyes condemned me while his voice wheedled: "Could you just run up to Badgers and get me some new shoelaces?"

The Woman, who knew nothing because Donnie had not told on me yet, laughed at my slavery: "Better get used to it, dearie," as if it were a woman's lot I had come into here. She could barely move around now, she was so pregnant, and I was her slave too. "Get me a nice glass of that orange juice, will you Lou?" Where's my magazine? What will we have for supper? I guess you'll have to go up to the store."

In the crispy middle of the night, on February 15, my mother's amniotic sac ruptured, signaling the onset of labor. I woke up hearing her high keening whimpers, "My waters, oh, Jesus, the waters . . ." Then I heard a lot of scrambling around for a towel, and the suitcase, as they got ready to leave for the hospital.

I came into the living room rubbing my eyes, acting more asleep than I really was. Mama was nervous, excited. "You go back to bed now, don't wait up, it's probably going to take all night," she whispered as she waddled off, strangling a towel between her legs.

I left a light burning and went back to bed and lay there in the dark thinking, waiting. I wanted to wake up Andy and Donnie and tell them, but they were such heavy sleepers. I was motionless, except for my mind, and all the world seemed to be at a loud standstill, too. I knew that every part of my sister was finished. She was full-term, a whole person. I had gone through all the stages of her development with her, bud by bud, in my mind. Her eyelids had unfused so she could be born with her eyes wide open. She was ready. It never occurred to me that she could be a he.

The light from the living room cast a vigilant blue glow. Would we all continue to live? I thought yes. But there was this possibility always niggling that something might go wrong. I said the same prayer over and over again, like a chant: "Dear God, make everything be alright."

I must have dozed off for a couple of hours, when I heard my father come in the front door. He tiptoed into my room and sat by me in the dim light. My eyes came wide open. I raised up quickly. He took my hand.

"It's over," he said, "we have a healthy new baby..." and here he stopped, teasing me, so that I had to beg him, "What? what is it?"

He smiled sanguinely, lifted my hand, held it delicately like it was a porcelain handle, "a girl," he said beaming, kissing my hand, "and your mama's fine."

We both hooted with joy. I made him tell me over and over, even though I could see how tired he was, what she looked like in every detail. Had he counted her fingers and toes? "Yeah, yeah, they're all there. Her hair is black, long black lashes, can't tell the color of her eyes yet. She's real pretty though." Then he seemed to be dozing and I poked him awake, and he got up and lumbered off to his bed and fell into an exhausted sleep.

I couldn't go back to sleep. I was too all-over excited and flushed with new energy. I laughed little ha-ha's that came from deep inside like a holy sort of joy, so filled with happiness I felt I might explode. I piled in on top of my brothers in their twin beds, first Andy, then Donnie, and tried to wake them up, which was never easy. I bounced on their beds and yelled: "It's a girl! We have a baby sister,"

"Yeah, yeah, that's great," they each mumbled, and went right back into their selfish sleeps.

My excitement kept mounting, I couldn't stop moving, spinning. I danced around the house on tiptoes interpreting the glee I felt, a sort of initiation-into-life dance I made up as I went along. Then I spilled out into the yard and did cartwheels in the cold dewy grass until I collapsed, dizzy and panting. Daisy peeked out from under the house where she was sleeping and watched me quizzically. I wanted to see my sister so bad, just hold her, but I had to wait four whole days till mama brought her home, and I didn't know how on earth I was going to do it.

I sat on the cold grass, the sun slowly coming up on my rapture. I stared at the horizon to calm down. Light melted onto the earth, gradually illuminating it in a windless, cool blessing, a dawning. This was eternity, I knew. Everything seemed to be out there for us, the living. God is infinite time—not one thing happening after another. God was on no clock, but seemed to have the time and interest to care about each and every little one of us. I confused myself with my new sister and thought that I was born too, I guess, right there at the pinnacle of her earthly entrance. It was like we two were one, part of the same dream prowling the dawn.

Roosters crowed and Blackbirds lined up on the telephone wires screeching, and it was like everything alive in the world was getting born on this day, again, too. Off in the distance, I saw lights coming on in friendly kitchens. The good smells of bacon and sausage whiffled in the air. I wanted to run around and tell everyone the news. I did figure-eights on my old blue bike, on the road in front of the Sea Breeze, still in my flannel pajamas, concentrating on my sister, dreaming about her, making plans for the future. Then I drove our old Chrysler fluid-drive back and forth in the gravel driveway, savoring its eau de seaweed, and listening to the gears click in—practicing. I'd be old enough to get a license in another year, when I was sixteen. Then I could drive my sister all over Miami and show her the sights.

When the sun was full up, I got dressed and raced over to Shelby's to tell her the news, and I got a shock—she had some news of her own to tell me too. It was news I didn't want to believe or even think about, and I tried to put it out of my mind.

They named my sister Emmaline Clair, for mama's dead sister. Those four days went by as slow as any summer. I cleaned up the house until it was spotless like Marie and

Skeeter's, and baked an applesauce cake for my mother. When they finally brought her home, I was stunned by her beauty. She looked exactly like the girl I had envisioned with wavy black hair, creamy skin, big eyes with long black lashes that winked at me, conspiratorially I thought.

My mother was cranky and kept on complaining about being so tired and weak she couldn't even make a fist. I looked at her differently now—impressed by her ability to carry this beautiful baby inside her and to give birth. Now I knew that I would always be allied with her at least by our femaleness—our gender was our big connection, and I finally knew what "come down to Earth" meant. She had shown me plenty.

Marie came over every day to help out. My caretaking of Emmaline, was full of frills and fancy, like Marie's. At first, mama was so exhausted she didn't even have the energy to begrudge us. After being up for night feedings she gladly let us take over in the daytime, while she slept to regain her strength. After school, I raced home and my living doll was just waking from her nap. Her diaper was soaked all the way through to her crib sheet. The whole set-up had to be changed. I gave her a little sponge bath in the kitchen sink, dressed her in a dry gown and diaper, the whole time humming and singing songs and asking her rhetorical questions she received with little gurgly sounds I pretended to understand. After I cleaned her up, my mother took Emmaline and breastfed her, a slow process I was impatient with.

When she finished, I took her back and burped her, and then I toted her all around the house like Baby Linda's were always toted, showing her the bookcase, the hiding place inside my closet where I felt safe, the bulls-eye mirror where she glanced at her reflection, her head wobbling against me. I loved her fragrance. She smelled essentially different from any earthly scent. A brand new incomparable sweetness transfused her body as if it was coming from heaven itself. On the inside of her little thigh was a port wine stain in the shape of a strawberry, luridly beautiful.

When Marie had been at the house it sparkled with her touch, all the surfaces clean and shining. There would be a pot of stew or soup simmering on the stove, a pie, or cookies.

Mama had learned the word aggravate from Marie and used it against her at the dinner table:

"Marie aggravates me the way she's always fussing around here. Every little thing has to be just so, unt, unt, unt. She's driving me crazy."

Pretty soon, Marie stopped coming over and the house reverted to its former loosely straightened up style, and mama dragged around trying to keep up with the laundry.

I felt less alone in the world because of little Emma and I made all kinds of vows to always protect her no matter what. I would have to get stronger for her, for my special intention of preserving her life and happiness. I didn't know that I would be preserving mine too, in the process.

Andy was solemn—he looked a little displaced. He had been the baby until Emma came along. Now he was reluctant to give up any standing he had in this competitive family of ours. He watched in silence while everyone fussed over Emma. Then he offered her his index finger and she gripped it tightly every time. Once I heard him tell her he was going to take her fishing when she was old enough.

Donnie acted like he finally understood the whole meaning of life, and was humbly submitting to something decent and good that was deep inside himself as well. He had a secure smile on his face and looked a lot different. Lifting weights and drinking milkshakes had built him up so his body was strong and muscular like an athlete's now. He even seemed to have forgotten about blackmailing me.

When Emma was six weeks old, my mother stopped breast-feeding, put Emma on the bottle, and went back on the bottle herself. She stopped washing and drank so much she passed out right after supper. The jar of medicine on her closet shelf was replaced with a bottle of Early Times. She stank. I was ashamed of her. I thought it was my fault for not helping out enough. I wished she would take care of herself, primp, be vain. This self-neglect was much worse. I felt all mixed up with her and afraid of catching what she had. She cried a lot and blamed it on her hormones. She said they were making her life a roller coaster, a living hell. She grew more and more on edge every day.

I raced home after school to take care of Emma, trying to counteract what was going on. Emma would be dirty, neglected, clinging to her stale milk bottle, her eyes sad from crying, until she saw me.

Mama was passed out on the bed. When she came to, her cold brown, pit-like eyes pierced me. She snarled at my fussy efforts to clean up, calling out her names for me: a pill, a pip, Miss High'n Mighty.

"Start supper, will ya. I'm too damn tired." she growled.

In the evening, we sat around our Muntz TV gazing at the flickering light, like Indians staring at a fire, the volume low so we wouldn't wake her or Emma, our throats constricted, unable to talk, a pall over our whole house no one knew what to do about.

44.

The shocking news I got from Shelby is that she is pregnant. She won't tell anyone who the father is, not even me. All she does is talk about love. She won't even tell anyone else she is pregnant except me and her sister. I didn't look too happy, and neither did Rene, so Shelby spared her mama and baby Linda the news, for now. She wasn't showing yet.

"Love is what you do, otherwise it's just a word, like a piece of paper," Shelby said, yawning and stretching out on her long white-sheeted cot.

I looked at her dark circles and wondered if Tall Paul was the silent culprit, a guy of action mostly.

"You love someone despite who they are and what they do, with all their faults, you love them anyway. It's too easy to love them because of what they are, you know, like if they're good looking or witty or bright, that's easy love," she said.

Maybe Billy Brown. I thought of that awful Cecil with his mean eyes and his big forklift and hoped to God it wasn't him.

"Who? Who do you love?" I pressed her, but she wouldn't tell me. She lay there thinking quietly, and yawning, yawn on top of yawn.

"What are you going to do?" I asked, craving a plan of some kind.

"Have it and hope for the best," she said easily, "it's a love baby."

As if that meant it wouldn't take up space, need to eat and have its diaper changed every hour on the hour. "Why don't you say who the father is and get married then?" I said, like it was the logical thing. Shelby fell silent, that habit she had of going way off, and I sat with her in the gloom for a time feeling fearful for her and betrayed because she wouldn't tell me. I thought we always told each other everything.

After awhile she came back all false-bubbly and said, "Emma will bring your parents comfort in their old age after you've gone on to your own life and family."

I wondered how she thought of that. It was like a dismissal. She closed her eyes and I saw how tired she was, so I went on home, without telling her about mama. At that moment her problem seemed bigger than mine.

As soon as I got there, Donnie made me cook him a grilled cheese. Then I started ironing a shirt he wanted to wear right that minute. He was back to finagling me. Worse than that, I hadn't seen Tim close-up since that night at the drive-in. He was back to acting afraid of me, and chasing tail probably.

Andy was playing with Emma on the couch, counting fingers and toes. Mama had left him to watch Emma while she went up to the grocery store. It was getting late and dark. I was in the middle of ironing the shirt when a panicky feeling hit me. I had to go find my mother.

"Hey!" Donnie yelled, as I ran out the door, grabbing the nearest sweater and scarf. "What about my shirt?"

"Iron it yourself," I yelled back.

"Okay, you bitch, I'm telling."

I ran up to Uleta, towards the damp lowness of the Greyhound Inn. It was a hazy, overcast night, and chilly. When I got there a skunk had sprayed around the entrance, probably riled by the ghost of my Blackie which I hoped haunted the place. The smell brought back the weather and all the feelings I had in the car in Baltimore ten years before. I saw again the back end of that tear-drop shaped trailer, torn asunder. How quickly life had gone by and taken us with it. Only emotions seemed resistant to change—they didn't grow up, nor grow old and die like we did. I could see the back of my mother's head through the foggy window, sitting at the red and white Formica bar, and it was as if I was in the back seat of the car again, about to bother her.

I had a feeling in my stomach that I recognized as dread and I wanted to keep on walking, just pass my mama by, now that I knew where she was, drinking the drink that owned her, and there was nothing I could ever do about it. I stood at the window, staring at the fray of daytime drinkers, all false-jolly or silently glum, and thought about fading. But I couldn't do it. I only knew one thing in my small-knowing soul—I had to get mama out of there.

"Ut-oh, here comes daddy's little girl," mama said as soon as I came through the door, "you caught me again!" A few people chuckled and looked around at me. My heart kept on pumping hard even though it felt like I had left it outside. I went up close to her.

"Come on home, mama," I said in a low, wobbly voice. I didn't want to embarrass her. I was shaking and felt like crying, but I wasn't going to let myself.

"Ah, don't worry so much, dearie, you're too serious. You just take these groceries and I'll be there in a little while, okay?" She said this tenderly, almost tearing up herself. She nodded towards the two bags sitting on the counter, and didn't take her hands off her highball. When I didn't move, she leaned close to my face and said in a harsh, whispery voice: "You're a prude, Lou, and a snob. You're just like my father."

"C'mon, mama, let's go now," I took her arm, lifted her off the stool, wondering how I could be just like her father who I had never even met. He was dead wasn't he? I thought she must mean daddy. She was always saying one of us was just like him.

"Hey, why don't you come down off your high horse." She spat out.

That's when I should have just gotten on my high horse and rode away. Instead, I coaxed, and got her out of there, but it was slow-going, down the road lugging two bags full of groceries, and pulling a reluctant drunk, angry about the interruption. She staggered, insulting me, and stank worse than goat's breath. There is a broadcasting of a smell and a drawing in of a smell and I was caught in the very middle of that process, getting washed in a rank odor that represented all grades of harm and ruin to me. She could cut the very ground from beneath my feet.

"You always stick up for your father," she said, accusing me, kicking sand on my shoes. "You should have had a father like the mean bastard I had. He never did anything but ridicule me."

I looked at her, unsympathetically, because I had a hard time believing. There was always the drink of distortion in what she said, and self-pity. Now she was talking with the front of her mouth, her lips and teeth pooching out the words.

"You and Marie always think you can do anything. Everything you do is just right. You think you're perfect, don't you?" she sighed, as though we made her tired.

Then I could see what was coming. I felt the snaky, green aura of it creeping on me like an ache. I didn't want to put the monstrous word on it.

Her eyes opened wide as she glared at my head: "What's that? You stole my scarf!" She flew at me and snatched her scarf off my head. "What're you wearing that for? It's mine! You pious little monster. You think you can steal anything I own, don't you? Answer me!"

When I didn't answer, she slapped me hard across the face, and I flung one of the bags of groceries at her. I couldn't help it—it was a reflex action. She was so surprised, her eyes got huge again and her color returned. It was like a declaration of war to her, and she started kicking, slinging her arms, pulling my hair and screaming, all at the same time, while I flinched and tried to pick up the spilt groceries. I still had the other bagful and held it up like a shield, fending her off. Suddenly I saw her as a street fighter in Boston, a scrapper, a survivor. She had savage abilities that weren't needed here, that I had only guessed at before. Probably everyone would understand her fine if she was back in Boston.

"You think I'm over the hill, don't you? I don't need any frills anymore. You want everything I own, even my husband. You think you're entitled, don't you?" She batted me a few times with a loaf of bread, which split open and the pieces went all over. I kept on walking as we fought, trying to get her home, my stomach churning.

Then she started dancing too, lifting her skirt up over her head, twirling around, flapping the empty bread package on my back. I saw she really was the last of the red hot mamas, oddly out of place, and in my eyes, vulgar and threatening.

"You can't stand this, can you? You can't stand for anyone to go so out of control huh?" she said this with menace, grinding her teeth, getting right up in my face with that licker breath.

It was true. I didn't like the feeling that any old bad thing could happen any old time. I was sick of how she controlled everyone with her reckless emotions, and her savage feelings. It was this means of control I couldn't stand, and finally I told her so. "You always have to be the boss of everything, don't you? The big woman. Run the whole show your way and to hell with everyone elses feelings!" I yelled it—what the hell.

"C'mon, keep going, that's good. Now you're showing some spirit!" she said, grabbing my ponytail and jerking me down the road, rough, manly, her voice had gotten deep.

I had to keep my temper. She was out of control enough for the both of us. My own breathing started to scare me as much as she did—it was hard, tumultuous and at the same time deprived me of oxygen, the way I remembered breathing just before I lost my temper.

307

"You think you're such a nonconformist, an artist! Aren't WE the high-fallutin' one? Well, you're not. You're unentitled, just like me. You're a fouled-up little twerp."

There it was again, that whole horrible feeling coming over me, and I couldn't avoid the word this time, and the awful outrage of it—that my own mother was jealous of me, that her jealousy trapped me, and bound me up in knots I could never untangle and get free from. I felt a deadening shame I didn't know how to endure. But there was something else going on besides that, and I realized with a sudden, utter helplessness that it wasn't about me at all. She seemed now to have turned into her father; her voice dropped low and her English was like madhouse Irish.

"We'll just see what you amount to, now, won't we? Why couldn't it have been you who died, instead of my sweet Claire?" She covered her face with both hands, muffling the voice, but I could still hear the low brogue demeaning her: "You're just a filthy little street urchin."

She didn't want me to see her crying, so she kicked me in the shins a few quick jabs so I'd look away, and then we came to the door of The Sea Breeze. She had the hiccoughs among her other losses of control. Donnie opened the door and she handed him the busted bread bag and flew past him, in to pee. "Here, hic," she said, "get her offa me. Hic."

Daisy was barking like we were all in danger. Emma started crying.

Andy could see that it was war and he looked scared. "Wait a daggone minute," he said, and he protected Emma in his arms, patting her to get her to stop crying. When she did he knelt down and hid her behind the couch. I put the groceries down and heaved a sigh, my heartstrings cracking like Palmetto on fire. By then mama was coming out of the bathroom hollering: "Hey, Donnie, where's those atheist books of hers? hic." Now the two of them would pare me down to size. I braced myself for the worst.

"Stop it" Andy hollered. But no one paid any attention to him.

Donnie looked at us disgustedly, "What's going on here?"

"SHE is too pious for her own good, hic. You know that, now what are you gonna do about it? hic."

Donnie looked mama over, squinted his eyes and said: "You're drunk."

"Oh so what, hic." She came over by me and jerked my ponytail up in her hand, and I hung there in her clutch. "SHE's the troublemaker, hic."

"Stop it." Andy hollered again, so loud the jalousie's rattled.

Donnie's face was turning a deep bruise color and the artery in his neck was sticking out. I could see his temper coming, and I wanted to be free to run, so I socked my mother on the arm, a crisp hit that made her let go. She clutched her stomach. "She hit me!" she said, incredulous. I stood my ground near the front door, guilty, ready for them, and glad I had legs to run.

Then mama changed her expression, looked at Donnie and sneered, "You know what my old man said to me once? He said I was not even entitled to his name. Can you imagine that? No right to his name even, like I was a nothing. Claire was all that mattered to him, the apple of his eye, just like HER." She poked her finger at me, and I blocked my face with my arms. She grabbed my ponytail again and this time swung me around with it. She was bawling now, kicking me and the groceries all around the room.

Emma started howling. Mama turned toward Emma. She started to go to her.

"NO" Andy shouted, and he picked up a can of peas and hurled it across the room and it struck the bulls-eye mirror shattering it to pieces. His blazing eyes were as big as his fists. I could hardly bear to look into the blotched oven of his face, and I knew with certainty that at that moment he could kill.

"We can't go through this any more!" he cried, punching the couch with his fists, trying to stave off his own rage.

Mama had stopped dead in her tracks, staring at Andy in disbelief. Donnie got hold of her arms, "Let go of Lou," he said, and shook me loose.

"What? Are you turning on me too?" She ground the words out under her breath and took a calculated swing at Donnie, missing. He led her towards the bathroom, holding her arms down by her side, and she babbled all the way: "You almost killed me. I had a hard time getting your big head out. After you, it was easy getting the other three out. Hey, where're you taking me?"

Donnie plopped her into the bathtub, clothes and all, and turned the water on, to her great surprise. She cussed and screamed, kicking the water all over, but she was too drunk to climb out.

"There," Donnie said, "take a bath" and he left her there, with the door open so we could hear her.

I went over to Andy who was lifting Emma out from behind the couch. She'd stopped crying, but was fussing a little, her feeding time had come. Andy gave her over to me, and I tried to catch his eye, to tell him wordlessly that it was okay what he did, good even to finally get mad, but he collapsed in a heap beside me and started crying. So I let him be, while I offered Emma her bottle. In a couple of minutes Donnie went back and turned the water off because mama had passed out. Daisy had finally stopped barking, and panted now, still excited, her eyes darting around the room to see what would happen next.

45.

We were slumped on the couch feeding Emma when my
father came in from work ten minutes later, in his dungarees,
carrying his metal hat in one hand and the *Herald* in the
other, crunching the Bulls-eye mirror-glass beneath his steel-
toed work boots.

"What happened here? Where's mama?" he said, alarmed.

"She's in the bathtub," we all said together.

He looked in on her and then came back to us.

"What happened ?" he stood over us, darkening with
embarrassment, looking tired.

"She went berserk," I said.

"Off her rocker," said Donnie.

"She had conniptions and was hitting Lou and spitting,"
said Andy, no trace of a stutter.

"Burp," said Emma.

Daddy got out in the kitchen banging pots around,
cooking dinner. He let mama stay where she was for a while
longer until she started moaning and waking up. Then he
washed her, dried her off and put clean clothes on her.

We all gathered round, long faced, while mama lyingly told
some of the truth. "He pushed me in the bathtub and locked
the door!" she wailed, "he knocked the breath out of me! He's a
conniver. Get him!" She wanted my father to hit Donnie.

I stood beside my father and shook my head. "PUT is the word," I said, "Donnie PUT her in the bathtub. She was out of control. There was no locked door."

"What do you know?" she snarled, "you punched me in the stomach!"

"The arm," I said to my father. "I wouldn't punch her in the stomach, she just had a baby."

"Oh, she's your pet. You believe everything she says." mama mewled out.

"Who broke your grandfather's mirror?" daddy asked us.

Mama said fast: "Donnie did it, swinging that bat."

"Nut-uh!" Andy yelled, "That id'n't right."

Donnie and I laughed.

"She just has to sleep it off," my father said, "help me get her into bed."

I fell asleep that night, heart-scalded and exhausted, but glad the worst thing that ever happened to us was over with. I could hear daddy out on the porch fanning his key of C harmonica, generating music in the world, the next best thing to light. I didn't recognize the wailing tune.

In the middle of the night Donnie came into my room and woke me up.

"Shhhh, don't wake the others," he said. "I just wanted to say I'm sorry. And I'm going now." Then he handed me a package wrapped in tin foil and I slid it under the covers.

"Wait," I said, pulling myself up, trying to get fully awake. "Where are you going?"

"Try-outs. I'm leaving school if I make it."

"But why now?"

"It starts tomorrow. I've had it planned for a long time. They wouldn't let me if they knew. I gotta go now. Don't tell them until morning okay?"

"But Donnie, you're only seventeen."

"You don't have any money, do you?" he asked quickly, and I had to laugh. I had fourteen dollars saved and I gave it to him.

"Jesus, where you been keeping this?" he said, and we both laughed.

"Well, I gotta go now."

"Bye, Donnie," I suddenly hugged his neck. He still smelled good and cozy, like a pencil eraser.

"Yeah, bye," he said and hugged me back. "Thanks for ironing my shirts."

I couldn't believe Donnie was being nice to me, and I started to cry. In the dim light I could see his eyes were looped in tears too, ready to spill over. He turned and went away quickly.

"Good luck," I whispered after him, and then regretted it because it was so incomplete. What I meant was I love you anyway, despite everything, and love go with you and part the waters. I unwrapped the tin foil package. It was my old Emerson I thought he had burned, and the Huxley. I would keep them hidden. They were good books, but they would remind my mother of her failures somehow. I put a wad of the tin foil in my mouth and clamped my teeth down on it until I got a scary buzz in my head and then I relaxed. I fell asleep with it in my mouth the way old Nellie Fox probably did with a chaw of tobacco, thinking about Donnie swinging his bat no more in the bulls-eye mirror.

46.

Donnie's leaving drove our slattern mama over the edge, into that nervous breakdown I never thought she'd have. I was wrong, she had never been bluffing. She lay in the bed motionless, and stopped talking too. Daddy carried her to the Doctor, and he admitted her into the hospital where they kept her for weeks.

Marie came over every day to help with Emma and the house. Sometimes Skeeter came too, and hummed while she polished all the green tile in the big bathroom. She loved to clean. Dot Murphy came by to help out about every other day. She was an Avon lady now. We all plundered around in her sample case of creams and make-up, and placed orders. Marie did the blowfish while she fed Emma, and bathed and dressed her, no doubt acting out all the love she had bottled up for her dead twin daughters. When I came home from school I took my turn feeding and burping and changing. Marie got supper going on the stove, and would usually be gone by the time my father came in from work. But he could always tell she'd been there—he knew harmony when he saw it. While we ate our supper, I'd load Emma up with baby cereal, applesauce, and six ounces of Carnation formula. And then I'd put her to bed. She'd sleep right through the night, usually.

Those were the most tranquil weeks of our lives, with mama and Donnie both gone. The Sea Breeze was purely a

Shangri-la. I had the solitude to stare out the big windows at the great outdoors, and feel my soul brim up in me again, to reclaim its spaciousness, feel what I had been missing in esteem, and peace.

Daddy spent a lot of quiet time with us, trying to get us to understand what had happened to mama. He wasn't sure we were old enough. All our hearts were exhausted, betrayed in one way or another. I was bleak from all the face slapping's of my life, which now came back to haunt me. In the trance of memory, my eyes flare and burn, and I relive the flood of humiliation inside my head. Mama had been cruel as only the weak can be. There is the strangest co-mingling of mama's slaps with Donnie's punches in my memory, as if I'd served as a target for both their angers. But both of them had saved me in their way too, mama had rescued me, and if Donnie hadn't hit me in the head with his bat I might still be half deaf.

The night he left, Donnie hopped a Greyhound bus and took it on the lam with the courage of a circus fire-eater. It was the end of March. When the bus finally stopped somewhere up around Stuart, he got off and hitchhiked the rest of the way to Vero Beach and Dodgertown. He lied about his age and tried out for the minor leagues. It didn't take him but a few days to dazzle them with his arm and speed and quick tobacco-spitting-good-ole-boy wit. He was a composite of all the famous baseball characters he'd ever seen or heard of, and now he was playing the role of a major league baseball star, that masked man. He had leap-frogged over the whole world of high school baseball, into the minor leagues—and he got a three thousand dollar bonus to do it, too. They signed him up and he became one of the boys of spring.

He called on the phone to tell us, all excited. Daddy wanted him to come back and finish high school, but Donnie said, "Are you kidding? I can do that any time. This is my big chance."

Now Donnie would play some baseball, instead of robbing banks. He'd channeled his craven need for love and attention into the true object of his desire: baseball. He had found a grand arena for himself, a game to play with the rest of the world that satisfied all his wildest dreams.

One Saturday afternoon when the weather had warmed up, daddy took me and Andy fishing. Emma was too young to go and stayed behind with Marie, who we now called Aunt Marie. We went out in his old dory boat, the Ellie-Nora, from Pirates Point at Hallover Beach, into the bay, and dropped anchor at a little island about fifty feet across. It had a couple of palm trees on it for merciful shade, and tons of shells engaged in the billion-year process of being ground by the tides into sand. It made me think of the process of growing up. At first we are like soft clay, we don't even know we are fixing to be turned into iron by the events of life, ironized so we'll be fit for living on, a life full of hazards. Made my jaw feel tight, like the tin foil and mama's slaps.

We waded around the shore line with our buckets until we found a good clam bed. Then we sat down, flat up on the ocean's floor in the warm shallow water, plunged our hands into the sand and dug out the clams one by one while we listened cooly to daddy trying to pow-wow with us, countering our mopey silences with his careful views.

"Your mother's feelings were terribly hurt when she was a child. She was showing you what her father had done to her, how he had destroyed her happiness and taken away any joy in herself that she might have had. It must have started when Claire died—a terrible shock to a family, to lose a child, But especially for your grandfather, because he adored his daughter, Claire, she was the apple of his eye." Daddy looked at me then, tears wobbling in his eyes.

I looked away, up. The sky was like an Xray picture, thin white clouds wafting like tissue and bone against a dense blue-grey background.

He went on: "When Clair died he must have been afraid to love your mama, who was just a baby then, probably afraid she'd die on him too. Almost all the children who got diphtheria in those days, died. There was no vaccine for it, no penicillin, and it was a terrible disease, high fevers, suffocation..."

"Mama loved Claire a lot too," Andy interrupted, serious, "she always cries about her."

"Your mama was only a baby like Emma, not even one year old when Claire died, so I don't think it's possible she could even remember her," said my father.

Andy thought back, "but she said...she loved...then why does she cry for her all the time?"

"Because it's as if your mama died then, too, and she cries for her own self as well."

"You mean because Grandpa wished she was dead instead of Claire?" I said.

319

"Right," said my father, surprised that I knew that.

"See, it wasn't happy for your mama, just a little baby, to be in a household where her parents were grieving for a daughter beloved for eight years and then taken away. They must have resented your mama just because she was still alive, and they probably neglected her too."

"But if you knew all that, why did you...?" I stopped cold. I had wanted to ask why he had loved me so much, but I suddenly saw the whole picture. From that instant when Grandpa had said to mama, "Why wasn't it you who died instead of Claire?" the whole course of mama's life was set in motion, and it was continued on by my father, who reinforced her feelings of worthlessness, by making me his favorite, the apple of his eye. But why did he do that? It seemed so wicked. Didn't he realize?

From the very beginning, he had picked me, for his side, like the captain of a team at school picks his favorites. And I went willingly, proud, never considering what it was costing my mother. Another abandonment. I could hardly breathe.

Now I understood why she called me Miss High and Mighty. But I was just a pawn. The rivalry with me had kept them together in some way now no longer mysterious at least to me. There was daddy loving me extra hard because he knew what an unloving father had done to mama. And it kept mama vying for him, jealous of a relationship she could never have. He teased out her envy. It was how they managed the hate and the love, and the poisonous memories that never would just grow old and die. And the alcohol led her right out of control, swept her to the certainty of this nervous breakdown.

I felt myself dissolve into those Xray clouds. I had been a mirror and a punching bag for my mother's own daughterhood all my life. I was suddenly angry at both of them and I started crying, salty oceanic tears. Did tears heal too, like spit? I was just a hostage of their marriage, of their feelings and life, and not my own person at all.

But strangely, I started to believe that anger could be generous too—it hurt, but it told me the truth. There was relief in the truth. It was the best gift of all. I knew the love of truth was the only thing that would give me the strength I needed to step through the mirror.

All I had to do was forgive—I saw that now. My adding machine for sins had to start subtracting. Not just for me, but for Emma to live too. It seemed to me that by forgiving my mother I was stripping her of her sins and mine too, and my father's and her father's, just the way Goatman had told me it worked so long ago.

Through the fog of my tears I heard my father talking about self-respect: "You have to get your own self-respect in this world. Sometimes you even have to fight for it." He was trying to reach me. "But it's a worthy fight. Your mother can't teach you self-respect when she doesn't have any. She didn't get any respect when she was a child, so how could she know what it is? You build respect for yourself by what you do. Do good things, and you'll like and respect yourself. It's just about that simple."

"How come she likes me so much?" Andy asked.

"Because you're neutral," my father said, with a snaggled grin, "and you're her little baby." He rifled Andy's red hair in the front, but Andy batted his hand away.

"Not any more." Andy yelled, and Daisy started barking like she was afraid we were going to froth up into another fight.

I didn't like my father very much just then, and he knew it.

I always thought I was lacking something other people had, except mama—she didn't have it either. And it didn't matter how pretty she was, she still needed this other ingredient to be happy, to get on in life. Now I saw what it was—self-respect. And Emma was going to need it too.

The following Saturday daddy surprised us by driving all the way to the Venetian pool in Coral Gables. I had been talking about this place for years, trying to get him to go. We sat in an oolitic limestone cave, under a waterfall, and had the place all to ourselves. The water was freezing and our teeth chattered as we talked, but we didn't give a damn.

I understood almost all of it now. How much mama's origins affected her– how she'd been descended from famine immigrants in Western Ireland, and the history that was behind her history tainted her, and then spilled into all of our lives. Mama had closed herself in with ghosts.

I was trying to untangle the knots in my own heart, to balance the love and hurt I felt, and my big question for daddy finally tumbled out awkwardly: "But, how do you? how can I...handle the...the jealousy?"

"Ah jealousy, it's born out of feeling excluded and deprived." He answered, shivering. He thought longer about it

322

and said: "It's the most corrosive emotion. You're thinking only about yourself when you're jealous."

"But mama is jealous of ME, and it hurts so bad." I hated to say this out loud, so I said it fast and low, but it echoed off the cave walls anyway.

"I know. It's ugly." Daddy splashed his face with water like he was trying to wash it away. "Jealousy can be the cess pool of emotions, but remember a cess pool is a breathing hole too. Try and think of it that way—as an escape hatch for piezons."

He meant poisons. He always murdered words to be cute, to take the edge off. But I saw what he was trying to tell me. We swam out of the cave, into the warm sunshine.

My father said the iron had entered mama's soul, like Julius Caesar, and I knew he didn't mean from the well water. It had entered mine too.

47.

Mama came home with coffee colored teeth, and a new gray streak in her hair, down the middle, like a skunk. Several doctors had treated her, and they all diagnosed the same: postpartum depression, and an allergy to alcohol. At least that's what daddy told us. She had to take a prescription for her nerves, hormones to stabilize her, and once a week, she had to go back and talk to one of the doctors for an hour. I knew this was the most painful part of all for her, taking her story outside the family.

That was the end of cocktails and Canadian Club parties at our house. Alcohol was poison to my mother. The food and drink that flows through our bodies makes up our minds for us, determines what we feel and think, just as I always thought. Even goats like good grass and hay, flowers and fruit. They don't eat tin cans like everyone says—not if there is something better. I wished my mother didn't hate guavas so much. She needed them, and dreams too.

Mama began talking to Andy and me again after school, telling us her stories—we both craved the story about the BB gun—Andy because it was funny, and me because it had a different twist each time. I had to ask myself all the time, what really happened? She told us about Irish history, how the English had ruled the Irish for so long. How they could have helped the Irish during the potato famine but chose to do nothing, and let the Irish suffer and die.

"The English will always get the backlash from that." mama said, "It was like a slap in the face. Where were they when they were needed?"

"Whyever did the English get to rule the Irish? Who did they think they were anyway?" I asked her.

"Oh you'll have to ask your father that one. He's black Irish ya know. His ancestors were all Fenians who fought against English rule. That's where you get your fighting spirit from." She said.

But I didn't think so. I got it from her.

And then she talked about her father a little, but in a new calm and distant way: "He was an Irishman from the old country. The boys in the family mattered most, my three brothers. Girls were nothing. Except for Molly, his firstborn, and Claire. Clair was different, his greatest joy in life."

I saw that she had that belief herself, in the unspoken superiority of boys. She had always expected me to subordinate my ego, my very presence to my brother's. My father didn't discourage ego in me, or strength, whenever I was alone with him, only when my brother's were there too, then I had to give in. This was an unspoken rule. Whyever do male egos have to be so protected like glass? from what? What is this weakness that empowers them to be bullies? I felt like I was asking impossible questions about the vast infinity of the universe, the answers unknown to everyone alive.

I tuned back in to what mama was saying: "He called me names, said he was ashamed of me. He made me stay outside when he went in to see his friends. I wasn't pretty enough, didn't have Claire's beautiful auburn hair, wasn't clean enough to go anywhere with him. He threatened to turn me over to the nuns, my own father, can you imagine?" She had big tears in her eyes. She'd buried the truth about Clair for so long I wondered if she even knew it. It was Andy said something:

"But ma, you were only a baby like Emma so how come you can remember Clair?"

"Oh he never let me forget her. He brought her alive for me every day, comparing my faults to her perfection. When I got older he said I was no good at all and would never amount to anything, I'd end up disgracing him."

It was as though all men were despots at heart—it was a given. They expected to have power and judgement over women.

"What did your mother do?" I asked.

"She was too busy to even know what he was doing to me. I was just one of five children she had to look after. She wasn't well and she was afraid of him, too. He could be so brutal, slap you in the face when you weren't looking. But I fooled him. I got out of there, went to nursing school. My mother helped me do that. She scraped together some money so I could escape. Her maiden aunt was the head nurse at Peter-Bent-Brigham and she got me into training."

Mama had her old bravado back. She had not yet acknowledged her breakdown to us. She couldn't. She ignored it, like a taint she thought no one could see. She had never admitted to anything in her whole life and always defended herself if somebody accused her of something. She claimed to have learned this from men, maybe her father. "Oh, men," she would say, "they never admit it if they're wrong, so why should I?"

But now I could see in her big warm brown eyes a plea for understanding, for forgiveness. Unspoken words have force too. I knew she was hugely proud, my rescuer.

I didn't care if she never apologized because my heart broke for my mother. The torture must have seemed never-ending to her. Maybe because Donnie wasn't there I began to realize that I was their problem too. I started seeing how my mother might have been a whole other person if she wasn't with my father, if I wasn't there to make her jealous, if Donnie wasn't there to play off.

She had given me her own sense of shame and failure, had shown me the terrors of cruelty, jealousy, bitterness, of the great going without that was the famine and the depression. She'd rolled everything together into one big pain. Often she'd shouted at us when we wouldn't wear our shoes: "Some kids don't HAVE any shoes." And that truly was the point we had missed.

I hoped she would never drink again, and I had enough hope for the whole world. But if she did, now I knew her demons didn't belong to me. I wasn't afraid of catching them anymore, or of getting mixed up with her. The savage connection that could have broken me was broken. I was free like a goat that ate through its own tether.

Oddly, the fact that my mother had gone so crazy told me I was right about art. Does passion grow when the will is thwarted? Maybe. But I knew why I wanted to make art now—it was to see the truth. Besides I was good at it, even though I knew I would probably always betray art with life. Art was in the air in 1955, there for the taking, just as science was. They weren't much different. The way scientists classified things in the natural world was the same as the way an artist created pictures of natural characteristics.

I watched mama rock Emma in her carriage while she talked, and I saw that she had gotten it all played out on me and now she could love Emma freely, without getting mixed up with her. Dimly in my memory was the comfort of her touch, the security I had gotten from her body in my early years, the time before she dumped me off her lap, the time before she started remembering what her father had done to her. Absence doesn't make the heart grow fonder, as they say. Absence lets you see what a person was truly like.

48.

The next big thing that happened was Aunt Marie and Badger got married, surprising everyone. Marie could now be found behind Badger's old wooden counter, selling penny candy to the kids and calling herself a Badgerette. She was in her glory and Old Man Badger beamed like he'd swallowed a jar of lightning bugs. "Doggonit, you're only young once," he said, "and if you do it right, once is enough." Then he cackled and beat the counter, and Marie did the blow-fish.

She told me Badger had a lifetime of troubles to forget because he'd been in the war, and she knew how to make him forget good. This time, you could tell, marriage was going to take, on Marie and Badger both.

And then I found Shelby again. It was on a rainy Sunday afternoon. My father and I were in the kitchen baking a lemon-chocolate cake from scratch, for something to do. Thunder and lightening split the sky, the air smelt like burnt sugar. Rene came up to the back screen-door dripping wet and lowing like the cow had done years before. It was the same kind of shock seeing her there too, but this time for some reason my ears turned instantly red.

My father had a new word for me: erythrophobia. We were on the phobias. It was the fear of blushing and I had it bad. Right then I decided that everyone blushed, but probably only people with translucent skin like mine showed their erythrophobia. It was sort of a fear of being exposed, of being caught hanging outside yourself with your raw feelings for all to see. It was the fear of walls coming down too, Humpty Dumpty's fear of being smashed to pieces. To me he always blushed as he fell. I never dreamed of falling from a high place though—I dreamt of jumping. I never get hurt. In dreams I find I can easily fly.

I gave Rene a towel to dry off with, and she planted herself just inside the door. She saw that she had come in the middle of something, and she held back from speaking, waiting for the right moment.

Daddy was mixing up the cake, and on his soapbox: "Blushing is just emotion showing. Nothing wrong with that." He smiled big, and went on, "a girl without freckles is like a night without stars." I blushed at that. "Redheads have startle ability. I bet the first time a person sees you they're startled, ha ha."

Then he said to Rene: "Redheads are not supposed to be placid either ya know?" and he gave her a wink.

He knew I took delight in him again. That I understood and didn't blame him. Whatever would I have done without him? He was just part of the equation, as we all were. Andy had told me a family was like a mathematical equation, with predictable outcomes. Andy, who held so much back, never wanting to tip the fragile balance had been the one to crash through the mirror first.

I realized that I had learned to hold in a lot of feeling in order to balance out my mother whose emotions and

330

nervousness dominated our house, even though she always felt she was not commanding enough attention.

Now she had simmered down, looked nonchalant, sitting in the living room reading her *Ladies Home Journal*, like nothing had even happened. She was still herself, funny and disapproving at the same time, though pleasantly doubtful now in the fixity of her mother role.

I turned all my attention to Rene, who was pale, yet her eyes were burning, and at last she spoke: "Can you come over and see Shelby?...she can't get up from the bed."

My father motioned for me to go on, it was okay- he'd finish the cake.

I followed Rene down the road in the warm drizzle, realizing as we went that somewhere along the line I had stopped my explorations around Uleta, and also that I had not seen Shelby for nearly two months. She didn't even know about my mother's breakdown. As we went, Rene was quiet, behind herself as if she had been struck deaf and dumb by what she'd seen, by some huge perdition I wasn't going to believe but she needed me to witness anyhow. She wouldn't tell me anything, no matter how much I begged. She just wanted to get me there.

I thought about Shelby's delicate bones, a glass support system for pounds of loamy flesh gone riot. And now she was pregnant too. Were her bones breaking again? I thought about her leathery skin that I loved so much and her big brown calf eyes. She didn't go to school anymore. The desk was too small and hurt her knees. Changing classes in the hallways was too dangerous, and too embarrassing. We passed the guava bushes, but there was no fruit yet. Too early. It came in, and ripened in the deepest part of summer. Now the bushes smelled like wild frangipani, a prelude of the cologne of fruits to come.

Rene led me off the road, into the jungle in back of the Brown/Holt Compound, deep in the mango groves, which were loaded with green and ripening fruit, to their white clapboard tenant farmer house, very like the one they'd lived in before the hurricane. Two police cars idled on the swept dirt yard outside, their radios crackling with scrabbled speech. I shivered automatically. Earl Wauldin sat cramped in the back seat of one, his hands in his lap handcuffed. He might as well have been blindfolded too, because he looked like he wasn't seeing out, but was looking inside the firmament that was his giantness, glaring quizzically into his own control center, wondering what went wrong.

Rene covered her mouth with one hand and whispered, mockingly: "My father, the great Earl Wauldin, has been arrested."

We entered the big, scrubbed clean, bare room with a kitchen at one end and no partitions, just white-sheeted cots placed under all the open windows. Fans were going on tabletops. Mrs. Wauldin had gotten pitifully thinner, her skin rippled like an old quilt. She was bowed on her knees at the kitchen table, her skinny head resting in her hands. Baby Linda, who was now a girl of eleven but was still called baby Linda, sat cross-legged on the shiny clean linoleum floor beside her mother, engrossed in a little game of jacks. She never missed, never looked up. Even though she was blonde, she had a dark, murky personality, and hardly ever moved out of sight of her mother.

A policeman stood over them asking questions: "Are you sure you want to do this, Mrs. Wauldin?" He wanted her decision on something, but she waved him off disagreeably, and cracked open her Bible.

Shelby lay across the room on a cot, made extra long by the addition of boards and a pallet. She had a thin, washed-out flannel blanket over her. When she saw me, she opened her eyes and smiled as if I was a Sunbeam. Rene and I sat on the edge of her cot, so we were shielding her from their mother who had begun reading out loud from her Bible, searching for passages she wanted the whole world to hear. She was always blurting out things from this book—we were used to it by then.

Rene and I dripped rainwater on Shelby and rubbed it on her arms and head and she liked that. She was so hot it evaporated in seconds. She pressed her face against the white pillowslip a few times, but always looked back at us with that modest smile she had. She arched her considerable body as if a great pain was making its way over it and had to be shed like snake skin. Everywhere the lusty sweet smell of mangoes assailed me till I was a little sick from it.

Shelby nodded to Rene, then turned her face into the pillow. Rene held my eyes, and told me Shelby had lost her baby, miscarried it, delivered it into the toilet. I shook my head at first in disbelief, and horror, and then I began acting like I knew all about how that could happen, and it was okay if it did. Every acorn did not become an oak. I stroked Shelby's forehead, combing through her matted hair with my fingers, wondering about the fetus. This must have been the third month of its journey. It must have been a little over an ounce but with all its buds, and a heart that beat 167 times a minute like a little bird's. I did not want to think about the eyes.

Besides the hum of the fans, we heard Mrs. Wauldin chanting in the background from Leviticus: "the Lord spoke unto Moses saying, 'Thou shall not lieth with...'" and she recited all the "lieth withs" from eleven to twenty-one and she still hadn't found what she wanted. She moved on to Numbers. That end of the house seemed oddly haunted to me, spooky and moldy like Mrs. Wauldin.

I chattered about the chocolate cake I had been making with my father to try to distract Shelby, while I held onto her big paw and patted it. Mrs. Wauldin started whacking the table in cadence with Matthew, Mark and John.

Shelby touched my arm and whispered: "It wasn't rape, it was just a little game... a ruse." I couldn't help grinning at that—it was like she was giving me a new word so I'd understand. She was that plain and sure. She went on talking low: "I was willing. I wanted to do it, to try it, you know? My papa looked for another giant for me but there was no one. We're dying faster than you are, so it's different. Papa wanted me to have the experience too. He was the only one I trusted, so we pretended he was just a boy my own age. It wasn't bad. I didn't think I could get pregnant, not ever."

There were more "lie-withs" in Deuteronomy and curses on the ones who did it. "Cursed is the one who lies with his father's wife, because he has uncovered his father's bed. Cursed is the one who lies with any kind of animal...."

As she read out loud looking for what she wanted, I gave Shelby my father's recipe for Lemon Chocolate Cake, every ingredient a little louder than Mrs. Wauldin. Then I moved on to Strawberry Rhubarb Pie, and I tried to make each ingredient as important as any word in that Bible. I knew I was making Shelby hungry, even though she probably didn't know what rhubarb was.

Mrs. Wauldin read on, behind my litany of ingredients, and we all kept secretly listening, even the policeman, for "a man shall not lie with his own daughter," but it didn't seem to be there, just daughter-in-law and sister, which was also referred to as a man's father's daughter and a man's mother's daughter, but never just a man's daughter. We could feel disappointment coming from Mrs. Wauldin's corner of the room and her wrathful indignation building, as if she had painted herself in. You had to feel sorry for her, clinging like that to a tricky book that could throw anybody. She thought it was all in there about fathers and daughters, in the shall-nots or lieth-withs or curseds, but it wasn't, or at least if it was, she couldn't find it. For a minute I was afraid she was going to froth up into one of her beseechings, but she stopped and scowled over at us like even she'd had a snoutful of scripture. She knew she was right but she couldn't prove it by the good book, and now it looked to her like God, her husband and Shelby were all betraying her.

She told the policeman to turn Earl Wauldin loose, take him to the bus station and get him out of town, gone from there. Otherwise, she'd press charges against him. After all, there was the law she could still use even if the Bible had let her down. The policeman left, and Mrs. Wauldin slid down on a cot, displaced into silence, and the whole house went quiet except for the fans and a great heaving swoon from Mrs. Wauldin's tired old body.

I didn't know why Shelby wanted me there by her for all this, when before she wouldn't even tell me who the father was. But all at once it occurred to me that I must really be a pill like my mother always said I was. And a pill I'd be, too. I ran back home, slipped into the kitchen, cut about a quarter of that lemon chocolate cake, and wrapped it in waxed paper to carry back to Shelby. Giants need a lot to eat. I would treat her like she had a cold, feed her tea and cake, my pill for all that ails the heart and body, a wilderness of sweets. I hated that the guavas weren't ripe yet.

As I left the house my mother called after me, "Hey, where are you going with all that cake?" I started to just run on, but instead I stopped and turned around and faced her. I had made a pact with myself to stop being secretive and not leave my mother out anymore, no matter what.

"Right now Shelby needs it more than we do, Ma," I said, and to my surprise, she said okay and waved me on.

Shelby looked at me with her doleful eyes. "It's the best chocolate cake I ever tasted," she said. Rene fixed cups of Lipton tea. Shelby always said Rene was a good sister. We tried to offer Mrs. Wauldin some, but she turned her back on us, rolled over on her cot, woefully tired. Baby Linda sat cross-legged staring out the window, indifferent to chocolate cake and tea and all of us.

I left a little while later, as Shelby was falling to sleep, and I hoped, to dream.

I didn't want to say it to Shelby, but I was furious with Earl Wauldin even though she wasn't. She was protecting him. I was shocked by his arrogance—by his trying to be a boy when he was a man first with responsibilities, a father. Shelby was barely sixteen. How could he?

I knew what happened wasn't something my father would ever do, but we weren't giants with short life-spans, just ordinary people with regular hopes. Even so, the idea that someone would be there to marry me someday was outlandish and incredible. I couldn't imagine it, but I now believed my father could. In a way, he'd always guided me with his unspoken hope. I didn't think Shelby and her father had that kind of hope.

Now, all they had was a humble penitence that almost seemed to make them innocent. Shelby hadn't been trying to hurt anybody, of that I was sure, especially not Mrs. Wauldin, who in all our eyes was Bible-whipped and had already quit life. It was hard to think of anything reaching her, even this, but it had. I tried to imagine the form and shape of her first attraction to Earl Wauldin long ago when they were young and wore all those stunning black clothes. What else could have attracted her if not his obvious giantness? Whatever had taxed her love so severely that all these years later it was as hollow-hearted as a goat's?

I didn't know how to think about it, only that I couldn't shove Shelby and Earl into some idea of normal family life. This all made my screaming family seem plain and common by comparison. None of us would fit into Mrs. Wauldin's biblical interpretation of the world either. We were all outsiders, captive within our crazy families.

Questions swirled around in my head. I needed answers beyond the ordinary, so in the gloaming of the after-rain, I headed up to Badger's to find Marie, who grew me up as much as anyone. I could always count on Marie to give me all the possible and unusual reasons for something. She told me everything whether I could understand it or not. Eventually I did. It was still dark inside Badger's Grocery Store, only it didn't smell like a mixture of cigars and cold lunch meat anymore. Marie had scrubbed and polished, removing the dull film of dust and dirt from everything, and now it seemed deeper inside the darkness, reflective even, Old English waxy smelling like the library at Guavonia. I wondered if the dirty pictures, the cigar box of rubbers and the half-pint were still under the counter. Even Badger looked cleaned up and cheery, his white wiry hair perked up on top of his head so he looked like an eccentric magician. He fussed over big loaves of bologna that had just come in, and when he opened the cooler I saw it had been cleaned out too. It might be safe again to buy meat from Badger's. For years, my mother had sent us a little farther up the road to Dick's Market for all our meat and chops. She said Badger's meat was stale and who knew how old. I saw how nice it was for him, Marie coming into his life organizing and beautifying everything.

I felt happy relief just being there, watching the two of them playing store. I remembered the day the Mole Lady had stepped from the shadows and showed me truth and beauty.

Marie read my face as she always did and asked me what was bothering me so much it was showing in my fingernails? She gave me an ice cold Pepsi out of the case, and I told her it was the Wauldins.

"Oh Lord, Honey, I been watching that for years. What happened now?"

I told her everything. Shelby said I could.

"Oh, law," Marie said, and sat down on her stool ever so slowly. Even in the darkness, I could see her blushing. She was quiet for a long time, thinking.

Badger had gone out back, to feed the mean watch geese, so we could talk freely. "Time flies like an arrow, fruit flies like a banana." He'd told us leaving, winking wildly. I sat behind the counter with Marie, while she reminisced about the Wauldins, and waited on anybody that came in.

"A long time ago Mrs. Wauldin, Esther is her given name, was beautiful. I don't believe she was born bitter, but after Shelby was born and then as the years went by and Shelby got so big, Esther changed from a shy, sweet, young married woman into an old fanatical witch. She was ashamed of having carried a giant in her womb and giving it birth. Imagine that, not proud, ashamed? She could have gone either way."

Marie started tapping her foot, thinking back, remembering. She did a couple of blowfish, and continued on: "She started hiding out in that Bible like a mole. She

339

rejected Earl and Shelby as if they were the devil's own and even ignored that sweet girl Rene, who was just as normal as she was. Only one she liked was baby Linda, who became like her shadow and never was alright in the head. Mrs. Wauldin hid behind that old religion of hers and pinched up her life until no one could reach her anymore. In a way, Shelby was shamed from her beginning, so shame isn't anything new to her. What she did with her father was bad, but it was probably the only comfort either one of them had in years."

Marie saw she had shocked me, that I didn't understand. She shrugged, looked up at the rafters, like she wasn't so sure her own self, and went on:

"Earl has the personality of a tree trunk and always stood alone, tall as an alp and just as cold. But he isn't really cold, it's defiance, from years of being made to feel like an outcast. He's afraid of people, has been his whole life, I imagine, everyone but his beloved Shelby. He could be different with her. It's sad that she got pregnant and miscarried, but I just don't think it's too awful surprising what they done—it's not like it was deceitful adultery just for the fun of it, and if that old Lady, Esther Wauldin needs to think it is, then it's just a word anyway. No sense being afraid of words."

With that, Marie hopped up and started fixing a sack of groceries for me to carry over to Shelby. Oh, I knew this was going to be Marie's greatest stage, behind the counter of this ordinary grocery store. After a lifetime of looking, she finally had the right man and the perfect stage. It was pure joy to see.

I talked about Donnie's leaving and signing up to play baseball, and she said, "He ain't got the sense of a fencepost."

But I thought she was wrong about Donnie. He had done the right thing for once—it proved he wasn't too crazy. I didn't talk about mama—it seemed disloyal and unnecessary. Marie knew it all already. Someday I might talk it over with her, but I didn't feel like it right then.

I went back to Shelby's that day with the groceries. I would go back every day for as long as it took, for as long as Shelby needed me. Her own mother still wouldn't even look at her. Marie had told me life was messy, you had to keep trying to straighten it up. It didn't take any brains or courage to suffer—that was something you made a decision to let yourself do.

49.

They found his body in the Oleta River. Even though he had been there for many days, there was no doubt it was the gangly body of Earl Wauldin. It was a miracle the alligators didn't get at him. No whole body had ever been found before, only pieces.

I told my mother the whole horrifying story about Shelby then. She wept for her, threw her magazine aside and ran her hands through her hair. She had none of Marie's sympathy for Earl Wauldin. She wailed: "Shelby's story is part of the soup we're all stewing in, a big old potful cooked up by MEN, the bastards."

I guess in her eyes I had gone past being too impressionable now. She seemed no longer afraid that I might be glomming onto other people for my own selfhood. She wanted me to know what she found out, that being your own person was an inside job, something you had to do by yourself.

I stayed by Shelby through the strange funeral service at The Higher Ground. There was no oversized coffin as everyone expected. Earl had requested cremation. Mrs. Wauldin and Baby Linda didn't even come. But most of the circus people were there, about half of Uleta. I sat between Rene and Shelby and we held hands the way we used to do, traipsing all around Uleta with hibiscus in our hair. It was the familiar Lord is my Shepherd service with a departure at the end. A quote from Genesis, chapter six, verse four. I guess the preacher could not resist:

> *There were giants in the earth those days; and also after that, when the sons of God came in unto the daughters of men and they bore children to them, the same became mighty men which were of old, men of renown.*

It was supposed to make Shelby feel better about what had happened I guess, but she had her own meanings, as well as a deep distrust of anything from the Bible.

She was doing all the condoling: "It's all right," she said to each person who came up after the service, "He never learned to swim. I knew he was dying. It's all right, he's at rest now."

Marie came over and hugged and kissed Shelby who she loved as much as I did. "Just get you another somebody," Marie advised her through a flood of tears. Then she held Rene for a long time, swaying and patting her back.

To me, Marie mused privately, "All those girls... imagine a man like that with raging hormones living in a house with all those girls. Well at least he had the good sense to die after what he did."

And then the letter from Earl appeared. Tall Paul had been its strange keeper. Earl had instructed him not to give the letter to Shelby until after he was gone—so Tall Paul had waited until after the funeral.

The letter told of a place, West of the Rockies, a little town called Goliath—chock full of giants. Everything in Goliath was scaled up in size and there was comfort. There were doctors who cared, and sociologists who studied colossal life. Boy giants abounded. This time, Earl had looked a little harder. There was money in the letter, enough for Shelby to go and start a new life there.

Two days later I saw her off on a Greyhound bus. Tall Paul stood silently beside Shelby—he came up to her broad shoulders. We didn't want to say goodbye and yet we had to. Shelby kept saying things like, "I'll write to you as soon as I get settled." But we both knew our childhood days together were over. Shelby had given me a chance to glimpse the mystery of who she was. All I had to give her was the Avon hand cream I had ordered for her chapped paws from Dot Murphy. And my love and undying friendship. She had that.

When the last moment arrived and she boarded the bus, to my surprise Tall Paul hopped right on with her. He was going too. They both waved out the window, Tall Paul's poker face looking almost smiley.

A couple of months after that, I went by the Wauldins to get Rene. We were going to a bridal shower for Sandy Yates. Mrs. Wauldin was silently ironing. She was veal-colored, and more unresponsive than ever. Baby Linda still played at her feet, and there was a newcomer: Bicycle Bill Knickerbocker, who seemed to have moved into the void Earl and Shelby created by their leaving. He lounged on Shelbys cot with his hands behind his head, his brown eyes, the same as Delora's, staring up at a spot on the ceiling. In a few minutes he fell to napping and I hoped dreaming of ways to keep them all alive. Having a factotum around lent a slight hopefulness to the scene.

Sandy Yates is pregnant and now she has to get married. They kicked her out of highschool for it. I wondered what Donnie would think if he knew, and if he was still in love with Sandy. Her husband-to-be is a Cuban refugee. More freedom lovers have started trickling into Uleta. Everyone here is from someplace else—we are all displaced persons, even my daddy. What is a rhubarb loving man doing in a guava wallow?

Sandy is teaching her boyfriend English and he is teaching her the Catholic Church. All she did was stay too long in a car with him, and bam, her whole life had been decided. But in a way, it was the calm abiding kind of thing that Sandy would do.

I sat at the bridal shower wondering what would happen to everyone. To Tim, Valarie and Chuck, Rene, Andy? Who was next? All at once it felt like a vacant space opened up in me—a willingness, and the certain knowledge that I'd have to go out from this heart of noplace to find any more heroes, to find what life might mean and who I could be in it. It was like I heard that lonely call of love in the wind, this time calling me. Shallow roots give freedom too, and now it seemed I had to figure out a way to get free, and a way to be useful in the world too.

At the shower, a new girl appeared, from Far Rockaway, named Rosalyn Falk. Her family had just moved into one of the new tract houses that took the pasture across from the Yates'. She was bouncy, cool, smart, and she had freckles and red hair. She brought with her a new book called: "The Catcher In The Rye." It would change all our lives.

So it was a combination of everything that happened, including Emma, and Rosalyn that helped me to see that I'd been playing too small. The same struggle I started with now had expanded to include a bigger world than Uleta, and the red, white and darkness of the Greyhound Inn. I started making a plan in my mind of leaving rubbery old Uleta, and the people who grew there like the fruit, abundant and exotic, of going off to college like the smart, rich kids did. I'd heard that Florida State University, way up at the top of the state, in Tallahassee, offered courses in the Circus. What better ilk for me?

But first I had to finish highschool. I'd get a job now that I was coming of age—you could get working papers at sixteen. I'd save the money to go. I'd study art, colors, fruit, flowers, biology, things I knew about, and loved, while I learned the trapeze. I liked having an advance plan, feeling emboldened with a future. I remembered a time when I didn't have any sense of a future coming up at all. Now nothing mattered as much as the future. Was future another name for fate? If so I was ready to go and meet mine.

Even my mother's world had expanded and she seemed to be finally leaving her childhood and the Irish troubles behind, and reaching into the future. Her eyes were wide and fresh. You can turn against yourself and still come back. I realized that having Emma was part of her and daddy's new life in Florida. Emma was their hope for the future.

Mama had even given up her futile cold war with strangers. When Desi Arnaz and his band came on the TV, wearing guayabera shirts and playing a continental, she got up and mamboed wildly around the room. Daddy dropped his newspaper and watched, I jumped in and danced with her, and she said: "C'mon dearie, put some oomph into it!"

As we danced around the room she suddenly stopped, her eyes tearing up, and she said: "If I could give you anything in this world, I would give you back your face before I ever slapped it."

50.

What an upside down time that was. We were drowning in feelings of one kind or another for months and months. And then in January of 1956, Elvis Presley came on the Dorsey Show, on a Saturday night, a half-hour before the Honeymooners and gave us a whole new bunch of feelings. He was up in New York doing this show with people who didn't know him very well. He wasn't known by Yankees. He was known mostly in the South, by us. Yankee journalists called him poor white trash, a rockabilly hick, but they also knew that no one had moved people like this since Jesus was a boy.

The truth was, Elvis couldn't stop moving—he could not sing standing still. "That is a fact." Grandpa Twombley had told us, "you can look it up in the Library of Congress someday under Elvis's name."

My generation was wide awake and eager for all life's processes. I was sixteen now. Marie pronounced me vivacious. Dot Murphy said her name for me, Bedelia, was a French name that meant strength. Mama said I had been conceived on Valentine's day, even though if I was a war baby. They all drank hot tea now, while they told me these things, clinking their cups like Mrs. Lentini, giving me a feeling of security, giving me back a portion of my lost heart, without knowing it. Or maybe they knew.

And here was Elvis gazing into the TV camera, his sleepy bedroom eyes half open, cool, charming. He moved his shoulders a little, settled his pelvis and relaxed his long wide-spread gabardine covered legs in position for the first beat: "Wellllll..." and he snapped his left knee almost imperceptibly, "since mah bebby left me/ah've found a new place to dwell/It's down at the end of Lonely Street/at Heartbreak Hotel." Then his whole body thrashed out the song to our amazed delight, while everyone screamed, and the camera held on Elvis only from the waist up. He sneered, drooped his melty eyelids and smiled out of the side of his mouth as he sang; while his body did a snake dance like nobody had ever imagined before except maybe in their own primal memory of their own conceptions. He flattened a note here and there but no one cared. He was practicing perfect and he would just get better and better, this messenger, this sexy baby-cheeked hunk who dared to rock and roll because it was the most natural thing in the world for him to do.

My mother blushed—yes she did—for the first time ever. When we caught her she clucked her tongue at how naughty Elvis was being. Emma started walking the very next day, a wiggle in her hips as she went from chair to table.

That summer a movie called "The Seven Year Itch" opened in New York City. In downtown Miami they put up a duplicate of the forty-foot high poster that had been erected in Times Square to advertise the movie: a giant cut-out of Marilyn Monroe with her skirt blowing up over her head. "That's the way everyone likes to think of me," Marilyn squealed, in a TV interview. She was always lamenting how everyone thought she was just a dumb blonde. But people couldn't have accepted her if she was a smart blonde, not then. Daddy said it was as if her image had been created just to give the lie to Hitler's blond super-race. And Marilyn was blazing the trail for smart blondes of some future generation.

My generation saw "Rebel Without a Cause," and we loved James Dean for the mysterious way we perceived him and ourselves to truly be: paragons of cool. We had grown up together, tensed up, as though we saw the future. Then shock of shocks—as swiftly as James Dean appeared, he disappeared, totaled himself in his fast car, and fell through a crack into eternity, leaving us with all our buds nipped. He had been too dangerous to live. The movie "Giant" was like his wake. He was so cool it was like he was there too, alive.

We didn't know where on the road Jack Kerouac was in 1956, but a whole generation waited in Miami for some kind of confirmation from him. No doubt they waited all over. Because that's what started happening all the time—the same thing simultaneously took the same shape around the world, and television magically showed it to us. Daddy said television was causing it. There was a build-up of energy you could feel drumming in your chest. We danced to, "I got a rocket in my pocket and I'm rarin' to go..." A few years later, John Glenn would orbit the Earth. I felt it was all connected—art and music and science—like nature, weather and bumper crops, cyclical.

So in 1956, music, movies, and television displaced nature in my world and I was not alone. It was happening everywhere. It wasn't about the nature out there anymore; it was about the nature inside us. It had always been about how we felt about ourselves; does anything in nature not feel good enough, besides people?

Even the Seminoles had moved into mobile homes and bought TV sets, curious to learn about other ilks. That was the year Goatman did not appear in Uleta. And the year Guavas started getting scarce—there were only a few good bushes left. And the year the bus boycott ended, so people could sit anywhere they wanted on a bus, no matter what color they were.

In the sky the constant sound of earth movers ricocheted off the clouds. Neon was still organic to me, the ultimate in manmade beauty. I looked around and suddenly all the cars were bright-colored and two-toned: turquoise and white, pink and grey, powder blue and cream. Who decides these things? Artists, that's who.

Sex became my number one interest, harrowing me, even though I'd never done it, never had "the experience," as Shelby called it. Tim had given up on me ever coming across. The sight of him still gave me butterflies in my stomach, but I was too afraid of getting pregnant. Something told me loving was better than being loved, though it was cold comfort.

Daddy had a new word for me: impetuous. "Now don't be too impetuous," he said, with a wink, "always study the situation." As if there were scientific reasons why we yield to love.

I wanted the earth to shake, to reflect the excitement I felt inside, and I wanted to be in tune with the beat forever. I thought I understood the smirky smile on Elvis's face, what he must be feeling in his heart's core.

In that one year he released twenty-two hit songs over the airwaves, one right after the other including: "I Want You, I Need You, I Love You," "Shake, Rattle and Roll," "Don't Be Cruel," "Tutti Frutti," "Money Honey," "Love Me Tender," and "Blue Suede Shoes." Each one brought a whole new set of rapturous feelings, triggered by his distinct voice. That year libidos all over the country woke up from a long sleep.

I remembered when nuclear fission could not prompt my father to build a bomb shelter. Once when we were looking at a film of Hiroshima on television he said TV was like the final wave of the A-bomb, and if we couldn't see it on television it would mean we had blown ourselves up with it. Now rock 'n roll inspired him to start building a new big porch onto the front of the Sea Breeze—for all the dancing we were going to do.

Acknowledgments

I am grateful to all the people who were there from the beginning, emboldening me: Shirley Rousseau Murphy, John Hildreth, Candace Moore, Shannon Gleason Grossman, Julia Bridger, John Tarlton, Phil and Madeline Van Dyck, David McCord, June Akers Seese, Terry Kay, Sandra Watt. Thanks to Gordon Lish, Catherine Lewis, Mollie Lyman, Karla Kuban and Karen Nelson for continuing to egg me on. Many thanks to Frank Bidart for his poetry and Kathy Yancey for her art. I appreciate my sister Jacqueline Martin, and my brothers Paul and George Gleason, who also lived the crucible of Uleta. The Squaw Valley and Sewanee Writers Conferences, and Emory University all came through with scholarship support. Thanks to my insightful friends in Book Club who have shown me what a reader wants. Thanks to the Linda's: Falk, Lenna and Rehler who have been my friends since The Uleta days—and the last class of the 50's. My husband, Ted Kelly for the very roof, and my extraordinary children and grands, Joseph Sean Torre, Nicole Torre Clair, David John Clair, Camille Louise, and Chloe Violette Theodora: you are gifts from on high.

- MTK

LaVergne, TN USA
09 January 2011

211718LV00003B/1/P